CW00832488

CAN YOU GET MY NAME IN THE PAPERS?

Harry Diamond

Foreword by
George MacDonald Fraser

Neil Wilson Publishing • Glasgow • Scotland

To Jackie

Published by Neil Wilson Publishing Ltd
303a The Pentagon Centre
36 Washington Street
GLASGOW
G3 8AZ

Tel: 0141-221 1117
Fax: 0141-221 5363
E-mail: nwp@cqm.co.uk
http://www.nwp.co.uk/

A catalogue record for this book is available from the British Library
ISBN 1-897784-52-X

Typeset in 10/13pt Bembo by The Write Stuff, Glasgow
Tel: 0141-339 8279
E-mail: *wilson_i@cqm.co.uk*

Printed by WSOY, Finland

CONTENTS

ACKNOWLEDGMENTS

IN the absence of the gift of total recall, I had to rely on many people to confirm dates, places and conversations. My grateful thanks therefore to Bill English, Bob Palmer, Andrew Miller, John Watson, Steven Inch, Mike Blair, James Rae, Jane Phelps, Jean McFadden, Peter Russell and Edward Brodie, among many others. I particularly thank my friend Ezra Golombok for his encouragement and advice at every stage in the preparation of the manuscript.

Harry Diamond
Glasgow, 1996

FOREWORD

by GEORGE MACDONALD FRASER

GOOD newspaper men and women (as distinct from mere journalists) are born, and of all the gifts which their fairy godmothers bestow, two are of priceless value: persistent curiosity and a brass neck. Of course, other qualities are useful, like literacy, a fast note, general knowledge, good memory, charm and stamina, but the lust for finding out, and the kind of sheer nerve that cannot be abashed, are essentials. Harry Diamond had them all, but those two in particular, as witness the facts that, on his first assignment for the *Glasgow Herald*, he was physically assaulted but still got his story, and on a visit to Parliament he warned Winston Churchill that his fly-buttons were undone. Any news editor worth his salt would have hired him on those two incidents alone.

What struck me when I first saw him on the *Herald*, where I was a young sub-editor, was that I'd never seen anyone who looked so like a reporter — the glittering eye, the sharp, hungry glance, the disillusioned cry, the weary raincoat, even the hat on the back of the head. I wondered if this might be a handicap, but concluded that it was probably an advantage. People tend to trust and confide in a man who looks what he is.

The *Herald* of those days was one of the world's great newspapers, the oldest daily in the English language (as Harry notes with pride), and his autobiography takes me back to it, with its vast dingy news rooms, the battered desks scarred by countless thousand cigarettes, the strange mixture of Dickensian dignity and frenzied efficiency, the urbane editor with his knighthood, the raucous pedantry of the chief sub-editor, and the unbelievable ordered chaos of two daily newspapers coming off the presses simultaneously. That was a time when news came first and comment second, when papers were modest in size, clean to the touch, and carried stories of sensible brevity, and when Fleet Street was a goal which had not yet become a playground for politicians' relatives and Oxbridge graduates who think their opinions matter.

Harry Diamond learned his trade there, as well as on news agencies, the *Mail*, the *Express*, and the dear old *Bulletin*. It stood him in good stead when he went into public relations, that gilded whirlpool (or so we imagined it) which drew so many good newspaper folk into its vortex, and where he made such a distinguished mark. 'Glasgow's propagandist' is how he describes his work as the council's PR chief, and the new and brighter image which the city has presented to the world over the past generation testifies to how well he did it. It used to be customary to mourn the loss of a newspaper man to PR, but in Harry Diamond's case one can say without too much regret that the *Herald's* loss was Glasgow's gain.

George MacDonald Fraser

Chapter 1

YOUR FLY'S OPEN, PRIME MINISTER

'THE Prime Minister's fly is open,' I whispered to my companion as Winston Churchill passed us in the House of Commons corridors. 'I think we should tell him.'

'You tell him, you're young and brash,' said my friend.

I padded quietly after the great man, hummed and hawed and coughed until he eventually turned round to see what all the row was about.

'Er ... excuse me, sir. I know you won't mind me mentioning it to save you some embarrassment but your fly is open.' I remember thinking rather irreverently that my suit was in better condition than the Prime Minister's but this was a very special occasion for me. I had taken my best suit to London to create the right kind of impression. This was at a time when I thought Members of Parliament were a superior form of homo sapiens.

Mr Churchill stared at me, looked down, and said in that slow, commanding, slightly lisping voice that had thrilled and inspired millions throughout the war, 'My boy, there is no harm in leaving open the door of the cage when the bird is dead.'

I hurried back to my colleague to report this piece of Churchilliana and before I knew it I was in the bar of the Mother of Parliaments telling the story to an ever-widening audience. Eventually I think there were more Members of Parliament in the bar than in the debating chamber.

I was in the bar for a fortnight being plied with whisky and I never did send a story back to my newspaper, the *Glasgow Herald*. Maybe that's why I was never sent to Parliament again. Not by the *Herald* anyway, but I did go back in later years for meetings with members in connection with public

1

relations work. Maybe it was unsophisticated but I always felt slightly awed at the thought of walking among the ghosts of people like Palmerston, Disraeli, Gladstone, Asquith, and Lloyd George.

Lord (Denis) Healey, one-time Deputy Leader of the Labour Party among many other things, told my story about Churchill, with a different punchline, on a radio programme in March 1994: 'A dead bird never flies out of his nest.' Lord Healey told me later that he couldn't remember who told him the story but he heard it when he was a young Member of Parliament in 1952, the year of my encounter with Churchill. It's always possible that the young MP was one of those who crowded into the Commons bar to hear me tell the story.

If I was brash that day in 1952 I certainly wasn't on the autumn day in 1944 when I walked through an old oak door on the third floor of a building in Buchanan Street and became the youngest reporter in the history of the *Glasgow Herald*, the oldest English-language daily newspaper in the world.

I was 17, pale-faced, skinny, and wore a brown velour hat with a wide brim like a refugee from an old Hollywood gangster film. The world was consumed with indifference at my elevation from telephone clerk and editorial messenger.

The war in Europe was going well for the Allied Forces and Prime Minister Churchill, later to be defeated in the 1945 general election (he made a comeback in 1951), was in Quebec talking with President Franklin Roosevelt of America about a master-plan to defeat Japan.

Another event took place in 1944 which caused no great excitement at the time but about which millions of words have been written since. Sir William Burrell, a Glasgow shipowner, gave the bulk of his art collection to the city, but more of that later.

I reported to the assistant news editor James Ross, a large, stout man who hurrumphed and mumbled like an Ealing Studio version of an Indian Army colonel and in whom the thrill of the chase had long since slowed to a crippled stumble. 'Take a desk somewhere,' he hurrumphed, waving his hand vaguely in the air.

I settled down at a heavily-scarred wooden desk in the middle of the vast reporters' room and waited for my first assignment. As I waited hour after hour for someone to acknowledge my existence I tapped at the ancient Underwood typewriter on the desk ... the quick brown fox jumped ... now is the time for all good men ... smoked cigarette after cigarette, made designs on the desk with a bundle of pencils. Every half hour I walked to a window and watched the pigeons battering themselves at the glass and cooing at each other, 'What's he looking at?'

The atmosphere in the reporters' room was not like the films I had seen.

No-one rushed round the room making wisecracks, waving scoops, shouting into telephones, and flicking fag ends and half-eaten sandwiches out the window.

I consoled myself by congratulating myself that I was there at all. After all, there weren't many half-educated, timid Jewish boys from Gorbals getting the chance to work for one of the world's great newspapers. I was inclined towards hyperbole even then.

I had been promoted because all the able-bodied reporters were in the armed services and there was an acute shortage of staff; so there I sat dreaming of sudden and dramatic stardom, and terrified in case it came.

What if something happened to one of our war correspondents, Charles Lynch, Eric Philips or David Woodward? Nothing serious of course. I didn't wish that on them. Maybe a slight touch of flu from a damp dugout or a wee bout of bronchitis from the dust of battle. Just enough to have him replaced for a week or two by a star-struck cub reporter.

I had been awake from 4am worrying about whether I should take a packed suitcase to the office just in case. As I sat listening to the sound of distant drums carrying the news of my exploits from continent to continent I heard Jimmy Ross calling my name through the haze.

Now at last I was to benefit from all the quiet studying in the light of the narrow sunbeams playing on the oak-panelled walls of my alma mater, Abbotsford Public School, Gorbals, that great hall of learning which had nurtured and encouraged men and women who had gone on to distinguish themselves in so many fields of human endeavour … housebreaking, arson, serious assault, fraud, prostitution.

I walked nervously the few feet to Ross's desk like Hercules on his way to confront Cerberus, guardian of the gates of hell. Here was the assignment that would launch me on the way to Fleet Street and beyond. Ross shuffled through some papers on his desk and handed me an envelope (not to be opened until I reached Calais?) and said, 'Pop over to the gas office and pay this bill for me, son.'

Later that day as British bombers flew out to pound factories in Stuttgart and Nuremberg, Jimmy Ross called me to his desk again. Right, this time. This is it. 'Here, see what you can get out of this,' he hurrumphed without looking me in the eye. A scrap of paper told me a woman had been knocked down by a runaway horse in West Nile Street and been taken to the Royal Infirmary.

To the *Glasgow Herald* that day this ranked on the Richter scale of news events somewhere between a rise in the price of yak's milk in Tibet and a tramcar breakdown in San Francisco, but I had been looking so miserable

Ross just had to give me something to do.

I got the lady's name from a friendly switchboard operator at the Royal Infirmary and went to her home in the Townhead district of the city. I groped my way up a dark, dank, evil-smelling close and came to a door with a brass plate which said that J Brady lived there. An overweight, unkempt Mr Brady with a face like a battered cardboard box and wearing an off-white undervest and baggy trousers, answered my knock .

'Good afternoon, I'm from the *Glasgow Herald* … '

Crash. Dust and plaster fell from the ceiling as Mr Brady said, 'Fuck off' and propelled the door at me at the speed of light. Fearlessly I knocked again.

'Fuck off Ah'm telling ye or Ah'll bash yer heid in.' Crash.

What's this? Phillip Gibbs didn't tell me about this in *The Street of Adventure*. Leonard Moseley and Alan Moorehead, two of my heroes of the printed word, had never been told to fuck off up a dark close in Townhead, or anywhere else as far as I knew. I couldn't go back without my story, a prospect which frightened me more than Mr Brady did.

Knock, knock. The door opened and a three-ton truck hit me full in the face. I shot across the landing, bounced off a wall, and slid down 14 stone steps bleeding profusely. I counted them later.

Hey, what the hell's this? It's not supposed to be like this. None of the books I had read about the glamour and excitement of newspaper work mentioned this kind of thing. Mr Brady had gone too far. He was now standing between me and the fulfilment of my function in life, to bring back the story. I walked painfully back up to Mr Brady's door and this time attacked the old-fashioned pull-type bell knob. As Mr Brady opened the door ready to kill me this time I held my hand up, palms outwards.

'Right, pal, you've had your fun. You're tougher than me. You can batter my head in but I'm not going away without my story,' I said. Mr Brady stared implacably for a few seconds wondering whether to pull off my head or one of my limbs. Then he grinned. 'Yur a persistent wee bastard, urn't ye?' and he pulled the door open wide. For the next 20 minutes he dabbed my battered face with a damp dishcloth, gave me a cup of tea in a dirty cup, and apologised repeatedly for 'hangin' one on me.'

He told me his wife had gone out to buy a birthday gift for a grandson and the next thing he knew was when the polis came to the door to tell him she had been knocked down by a runaway horse. 'Stupid bitch.' All good human interest stuff. 'Ye canny trust anybody these days,' he said. I don't know whether he meant his wife or the horse.

Eventually the blood stopped flowing and we parted on the friendliest terms, although we didn't promise to write. I went back to the office to write a gripping drama about Mrs Brady's encounter with a runaway horse.

Ross wasn't at his desk so I handed my story to Jimmy Harrison, who was second in command in the reporters' room. Harrison was rumoured to have spent three weeks in the army before being discharged with flat feet or some similar fatal disease. I remember him as a gaunt, granite-faced man whose soul had transmuted to iron filings.

'What happened to you?' he said when he saw my battered face. I was surprised he even asked.

'I fell.'

Harrison muttered something that sounded like 'stupid bugger', read my story, looked impassively at me and grated, 'Not quite our kind of material, is it?' and dropped it into the wastepaper basket.

I didn't get any more assignments that day, so at the end of my shift at 10pm I went home to commit suicide. I thought better of it when I got there and decided to give it another go next day.

The second day wasn't a whole lot better although I do vividly recall two things I was sent to cover. One was the annual general meeting of Glasgow Foundry Boys Benevolent Association, presided over by Bailie Edwin J Donaldson. The *Herald* didn't miss anything of social significance in those days.

The other was Mr John Agnew's 100th birthday party. Not many hard-working men reached their 100th birthday when I was a young reporter. Of course I asked him to what he attributed the fact that he had reached 100 years of age. A far from doddering Mr Agnew put down his pint glass, took the stained clay pipe out of his mouth, and said, 'To the fact that I haven't died yet, son.' I'm not sure I ever heard a better comeback than that for the rest of my journalistic career.

I had had a couple of jobs before I joined the *Herald* group. One was in the office of Mr Reginald Oliver Elderton, stockbroker of Queen Street. Mr Elderton was a tall, thin, round-shouldered man who rarely smiled and laughed only once in the year I worked for him although he was not unkind, except financially, to me.

On the last day of the month he strode purposefully in the front door of the office and, without pausing, placed three pound notes on my desk and raced into his own office as if he felt guilty about paying me such a lowly sum. That's how it looked to me, anyway. Some months had five weeks but I still got the same £3. A canny man was Mr Elderton. I know I gave the £3 to my mother but I don't remember how much I got back. I do know I never really went short of anything, perhaps because I didn't smoke or drink or go with women. There wasn't much else a lad could spend money on.

One of my jobs was to type contract notes for clients. One was for an elderly widowed lady in black lace who was driven to our office in a large limousine despite the war and shortage of petrol. I was always amazed at the number of widowed old ladies in black lace who were driven about in limousines. I used to wonder what had happened to their menfolk. I had visions of cellars full of their corpses wrapped in tarpaulins.

I laid the contract note on Mr Elderton's desk and left. Moments later I heard the cackle of laughter from his room.

'Harry, son. Come in here a minute.' My real name is Henry but I was called Harry all through my working life. I don't know why.

Mr Elderton handed me the contract note and said, 'Read it.' I had typed '100 Ordinary Shares of Phillips Rubber Souls …'

In the year I was in Mr Elderton's office I read every book about journalism I could get my hands on. Many of them made the point that a reporter needed a good knowledge of shorthand so I studied Pitman's shorthand in the evenings and by the end of about three months I could take down most of a radio talk, but I also had to get glasses as I nearly went blind.

A job came up in the office of Mr William Campbell Balfour, who ran a tiny news agency up a close in West Nile Street with the rather pretentious name of Scottish Newspaper Services. When I told Mr Elderton about it he asked me not to go. He told me he had no family and when he could no longer carry on the business it would have to close because there was no-one else there. He did have a clerk but he was older than he was. Mr Elderton said if I would stay he would propose me for membership of the Stock Exchange when I was old enough and I could carry on the business. I was too young and stupid to appreciate what Mr Elderton was offering me and my mother and father didn't even know what a stockbroker was so they couldn't advise me and I left.

Mr Balfour, to whom I referred disrespectfully as WC, was also a tall, thin man but with absolutely no sense of humour. His main income was derived from stealing the more salacious court stories from the daily newspapers in Scotland and sending them by teleprinter to the *News of the World* in London with which he had some agreement.

He also insisted that I had to have at least one idea for a news story every morning, gleaned from voracious reading of the dailies. Mr Balfour looked unmoved by any human emotion as morning after morning I produced the most bizarre ideas for stories, none of which came to anything.

The only other employee at the time was Cliff Hanley, who later achieved fame as an author, broadcaster and wit. Cliff was very encouraging to me in those early days and is still a friend of mine even if we don't see each other all that often. He lasted longer than me in Mr Balfour's office. I was fired after a few months for, among other things, not ensuring there was a warm, welcoming fire in Mr Balfour's room when he arrived in the morning.

Mr Balfour called me in one day and made the longest speech I had ever heard him make. 'Harry, son, I'm afraid I have to let you go. Through no fault of your own you are just not the stuff that journalists are made of. That's no reflection on you at all. There are many successful men who would not make good journalists. I think you should go into a shop and work yourself up to be a business tycoon.'

These were just about the most insulting and wounding words that one could make to an aspiring James Cameron. Mr Balfour didn't approve of tycoons, never having become one himself.

Cliff Hanley told me later that the real reason for my departure was that Mr Balfour wanted to employ the son of a friend. Some years later I met a rather run-down Mr Balfour in a coffee shop. He didn't recognise me, so I sat down at his table, introduced myself, and told him about the advice he had given me.

'Did you take it?'

'As a matter of fact, no. I'm Chief Sub-editor of *The Bulletin*.' (Another morning newspaper in the *Herald* group.) Mr Balfour was unimpressed.

Somehow or other I had known I was not going to spend much of my young life in Mr Balfour's office, so every lunchtime for months I went round to the *Herald* office to ask for a job. At one point I was asked into the office of an accountant who asked me to add up a column of figures. I added three columns of figures three times and got nine answers. 'Don't call us, we'll call you,' was the gist of his parting comment.

The day after I was fired by Mr Balfour I went to the *Herald* office again. The lady in charge of office boys, Miss Charlotte (Lottie) Anderson took me to see Mr T P Inglis, Editor of the *Evening Times*, who for some reason was the only man authorised to take on office boys.

'This young man has been coming in every day for months asking for a job,' said Lottie. 'I don't know what to do with him.'

'Give him a job, then' growled Mr Inglis, and I was on my way. The job description was telephone clerk, which embraced quite a number of functions, including running to the canteen for cigarettes and bags of chips for eternally ravenous sub-editors. The main function though was to take stories in shorthand from reporters on the phone, transcribe them, and give them to the chief sub-editor.

After the stories were emasculated or otherwise distorted (I'm writing as a one-time reporter now!) by one of the sub-editors he would shout 'up' and one of us would put the small sheets of copy paper in a carrier and insert it in a pneumatic tube which carried it to the caseroom to be set in type. In those days I had a tendency to run everywhere like Sammy Glick to prove how enthusiastic I was. Once I grabbed a story from a sub-editor and thrust it into the pneumatic tube without a carrier. Minutes later the story that was to have led the front page floated gently over the rooftops of Buchanan Street. The loose pages had filtered out through a grating.

A substitute story was found on the spike which was used to impale discarded stories. John Downie, a night editor under whom I once served and who was one of the best journalists I have ever known, used to park his sandwiches on the spike.

My newspaper career was nearly cut short one day when I raced along a corridor, slammed open a door of the sub-editors' room and hit the editor full in the chest. He sat heavily on the floor with his pipe half way down his throat. Miraculously I survived. Mr Inglis was a tolerant man.

Soon I was allowed, along with others of the brighter telephone clerks, to cover police courts in the morning where the lesser dramas and comedies of the human dilemma were played out. One magistrate, a local councillor who had a liking for Scotland's national drink, was still suffering from the effects of a reception he had attended the previous night.

Staring with bloodshot eyes at a wee man who had been found drunk and disorderly after his own version of a good night, the magistrate mumbled, 'You're sentenced to death.' The normally dignified, soft-spoken assessor who was sitting with the magistrate turned pale and exclaimed, 'For Chrissake, you can't do that! Fine him half-a-crown.'

'Er … sorry … fined half-a-crown,' repeated the magistrate dutifully.

Another time a group of thugs who had terrorised the neighbourhood were told by the magistrate, 'This type of behaviour cannot be tolerated in the streets of our city. I shall make an example of you all. You will each pay a fine of half-a-crown', (12½p in today's money). Thus was law and order restored to our unruly streets.

More than once I was threatened with a cement overcoat and dumping in the Clyde if I published the name of some villain who had appeared in court but I always survived to write another day. I was a telephone clerk for only a few months when I was promoted to reporter.

My first few weeks as a reporter were less exciting than my months as editorial dogsbody. The paper was thin, much of it filled with the progress of the war, and at home the *Herald* seemed to concentrate on covering meetings of one kind of another. I got the less interesting ones to cover, which rarely saw the light of day. A few months later I was called up for the army and was away for more than three years.

Chapter 2

MY DAD WAS
AN ALIEN

UNTIL the age of 18 I celebrated my birthday on 14 December because that was the date my mother told me. My birthday turned out to be 15 December. I found that out when I got a copy of my birth certificate before I joined the army. I always thought my mother's name was Minnie, but when she died I discovered among her papers that her name was really Millie. My father was always known as Joe. His real name was Julius.

Sometimes people of my faith are given a new name when they are very ill in the hope that a benevolent Almighty will make him or her better and give them a new start, so to speak, in their new name. It's a nice idea but didn't apply in our case. Accurate, reliable information was not a highly-regarded commodity in my family.

I was born in December 1926 in a room near Queen's Park which my parents rented when they were married in March of that year. The *Glasgow Herald* still carried only advertisements on its front page, including births, but not mine. The people from whom I sprang didn't read the *Herald*. In fact few of them could read at all.

A few months after I was born my family moved to a small flat in Abbotsford Place, Gorbals, where we lived until I came out of the army in 1948. I have read several books about Gorbals, most of them sentimental, nostalgic drivel. My Gorbals had ignorance, stupidity, every disease known to mankind (and a few still to be identified), malice, violence, illiteracy and unbelievable cruelty to partners and children.

Most of the people I knew lived in grim, dank-smelling, dingy tenements although they did look after their own homes well. There may have been good times but I don't remember many of them. I do remember we kept odd bits of furniture in the bath because there was no hot water unless we boiled it in kettles and we would have to boil a hundred kettles to fill the bath. I remember the bed recess in which my younger sister Sheila and I had to sleep until she got too big to go into the same bed as me. Then I had to move to a bed settee in 'the front room,' which also served as the dining room although it was never called that. We didn't dine in those days. We just ate.

I remember that Sheila and I went to sleep every night to the accompaniment of drunken singing from the public house next to our close. I remember the smell of damp plaster in the close, gang fights, boys snatching my cap off my head and throwing it about the street as I was on my way to *cheder* (Hebrew School) every evening. I attended Abbotsford Public School from 9am until 4pm and *cheder* from 5pm until 7pm and then had to do homework from both schools when I came home. No wonder I learned very little from either.

I remember falling over a body lying face down in vomit in the close one night and running up the stairs to tell my father. He came down, turned the man over on his back and said, 'That's Benny Lynch, son. He used to be a famous boxer.' Lynch was dead drunk. My father dragged him clear of the vomit and propped him against a wall.

I've also read a lot about the new Gorbals with its luxury flats occupied by lawyers, doctors, journalists and, according to one newspaper, even a judge, but I'm unimpressed. There isn't enough money in the Royal Bank of Scotland to persuade me to live there again, which I suppose is not a very sensible comment as no-one is asking me to live there.

I have to laugh when I think of the difference between public schools in Scotland and England. In many autobiographies I have read people have written about how their school contemporaries later became famous lawyers, doctors, army generals, politicians, and film, stage, and television stars. As I've said, my contemporaries took totally different directions.

Some years after I left school I met one of my old teachers and he asked me what I was doing for a living.

'I'm a newspaper reporter,' I said proudly.

'I always knew you would come to no good, Diamond,' he said.

I always told interviewers I was the first person in my family to be born in Britain because it sounded more interesting. The truth is my mother was born in London but her parents and my father and his parents came from Lithuania at the beginning of this century, as did so many others at various times, to escape the clutches of malevolent Russian rulers who had dominated Lithuania since the end of the 18th century.

Because my father was registered as a Russian alien during the 1939-45 war he had to observe a curfew decreeing he had to be home by 10pm. One night a policeman stopped him in the blacked-out street and asked him for his identity card. Minutes later he was in the local jailhouse. The desk sergeant phoned a neighbour of ours who was wealthy enough to have a telephone and I raced down to the police station to rescue my bewildered father.

Another night he was stopped by two hooligans who demanded money. My father was a better actor than Laurence Olivier. He turned his coat pockets inside out and told the hooligans a hard luck story about not even having enough money to get a bus home. The encounter ended with them giving him a shilling for his bus fare and a couple of cigarettes. As it happened he was near home so he saved the bus fare. A shilling is equivalent to five pence today but in those days you could do quite a lot with it.

My father claimed to have been a soldier in the 1914-18 war but was very vague about his unit or regiment. He used to tell me he was in Maryhill Barracks, Glasgow, when the war ended and he and some mates just walked out and went home without being officially discharged.

He never bothered to become a naturalised British citizen because it would not have made any difference to his life, but it did have an effect on mine. In the days when I still had an ambition to become Scotland's Walter Winchell the BBC rejected my application for a job on the grounds that my father was an alien. Nowadays, judging by some of its programmes, you have to be an alien to get into the BBC, or at least have a near relative from outer space.

I don't want to be judgemental about my parents because I loved them both and they loved me and Sheila but they certainly didn't get on with each other too well. They just couldn't communicate. My mother wanted my father to 'make something of himself' but his mind just didn't work the way my mother wanted. Apart from his work as an upholsterer, at which he was an acknowledged master, he was an incurable gambler, his only interests being cards, dogs and horses. Sometimes when we were out together and someone passed in a Rolls-Royce I would say to him, 'Look, Dad, there's a bookie driving your car.' He always laughed wryly.

My father didn't like responsibility or making decisions. One morning before he went to work my mother gave him a slip of paper with an address near Queen's Park. 'Come to that address after work, Joe,' she told him. 'We're moving.'

Not once in our lives did Sheila and I ever go on holiday with our parents. In fact I don't remember us going anywhere as a family, to a cinema, or a picnic or the circus or any of the places other families went. On school holidays my mother took Sheila and me to her family in London. My father stayed behind and passed the time in whatever way he could.

My mother's mother and father had a grocer's shop in Bow in the East End of London. Their name was Steinberg, which was printed in large letters above the shop. One day when I was playing on the pavement at the door of the shop a parade of Blackshirts, the gang of thugs led by Sir Oswald Mosley, founder in 1932 of the British Union of Fascists, marched past the shop. As they passed, one of their number stepped out and hit me hard on the face with the back of his hand sending me reeling across the pavement. My face stung for days afterwards.

My mother and father had a battle every Friday night when he handed over his wages. She wanted to see his pay packet showing the amount and overtime if appropriate and he stoutly resisted what he considered to be an invasion of his privacy, not to mention a slur on his integrity. This was a common attitude, even among the indigenous population. Men just didn't want their wives to know what they earned because they feared being left with less than they considered their due.

For many years I used to fantasize about winning a lot of money on the football pools and going into the workshop where my father worked, taking his hammer and scissors from him with the words, 'You won't need these any more, Dad,' and throwing them through the nearest window, without opening it first. I still have a sentimental attachment to his hammer, which I have carefully preserved.

My mother once persuaded him to go to night school to improve his English. His spoken English was quite good, if rather fractured, but his attention span for the written or printed word was short. His teacher was fired a few weeks later for going to the dog track with my father instead of looking after his classes.

I still remember the very first thing I had published. It was a few lines to the effect that £25 had been raised for charity at the wedding of a friend. I went down to the machine room, as we called it, to watch the huge rotary presses thundering out thousands of copies of the paper, each with my wee story in it. I was tingling with excitement.

A friendly machine man gave me a couple of copies of the paper and I raced home to show my parents. My father mouthed the words slowly and looked blank. My mother's comment was, 'That's good, son.' I know they were pleased for me but they didn't understand the implications of what I had done. I had written something that would be read by hundreds of thousands of people all over the country. I have never lost the feeling of excitement at seeing something of mine in print.

My father was an unschooled man and good-natured with a keen sense of humour and was a marvellous story-teller. If I have any talent in that direction I am sure I inherited it from him. He used to tell the story of how, when he was about 12, he and his parents and a lot of other refugees fled from their village home in Lithuania to travel to Britain. At the port of

Hamburg they were all ushered into a giant shed where he accidentally leaned against a wall switch. Lights went on all over the place and everyone ran out of the building shouting 'Fire! Fire!' because they had never seen electric light before!

My father's family name was Chatzkind, not Diamond. That came from the fascia board of a shop at their port of entry to Britain. An immigration officer who couldn't understand what they were saying bestowed the name on them. My father couldn't tell me what port it was.

When my parents died, I wept — not so much because I had lost people I loved, but because I think life was not kind to them. Because of the many frustrations in her life my mother spent day after day lying on her bed with a vinegar-dampened cloth round her head in the belief that this would take away the nervous headache she always seemed to have. It never did. One day in 1966 a telephone operator told me my mother was trying to reach me. I went round to her house, let myself in and found her lying on the hall floor in her nightgown with the telephone in her hand. I telephoned for an ambulance and took her to the Victoria Infirmary.

I walked up and down for half an hour until a young doctor came out and said, 'Your mother has just had a bad turn. You can take her home now.'

'I'm sorry, I can't do that,' I said. 'She is living alone at the moment and is obviously not fit to look after herself. Besides, I don't think she has just had a bad turn. I would like someone else to look at her.'

The young doctor called someone else and I walked up and down for another half-hour and the second doctor came out to tell me my mother had had a stroke and would be kept in.

'Why didn't he know that?' I asked, indicating the younger doctor. 'Everyone has to learn,' I was told. I couldn't trust myself to say anything so I just went away. A few weeks later I arranged for my mother to go into a nursing home. She was there five years before she died.

Four years later I visited my father one afternoon and found him sitting in a chair staring silently into space. I tried to talk to him but there was no answer. I called a doctor who told me my father was senile, at which I blew up and told him, 'You are more bloody senile than he is. Last night he was in very good form and you don't become senile in 24 hours.' I insisted on his going to hospital where he was diagnosed as having had a cerebral haemorrhage. He died a few hours later.

Sheila, whom I loved very much and who was seven years younger than me, died at the age of 45 from cancer, leaving a 12-year-old son, Mark. One afternoon a hospital nurse phoned my office to tell me she was in a coma and I went to the hospital and held my sister's hand until her breathing stopped almost 12 hours later. She didn't even know I was there. My younger son Michael arrived early in the morning to keep me company and was with me when Sheila died. I was very grateful for his presence.

I still miss Sheila very much after 20 years. Rightly or wrongly she looked on me as some kind of hero because I helped her in a number of ways throughout her life when things weren't going too well. I wish she were here now so that I could weep on her shoulder when things aren't going too well with me. My nephew Mark is married now and lives in London with his wife Bella and their young son Zachary. They are very happy and live a sensible life and I keep in touch with them.

Both my parents had brothers and sisters. My father's two brothers, Jack and Henry, were mean-spirited men. I don't know exactly what they did for a living but I know it was probably something on the edge of the law. Jack gave me a wristwatch that didn't work for my bar mitzvah and Henry gave me a gold ring that was so thin it blew off the kitchen table one day and I never found it again.

Henry did some dealing in gemstones and when I was getting engaged I asked him if he could get me a diamond ring at a reasonable price. He came back a week or so later with a ring for which he charged me £80. It was every penny I had. Another couple of weeks later a friend asked me, 'Did you like the ring I gave your uncle for you? It's good value for £60.' Never give a sucker an even break, even if he is your nephew.

Henry lived very near me in the years when I was a newspaper reporter. Often the night news editor would send a taxi for me in the middle of the night if a story broke. Unfortunately he would give the taxi driver my uncle's address so Henry was awakened by thunderous knocking at his door and would appear, in a foul mood, in his long drawers.

'Taxi, Mr Diamond,' the driver would say and Henry would slam the door wordlessly and let the driver wait for ages until he finally got fed up and went away. Henry would never tell the driver he should go to my address a few hundred yards away and I never seemed to be able to get it over to the night news editor that he was giving taxi drivers the wrong address.

My father had three sisters. Two of them were crumpled, defeated little creatures from what I remember of them. The third was very well-off indeed by our standards. They couldn't talk like normal people; they bludgeoned you with words spewed out at a high rate of decibels. Some of their children were the same. Whenever I came in contact with them I felt disorientated, as if I'd walked through a mysterious, hidden door and landed in a madhouse.

The well-off sister lived with her husband and children in a big house a world away from places like Gorbals. How they became wealthy I don't know, although I suspect she married someone with money or the business acumen to acquire it.

Money was the yardstick against which people like my aunt judged their fellow humans. It didn't matter how intellectually impoverished her friends were as long as they had money. Music, art, literature meant absolutely nothing to them. They could go through a lifetime without reading a book or going to a concert.

My aunt had a friend who owned a chain of cinemas. When Sheila was married in the 1950s my mother worked very hard to scrape enough money together to give her a 'good' wedding. My mother and I agonised for weeks on who to invite to the celebratory dinner because we had only a limited amount of funds. My father had no opinion on the matter.

Just as the dinner started my aunt swept regally into the hall with her wealthy friend, who had not been invited and for whom my mother had made no provision. She stayed anyway. A week or so later she sent a gift for my sister, a set of highly-tarnished electro-plated teaspoons in a well-worn box. My mother didn't know what to do. She didn't want to let Mrs Thing away with her insulting behaviour but neither did she want to start a family feud. I had no such inhibitions because I was angry that my mother and sister had been hurt so I typed a note to Mrs Thing and took the teaspoons round to her hotel with a note that read, 'As you were not invited to my daughter's wedding we do not think it is appropriate to accept your gift, which I now return secure in the knowledge that it did not involve you in any great expense.' I had a way with words even then. My aunt went berserk and didn't talk to any of us again for a long time, which was no great loss.

One of my father's sisters had a son who was generally acknowledged to be 'intellectually challenged' to use a modern euphemism. He refused to have anything to do with anyone in his family, which on second thoughts may have indicated he wasn't so odd after all. Although he was in business and could hardly be said to be penniless, he was once taken into hospital with malnutrition. His wife, who was no intellectual heavyweight either, wore a black eye patch but kept forgetting which eye it was supposed to protect!

My mother's family were very different, although there were one or two eccentrics among them, too. One uncle took out his hearing aid so that he could hear better when someone was talking to him, then he would put it back when they were finished.

Most of them were kind to me and my sister Sheila and we both had great affection for them. My maternal grandmother was a kind, good-humoured, handsome woman. I enjoyed talking to her in Yiddish. The family were amused when I talked to her about one thing and she would give me a totally irrelevant answer because she really hadn't heard what I'd said. My grandfather was a good man, too, and I enjoyed playing dominoes with him when I was a boy. Both grandparents died in 1947 when I was a soldier in Egypt but I wasn't told until I came home as the family didn't want to upset me when I was so far away. I have only a faint recollection of my father's parents.

My mother's sister Debby and one of her three brothers, Myer, are still alive. Aunty Debby was 94 in November 1995. Any time I feel depressed I only need to phone her to feel better again as she is the only person in the world who thinks I can do no wrong. There aren't many of her kind left.

Chapter 3

I NEARLY BECOME A RUSSIAN

THE war broke out four months before my 13th birthday. I remember the sirens sounding almost immediately after the Prime Minister, Neville Chamberlain, announced on the morning of Sunday, 3 September, 1939 that we were at war with Germany. Everyone thought we were going to be bombed out of existence before the week was out.

The war didn't affect me all that much until a month later. There was an air of tremendous excitement when I arrived at school that Tuesday morning. We were being evacuated. My mother had dressed me in my new dark blue suit and sparkling white shirt so that I would be put in 'a good respectable home'. Two or three other boys and girls had also been spruced up for the occasion but all of us came from working-class families and some of us looked rather more respectable than others.

I didn't feel very brave about the whole business and looked round anxiously for some particular friend to keep me company. Then I saw Hertzel, a classmate of mine, and a wave of relief surged over me. I stuck to him like glue and suddenly we were on a bus.

A teacher stopped at our seat to speak to us. Hertzel told her my mother had told him to look after me. I was a bit indignant about this bare-faced fib but I let it pass. Even at the age of 12 Hertzel had a sharp brain and a ready answer to all emergencies. His silver tongue later helped him to accumulate a considerable amount of money but he was a firm believer that you can't take it with you and lived his life accordingly.

The bus started off amid cheers — we had embarked on our great adventure. My mother had looked at the gas mask and label round my neck without comment. It was a long time before I felt I knew what was going through her mind.

Before long Hertzel and I were sitting on our luggage in Newmilns town hall in Ayrshire with the other evacuees. Natives of the town walked slowly round eyeing us critically and from time to time muttering to an official, 'I'll take that one.' I felt like something in the autumn sales.

Panic swelled up in me when someone pointed at Hertzel and ignored me completely, but my friend stood by me staunchly. 'I'm sorry, you'll have to take us both or I can't go,' he said. No-one contradicted him. They must have sensed he was a formidable opponent.

The next thing I recall is walking along the town's main street with Hertzel. A middle-aged, dignified-looking man recognised us for what we were and stopped us. It crossed both our minds in the same instant. This looked like the type of person we would like to be billeted with.

It was Hertzel of course who blurted it out. 'Would you like a couple of evacuees?' The man smiled and explained why he couldn't take us. I forget the reason. He told us he was the Provost of the town and we were aghast at our impertinence. At least I was, I'm not so sure about Hertzel.

We went back to the town hall and sat on our suitcases again. Eventually a young woman smiled at us and said, 'I'll take these two.' Our white shirts and new suits had done the trick. Away we trudged with our luggage to Mrs Campbell's neat little house at the top of a steep hill.

After we got installed Hertzel and I went out again. His mother had given him half-a-crown (12½p) to last him until she came to see him at the week-end. Hertzel made straight for a café and bought ice-cream, for himself. And he kept buying ice-cream, for himself, until the half-crown melted away too. Not surprisingly he got a tummy-ache. That night when we went to bed the pain of Hertzel's tummy-ache transcended all the terrors of war and evacuation.

Our hostess had the cure. She brought Hertzel a heated dinner plate and put it on his stomach. We got burned a couple of times when it fell out of its cover but eventually Hertzel's tummy-ache subsided. Next morning we went to our new school and for a while I felt as though we were on a different planet. The Ayrshire brand of English differed greatly from that of Gorbals. I am prepared to admit that neither reflected much credit on their users.

I stayed in Newmilns a month and my mother came to see me every week-end. One day a parcel of foodstuffs and sweets arrived for me from my Auntie Debby in London and that evening I asked our hostess if she would put up the black-out curtains on the window of our bedroom so that Hertzel and I could open my parcel. Mrs Campbell asked her husband to do it and an argument started. It ended when Mr Campbell set about his wife with a dog chain.

When my mother came at the week-end I asked her to take me home. Hertzel stuck it out for another month before the call of the city jungle proved too strong for him. I had not heard anything about Hertzel for some years until a relative of his phoned me in April 1995 to tell me he had died. Another link with my youth had gone.

When I came home from Newmilns all the able-bodied teachers in my school had been called up for the armed forces and we were left with a few elderly, rather world-weary souls whose years of struggle with young Gorbalonians had taken a heavy toll. It soon occurred to me that I wasn't learning much that would help me to make some kind of meaningful life for myself. That occupied a lot of my thoughts. It seemed to be that all the adults I knew had menial jobs in tailor shops, furniture or tailoring workshops and butcher shops.

On Friday, 14 December, 1940, the day before my 14th birthday I arrived home from school, threw my schoolbag into a corner, and announced to my mother, 'I'm not going back.' Unskilled jobs weren't all that difficult to get in those days and I got a couple of them, but I didn't keep them for long. One was in the darkroom of a photographer, another was in a garage.

After work most days I walked down to Gorbals public library and buried myself in books. There were rows upon rows of them on such a bewildering range of subjects and I used to think how clever all these authors were to write a whole book about all these interesting things. I wasn't very discriminating in my reading.

I read for hours about strange, faraway lands and peoples and about the seas and stars and deserts and about explorers and doctors and scientists and lawyers and archeologists and animals and anything else that would take me away for a while from the grey streets and black buildings.

I vividly recall walking the half-mile or so home when the library closed dreaming of being somebody of importance with a big office and a big desk and telephones and people constantly coming in to ask my advice. I knew from the all the books I was reading that there was a better life out there somewhere and I was determined to try to achieve it. Young and unsophisticated as I was I also realised that life was no rehearsal. This was the real thing and you get only one chance to make something worthwhile of it.

Then I chanced on books on journalism and the characters that followed that profession and the adventures they had and the people they met and I decided that was for me. It was a curious ambition for a boy whose family were barely literate. In later years when I was interviewed by other journalists

I always said I became a journalist because I had seen films with Humphrey Bogart or Lloyd Nolan or George Raft as a wisecracking, daring crime reporter who helped dumb cops solve gruesome murders. I'm not even sure these actors ever played newspapermen. I never did reach the heights of the newsmen I read about in those early days in Gorbals library but I did achieve a certain status and reputation over the years.

I have never regretted going into journalism, even if it's not the most respected of trades. In later years I have regretted never having taken piano lessons but I'm not really envious of musicians, painters, architects or men who build great bridges. I am happiest when I'm putting words down on paper, even if I'm not a Norman Mailer, Gore Vidal or Morris West. I can still do things with words that many other people cannot do. Writing also helps me considerably by making me concentrate so that everything else — anxieties, chores, worrying about trivialities — is driven out of my mind for a while.

The war that was supposed to be over by Christmas lasted six years and before it ended I was a soldier. My mother and father understandably didn't want their son to go into the army. They were convinced that anyone who went into the armed services was given a uniform and rifle and sent out the following day to be killed. My mother tried to think up all kinds of devious schemes to keep me out. At one point she tried to persuade our family doctor to give me a letter to take to my medical to say I wet the bed. Someone had told her they didn't take men with that particular complaint. Someone else told her to get me to swallow some chewing gum before I went for the medical. This was supposed to show up in X-rays as an ulcer. Of course I wouldn't play along with these ploys. Not that I wouldn't have been happy to stay out of the army but I did have some pride.

Even when my parents died many years later they still did not know that I could have stayed out of the army. When I went to register for service the clerk told me I could stay out because my father was registered as a Russian alien and I would automatically revert to his nationality when I reached the age of 21. If I went into the services I would become a fully-fledged British citizen at 21.

'Get me in quick,' I told the clerk, 'I don't want to be a bloody Russian.' As I said, my parents never knew about this exchange. They would have been happy if I had become a Martian if it had meant staying out of the services.

My father saw me off to the Black Watch barracks in Perth that Thursday morning in 1945. He arrived home with a badly bruised face. After my train drew out he walked out of Central Station with his eyes fixed disconsolately on the pavement and walked into a lamp post, almost knocking himself out.

My army career was undistinguished but interesting. For a time I was an army boxer and once created a sensation by hitting an opponent. My sergeant nominated me for several inter-company boxing matches to get back at me for a run-in we had on parade one morning. Passing along the ranks he stopped at me and made a number of uncomplimentary remarks about my appearance.

When he was finished I said quietly, 'Have you ever considered consulting a taxidermist, sergeant?' Sergeant McCann of the Black Watch glared at me and passed on. About 15 minutes after our parade was dismissed I was lying on my bed when the door of the barrack room burst open and Sergeant McCann marched up to my bed and bawled, 'On your feet soldier!' I was marched to the adjutant's office where the sergeant reported me for everything but mutiny on the high seas. Apparently he had gone to the barracks library after the parade and looked up the word taxidermist.

'What exactly did the accused say to you sergeant?' asked the adjutant.

'He told me to get stuffed sir,' said Sergeant McCann.

'I did not, sir,' I said indignantly.

'What did you say then?'

'I asked the sergeant if he had ever considered consulting a taxidermist, sir.'

The adjutant's face contorted as if he were trying hard not to choke and he sentenced me to seven days' confinement to barracks.

On leave one week-end I was walking with my mother when we met an elderly Jewish friend of hers who said questioningly, 'You're in de army?' and added, 'You must know my nephew Sidney. He's in de army also, a tall fair-haired, good-looking boy, yes?' There didn't seem to be any point in telling her there were quite a number of guys in the army I hadn't met.

I did my training at Queen's Barracks, Perth and halfway through my training was sent to an army physical training camp at Shrewsbury, Shropshire, to be 'built up' a bit. I wasn't the weediest soldier in the British Army when I was called up but I wasn't far from it. When I went back to Perth after the three-month course I was a great deal fitter and stronger.

Back at Queen's Barracks I saw a notice outside the adjutant's office asking for volunteers to learn shorthand and typing so that they could be sent to the British Embassy in Washington DC. I immediately volunteered as I was already a good shorthand typist and was transferred to the Royal Army Service Corps and posted to an army transit camp near Little Budworth in Cheshire as a clerk. This was the army's version of logic. A number of former joiners, plumbers and coal merchants joined the shorthand/typing course and were later sent to America.

A couple of years later my knowledge of shorthand and typing got me posted to Egypt as secretary to the Deputy Assistant Adjutant General, Middle East Land Forces at Fayid in the Suez Canal zone.

Much of the 12 months I spent in Egypt was occupied typing letters to generals in surrounding military theatres. My boss, also a general, had a flawed knowledge of the English language.

'How does that sound, Diamond?' he would say when he had dictated a letter.

'May I speak freely sir?' I enquired politely.

'Of course.'

'Er ... let's say it's not a model of lucidity, sir.'

'Impudent bugger. You write the bloody thing then.'

So from that day he told me what he wanted to say and I drafted the letters, which is how a private soldier in the British Army came to issue orders to generals throughout the Middle East. A lot of my time, too, was devoted to maintaining a stock of tennis balls, racquets, and other vital sports supplies for officers' clubs during my tour of duty in Egypt in 1947.

I was introduced to the wonderful world of sex by a persuasive Egyptian belly dancer with a large family to support. I was a poor pupil, probably because I was scared sti ... er ... silly. Many years later when I was entertaining my colleagues in the dining room of the City Chambers with this and other stories I declared, 'I don't think you guys appreciate that people like me came out of the army trained killers!' I couldn't understand why they burst into hysterical laughter.

The year before the State of Israel came into existence in 1948 was not a good time for a Jewish soldier in the British Army in the Middle East. The British detested the Arabs and the Jews, the Arabs detested the British and the Jews, the Jews hated the British and the Arabs, and I was in the middle of it all.

There weren't all that many places to go in the immediate vicinity of my camp at Fayid, but I seem to recall looking furtively around whenever I wandered any distance from my tent in case someone decided to take a shot at me. It wasn't unusual for me to get the blame for Haganah or Irgun exploits. Haganah (the Hebrew word for defence) was the forerunner of the Israel Defence Forces. It was formed in 1920 in response to Arab attacks and British inability to defend Palestinian Jewry.

Irgun Zvai Leumi (national military organisation) was formed in 1931 because its leaders felt that a purely defence orgnisation was not enough. The organisation's objective was to obtain the admission to Palestine of Jews from the death camps of Europe. Later it focussed its attacks on the British

Mandatory authorities.

One of Irgun's exploits while I was in Egypt really generated hatred of anyone vaguely connected with Jews or Israelis: the hanging of two British Army sergeants. This was in response to the hanging of four Irgun men in Acre prison by the British authorities. It was a bad time for everyone in the Middle East.

While I was engulfed in indents for tennis balls and racquets my co-religionists who had survived the holocaust in Europe continued to arrive in Palestine, despite British efforts to keep them out. Then an event took place that shocked the world and reinforced the British government's decision five months earlier to hand over the Palestine problem to the United Nations. This was the voyage of the immigrant ship *Exodus* from France to Haifa and its enforced return to Germany with more than 4,000 Jewish refugees from all over Europe. The story of the voyage was to have echoes in my life 40 years later.

Chapter 4

CRIME
REPORTER

I CAME out of the army in February 1948. I had turned 21 only a couple of months earlier. The picture of my mother and Sheila waiting on the platform as I came off the train at Glasgow's Central Station is still vivid in my mind. Sheila hadn't seen me for more than a year and shyly hid behind my mother. We all hugged and kissed and went home to Gorbals. I also vividly recall the claustrophobic feeling that engulfed me when I went up the dingy close to our first-floor flat with its odd bits of furniture still in the bath.

I had spent three years in wide open spaces, seen Notre Dame Cathedral overlooking the Seine and the Great Sphinx and the Pyramids and Cairo and although I was glad to see my family I was also overcome with gloom at the thought of living in a place like Gorbals. I suppose like many other men I could have left home again to seek my fame and fortune elsewhere but I wanted to be with my family after such a long time away from them. I also missed the cameraderie of the barrack room and the tent.

A week or so after my return I went back to my old job as a junior reporter on the *Glasgow Herald*. Not long afterwards a banker was found dead early one morning in the garden of his elegant home in Bearsden. Every paper in the country had the story except mine. The Crime Reporter had fallen down on the job, an unforgiveable crime even on the unsensational *Herald*.

Tom Chalmers, the News Editor, called me to his room, a tiny space with a roll-top desk at the end of a large, gloomy room which reporters shuffled in and out of at all hours of the day and night. Chalmers was something akin to the Almighty in the Outram Group. That's the way he looked to me anyway from my vantage point as a lowly junior reporter.

Many stories circulated about how he had lost an eye but I never met anyone who could tell me exactly how it had happened. He wore a black patch like a pirate because, it was said, his glass eye exploded one day and nearly blinded someone he was talking to. Chalmers was the kind of man about whom stories like that were told.

'How would you like to be Crime Reporter?' he said.

The job required me to write three versions of every story, one for the *Herald*, another in a less formal way for our sister morning paper the *Bulletin*, and the third in a 'punchy' style for the group's evening paper the *Evening Times*. I was young and keen and touchingly grateful for the chance to show what I could do. It was also very good training. I can still write in a variety of styles, sometimes unintentionally, as you will possibly gather if you read the rest of this book.

Jimmy Paton, Chief Reporter of the *Bulletin*, vetted my stories before they went to the chief sub-editors of the two morning papers. It was Jimmy Paton, a good-humoured, fresh-faced man who came to Glasgow from Dundee in 1926, the year I was born, who taught me how to write a news story; that it should start in such a way that the reader will want to read on, and that it shouldn't ramble and be cluttered with unnecessary verbiage.

The title Crime Reporter was a bit grand for what I had to do. My job was to go round all the main police, fire and ambulance stations and hospitals in the city to try to pick up any kind of stories that were going. The hospital casualty departments were real war zones, especially the Victoria Infirmary, which was nearest to the notorious Gorbals. On Friday nights the Infirmary was packed with the victims of drunken battles. There were men and women waiting patiently on benches with broken legs, arms, jaws, and strips of pillowslips, curtains, and shirts stemming the blood from head wounds.

All the other newspapers in the city also had reporters doing the same nightly rounds as myself and the competition between us was fierce. I soon learned not to ask a question I had heard in many Hollywood films, 'Any statement for the press?' The answer one was most likely to get in the environment I worked was, 'Fuck the press.' One had to be direct in one's questions; and they had to be formed in a way that brought out the answer one wanted.

One night I went to see a robbery victim, a woman who operated an unlicensed money-lending business from her tenement home in the Bridgeton area of the city and who had been robbed earlier in the day. I knew she wasn't likely to be very forthcoming about how much the robbers had taken as she didn't want anyone but her clients to know about her business.

The door opened about two inches and one eye peeped out suspiciously. The conversation went like this:

'I'm a reporter missus. I hear you were robbed of a thousand pounds today.'

'It wiz £75.'

'It was three thugs, is that right?'

'It wiz only wan.'

'A wee fellow.'

'He wiz a big fella.'

'I hear he punched you in the face.'

'Naw, he jist pushed me into the hoose and demanded money.'

'That was the fourth time you've been robbed in a couple of months.'

'It wiz the second this year.'

The woman then slammed the door with the words, 'Ah'm telling you reporters nothin'!'

My nightly ritual started with a phone call round the potential news sources when I came on duty at 7.30pm. There were two telephone boxes, each about the size of a broom cupboard, built into a wall of the reporters' room. Each cupboard had a shelf on which rested a 'candlestick' telephone with a tubular-shaped earpiece that clipped onto the side of a column with a mouthpiece at the top. Not the kind of thing you would use to talk to an astronaut. The air, if that's the right word, was heavy with stale cigarettes and perspiration.

Immediately after the calls, which took up to an hour and yielded almost nothing, I did the rounds by car, came back for a meal if the volume of work allowed, rushed out again to do another round, and so on until about 2am, which was the deadline for the morning papers unless something really big broke.

Many nights I was so strung up with excitement and the desire not to miss anything that I raced up to the office canteen, bolted down a pie and greasy chips, rushed out again and brought it all up on the pavement.

Because of my frequent nocturnal visits to police stations I became friendly with many police officers, but I also became known to many ladies of the night who had been hauled in for 'hawking their mutton,' as it was inelegantly described by the hardened coppers.

This had unfortunate consequences sometimes. One evening after leaving the Empire Theatre I was walking down a busy Renfield Street with a well-brought-up young Jewish girl of whom I was very fond when we passed one of the ladies at the St Vincent Street coffee stall, which served as a kind of headquarters for prostitutes. She had a cleavage like an elephant's arse and a complexion to match.

'Helloooo rerr, Harry,' she drawled drunkenly.

'Friend of yours?' said my well-brought-up young Jewish girl, icily.

'You meet all kinds in my job,' I said nonchalantly.

'Huh, huh,' she said without much conviction.

A couple of weeks later we were walking down the same busy street when a police car, siren tearing the evening air apart, screeched to halt beside us and two policemen leapt out. 'That's him. Get him!' Each of them grabbed an arm and bundled me into their car, which raced off leaving a bewildered young lady on the pavement,

The car sped round a corner, stopped, and soon the young lady arrived at the corner drowning in tears. One of the coppers said, 'Talk your way out of that one, son!'

They watched my fruitless efforts for a couple of minutes and then had to intervene to tell the girl it was just a joke by a couple of friends.

Joke or no joke it was too much for the girl's mother who forbade her from going out with me again. It was bad enough being hailed by prostitutes, but being grabbed by policemen in front of everyone in the street was just too much. Besides, how could she boast to her bridge friends that her daughter was going with a junior reporter, not a lawyer or a doctor or an accountant?

The girl's mother wouldn't have been terribly impressed with another encounter I had. About 2am, on a very dark, wet morning I was driving to police headquarters in Turnbull Street when I saw a tall, slim, well-dressed young woman with a hand to her head swaying at the edge of the pavement. The world's dumbest reporter immediately thought, 'My goodness, a lady in distress. I must try to help her.'

I drew up beside her but before I could get out to enquire what was the matter the young woman was in the passenger seat. 'Take me up to St Vincent Street,' she drawled drunkenly. Jeez, what have I done, I thought. Where the hell did my brains go?

'Look, I'm a reporter and I'm going to police headquarters. You'd better get out.'

'Take me up to St Vincent Street,' she drawled again. 'I'll make it worth your while.'

A hand shot down to the front of my trousers. I pulled the hand away and told her again to get out. She wouldn't go, so I started the car and raced for the police office. The hand came back and wriggled past the buttons. Trousers didn't have zips in those days. For several hundred yards I tried to steer the car through the darkness and fight her off while she juggled with my crown jewels.

I couldn't be too tough with her as she would undoubtedly have created a helluva row in the street and I could have been arrested, even if I did have friends in the police. That would have been just great, the *Glasgow Herald*'s crime reporter in the pokey for fighting with a prostitute in the street in the middle of the night!

I raced into the police forecourt, jumped out of the car, almost leaving some of my vital organs behind, and ran into the office. Gasping for breath I told the lads what had happened and appealed for help.

'You must be joking,' said the desk sergeant. 'You have a good time and then want us to get rid of your lady friend. That'll be right.'

After a bit more pleading, however, a constable came out, dragged the woman out of the car, and told her to beat it before he locked her up. Even the world's dumbest reporter learned a valuable lesson that night.

Another night I was sitting in a deep armchair interviewing a very attractive young woman in a dressing gown about a stairway collapse when she came over and sat on the arm of my chair as I scribbled away in my wee notebook. At one point I turned to ask her something. The dressing gown had opened wide and my nose collided with her left breast. I jumped up as if I had been attacked by a scorpion and fled. When I told my colleagues about the incident their comments were pretty ribald. You could say they unanimously agreed that Mr Balfour had been right. I just didn't have the qualities of a real journalist.

For two years I raced round the city every night covering murders, accidents of every kind, fires, floods, gassings, bank robberies and jewel thefts. There was laughter, excitement, drama, and tragedy. Once I walked down a tenement stairway with tears running down my face. I had just talked to a couple whose daughter had been burned to death earlier that day, her fifth birthday, when her birthday dress had caught fire from an electric-bar heater. It was bad enough having to interview the parents but I also had to ask them for a picture of their daughter.

Understandably they refused, but as I was walking downstairs the mother came after me and handed me a beautiful picture of the girl with the words, 'You're only doing your job, son.' I can still see in my mind the child's picture on the front page of the *Bulletin*. That was the stuff of which human interest stories were made, and still are I suppose. If anyone in that family is still alive I hope they forgive me for my intrusion in their grief.

On another occasion I interviewed a woman whose young son was drowned in the Forth and Clyde Canal. When I muttered a few words of condolence she said, 'There's plenty more where he came from.' I didn't write that comment into my story.

I quickly learned to take a professional view of what I was doing, which meant distancing myself from other people's tragedies like a doctor or an ambulance man or a lawyer. I could still feel sorry for them but not to the extent that I worried about their problems. I had to develop a protective barrier.

One night I went to see a member of the famous Bluebell troupe of dancers whose trousseau had been stolen from her car. When I announced my identity at her front door she said, 'I'm sorry, I've sold my story to the *Daily Express*.' I talked my way into the house anyway and found sitting in the lounge the *Express* reporter, a young man named Magnus Magnusson, to whom she had sold her story, for five shillings. The three of us sat and talked and eventually I got my story, for nothing. Good thing, too. If I had tried to outbid Magnus I would have had to go to the international court at The Hague to get my money back from Tom Chalmers.

A fire in which 13 girls died stays in my memory for a number of reasons. Solomon Winetrobe, a 29-year-old ex-paratrooper, was manager of the stock records department of Grafton's fashion warehouse in Glasgow's busy Argyle Street when fire broke out one afternoon in the spring of 1949. The flames quickly spread through the building. Winetrobe was on the fourth storey along with some girl workers. Their route downstairs was cut off by the flames.

Winetrobe climbed out of a window on to a narrow ledge, grasped a rain pipe with one hand and with the other helped four girls out to the ledge and on to the roof of an adjoining cinema where his assistant, George Platt, grabbed at the girls and pulled them to safety. All of them then went down a fire-brigade ladder.

That night when myself and other reporters were fitting the many aspects of the story together I discovered that although we had received an account of Winetrobe's bravery from the Press Association, we didn't have an interview with Winetrobe or Platt.

This is where I had the kind of break that comes to a reporter only very rarely. The moment I heard Winetrobe's name I knew where to find him because his younger brother Raymond had been in my class in primary school and was my closest friend.

I went to their tenement flat in Gorbals, not far from my own home, and the boys' aunt opened the door.

'Aunty Sophie, I have to speak to Solly,' I pleaded. 'I have to get an interview with him for my paper.'

Aunty Sophie was unimpressed. 'You can't. He's sleeping.'

'Aunty Sophie, I can't go back without seeing Solly. My Editor will throw me out. I might even be fired.'

Aunty Sophie was still unimpressed. 'He has been through a terrible ordeal. The doctor has given him some sedatives. I can't wake him up.'

At that point Raymond, who had been out with me on assignments from time to time, came to my rescue and persuaded his aunt to let me in. It took us some time to wake Solly out of his heavily-sedated sleep but eventually he came to just enough to tell me in a whisper about his eventful day. My story of the fire and Solly's heroism took up the whole front page and most of page three.

Later that year Winetrobe and Platt were awarded the George Medal, the highest civilian bravery award. In February 1994 I went to Solomon Winetrobe's funeral. Much of the material for the obituaries which appeared in *The Herald* and other newspapers was taken from my original story.

Another fire in November 1968, long after I had left the sound and fury of daily newspaper production, had a profound effect on my father. Among the people killed in an upholstery warehouse in James Watt Street was Harry Ure, one of my father's closest friends who had come to Britain as a refugee about the same time as he. Twenty-two people died that night in the worst fire disaster in Glasgow since the 1939-45 war.

As Night and Crime Reporter I very often had to phone my stories from dark telephone boxes because there wasn't time to go back to the office to write them. My fingers were often burned by matches as I wrestled with the telephone and my notebook. Most of my travels about the city were done in the office car but once when it was not available I became the only reporter of a major newspaper group to be sent to a murder scene on a tramcar. The *Herald* believed in carefully husbanding its financial resources.

Friendly policemen phoned me at home when I was off duty to tip me off about a good story. One Sunday morning I received a cryptic message to go to a bank in Bridge Street. During the night some bandits went into an office above the bank, drilled a hole in the floor, put an umbrella through the hole and used it to catch debris as they widened the hole enough to wriggle through. Years later a very successful film about a bank raid was made. The method was exactly as I described it in my story.

The night job I had been doing was regarded as an apprenticeship and eventually, after I had served my time so to speak, I was transferred to the staff of the *Bulletin*. My job doing the rounds at night went to a clerk from a city-centre unemployment office who quickly became popular with the city's police and banditry because they knew he could be relied on rarely to reveal what either of them were doing.

One afternoon when I reported for duty Tom Chalmers handed me a brief teleprinter message from the Press Association. It said 'Attorney General announced in House of Commons no criminal proceedings against people who took Stone of Destiny from Westminster Abbey.'

It was the signal for every major every newspaper in the land to publish the stories they had been compiling for just such a day.

'See if you can find these people and get their stories,' said Chalmers.

'OK, where are they?'

'You're the reporter, you find them.'

It had taken months for an army of police on both sides of the border, and an even bigger army of reporters, to find the four students who created a sensation on Christmas Eve, 1950 by taking the Stone of Destiny, on which the ancient kings of Scotland were crowned, from Westminster Abbey.

By the time the Attorney General, Sir Hartley Shawcross, made his statement in the Commons on 1 April, 1951 the Scottish-based newspapers, and most of the London-based nationals, already had the students' story. But not the *Glasgow Herald*. The *Herald* didn't believe in devoting large resources to any story, let alone one which was tainted with Scottish nationalism, which the *Herald* hierarchy considered to be the province of the crank and the politically insignificant.

Sir Hartley's reason for taking no action against the students was that he did not think it was in the public interest that he should direct criminal proceedings to be taken. 'I have no desire to provide these individuals with the opportunity either of being regarded by their followers as martyrs if convicted or as heroes if they are not convicted.'

It has to be said that quite a lot of people didn't care a lot either way. Home Rule for Scotland meant nothing to them. One woman interviewed by a *Herald* reporter said, 'Devolution? Is that not something to do with Darwin?' Despite the disproportionate amount of clamour generated by a few people nowadays I still don't think most Scots would be better off with their own parliament.

There were another couple of reasons why young Diamond was given the job of finding the students. I had better police contacts than anyone else, having been crime reporter for two years, and the brutal truth is that, despite its long and distinguished history and the many talented journalists who had worked for it, there were not many *Herald* men accustomed to running about with notebooks and pencils looking for delinquent students. They were more used to spending most of their days covering meetings of one kind or another where the main qualification was the ability to take lengthy shorthand notes and transcribe them afterwards. The kind of thing I had been doing was alright for the lower orders of journalism but not for the superior men of the *Herald*.

So young Harry was given the task of finding Ian Hamilton (a Queen's Counsel for many years now), Gavin Vernon, Allan Stewart and Kay

Matheson. And I had only two or three hours to do it as all copy had to be in the caseroom by 8.30pm to catch the first edition.

I started my search at Glasgow University but discovered that Hamilton, Vernon and Stewart had been there talking to the reporters in the students' union but had gone. No-one knew where.

Filled with fear of failing to get my story, a capital offence in journalism, I went on a pub crawl in Byres Road. Someone up there must have been looking after me because I found the students after about the fourth pub and got my story, which of course led the front pages of both the *Herald* and the *Bulletin*.

Curiously enough, the Editor of the *Bulletin*, J M Reid, was a strong supporter of the nationalist movement and this was reflected in the newspaper. Although I was a *Bulletin* reporter and sub-editor for some years I did not agree with my newspaper's political views. It was not that I was interested in politics — the subject bored me rigid and it still does — but I was so often sent to cover Scottish Covenant meetings on a Saturday night and listen to people like 'King' John MacCormick, Chairman of the Scottish Covenanters, Oliver Brown, Roland Muirhead and others when I should have been out with my pals or a girlfriend.

For a time I raced all over the country writing stories about idiots blowing up letter boxes because they had little plaques on them with the letters 'EIIR' (Elizabeth Second Regina) when the idiots claimed that she was Elizabeth the First of Scotland and Elizabeth the Second of England only.

On two or three occasions I was enlisted by Special Branch as a secret intelligence agent. The spooks couldn't go to certain meetings of the nationalists because they were too obvious, but no-one in their mind could suspect me, a pale thin, timid reporter. My job was to tell Special Branch who was at the meetings and what they said.

Sir Victor Warren, Tory Lord Provost of Glasgow (they were called Progressives in those days) and an implacable foe of the Scottish Nationalists, had the front of his house daubed with the words, in very large letters, 'LONDON'S OFFICE BOY, SCOTLAND'S QUISLING', and in even larger letters underneath the word 'TRAITOR'. A picture of this piece of vandalism appeared in the paper with a sinister-looking figure in a dark hat, long coat and gloves peering at it closely — Harry Diamond.

Warren had been elected Lord Provost on 6 May, 1949 by one vote. Although Labour had a majority of members in the council they took the huff at an opposition member being elected Lord Provost and gave up control of the city after a rule of 15 years.

In the middle of all this I remember two stories I had to write, much to the amusement of my colleagues. One was about a live monkey and a book-keeping machine which were among items handed in to Glasgow Police lost property department and the other was about a man who was taken to hospital with a fractured skull after a cistern fell on his head when he pulled the lavatory chain. This was not the kind of thing that brought down governments or got presidents impeached but it was fun. Apropos nothing, the entire day's radio programmes occupied four single-column inches in those days. Television was yet to come.

In the years that followed I covered disasters on land, sea and air, and wrote about royalty, prime ministers, princes of industry and rogues, some of whom were indistinguishable from one another. I interviewed film and stage stars like Dean Martin and Jerry Lewis, Abbott and Costello, Danny Kaye, Johnny Ray, Guy Mitchell, playboys, playgirls, sportsmen, millionaires, paupers, crooks, cranks with talking dogs, and people who claimed to be the reincarnation of everyone from Henry VIII to Count Dracula.

Reporting a royal visit I wrote that the Queen wore a hat and coat and when I couldn't explain them in detail our women's editor exclaimed contemptuously, 'You stupid boy.' Years later when I was chief sub-editor I had to tell her to change a horse-riding story which started, 'Miss Charlotte Drink-Waters was mounted last night by Colonel Featherstonehaugh-McGinty ... ' The names have been changed to protect the guilty. I had a helluva job trying to tell her why she should change the introduction but I didn't tell her she was a stupid woman. She was just pure minded, a characteristic not common in newspapers.

Once, I was at a wedding reception with my mother when a friend of hers looked me up and down with a critical eye and asked,

'Voddus he do?'

'He's a reporter,' said my mother.

'A porter?' said her uncomprehending friend. 'Vot kind of job is dat for a Jewish boy?'

In the early 1950s I met my first hard-boiled American colleagues when a wee man the newspapers described as an 'odd job man' from Maryland woke up one morning to discover he had become Sir Adrian Ivor Dunbar when a distant relative died in Wigtownshire. Sir Adrian hurried to Scotland to claim his baronetcy followed by a posse of journalists. My news editor sent me there, too, to chronicle Sir Adrian's adventures.

Among the Americans was Bob Musel of the Associated Press of America, a short, burly man inseparable from his black, wide-brimmed hat and black raincoat. Bob could have stepped straight out of a Hollywood gangster film. Despite his sinister appearance he was a talented, good-humoured man and his daily despatches on the comings and goings of Sir Adrian testified to his gifted imagination. I learned a lot from him! Bob was also a song-writer. One of them was 'Pappa Piccolino', which had quite a lot of success on both sides of the Atlantic.

I have met many American journalists since then and have even been interviewed by a few of them, and almost without exception they have been men and women of exceptional ability and great fun to work with. Some of them have become personal friends like R W (Johnny) Apple of the *New York Times*, Stanley Meisler of the *Los Angeles Times*, Bob Erburu, Chairman and Chief Executive of the Times Mirror group, and Israel Shenker, author and former European correspondent of *Time* magazine who now lives in Scotland.

In 1985 Johnny Apple wrote to tell me he had been appointed chief correspondent in Washington of the *New York Times* and added, 'Wherever again will I be associated with a success story like Glasgow and the Burrell?'

In 1988 I met an American couple, Harvey and Myrna Frommer, a husband and wife writing team, who came to Glasgow to write about the Jewish community of Scotland. I was with them only a few hours showing them something of the city but we formed an enduring friendship. In August 1995 I went to New York at their invitation and stayed with them in their home on Long Island for a couple of weeks. They were generous with their time and lavish with their hospitality and I spent one of the best holidays of my life with them.

None of the stories I covered as a reporter reshaped the world in any way but I enjoyed it all, especially when I saw my name on a story. That made me a celebrity in the particular level of society in which I lived and moved.

For a few months my name and a caricature of me appeared every day as the paper's gossip columnist. 'Diamond's Diary' my page was called. The cartoon was drawn by a very clever cartoonist named John Jensen and portrayed me with a rather prominent nose. The caricature also appeared on posters outside newsagents' shops throughout the country. One day my mother came back from her daily errands furious with indignation because, she said, I was plastered all over the country looking like a big-nosed, chinless idiot.

She wanted me to sue the paper for defamation of character! I told her, 'Don't you mean definition of character, mum?' but this went over her head. I tried to explain that the paper was making her son famous but she was unimpressed.

I wasn't a great success as a gossip columnist as I was no William Hickey and had no desire to spend my nights in restaurants, receptions and night clubs and looking through keyholes.

Chapter 5

THE IDIOT WHO CUT HARBEN'S RECIPE

IN MY day it was the ambition of most young newspapermen in the provinces to graduate to Fleet Street, where all the famous national newspapers were located. I remember one day during the 1939-45 war walking there with my cousin Frank, an accountant, when I looked up at the *Daily Telegraph* building and said wistfully, 'Some day I hope to be up there.'

'Fire watching?' said Frank.

I never did get to Fleet Street but I did get near it. During one visit to London some years later, after I had become a sub-editor on the *Bulletin*, someone told me that Jimmy Drawbell, Managing Editor of *Woman's Own* was always on the lookout for bright young men, especially Scots. He himself came from Edinburgh or thereabouts. I managed to get to see Drawbell, who was known as king of the women's magazines, and to my great surprise he offered me a job as Deputy Chief Sub-editor. Drawbell had wrought miracles with the magazine, taking it from a circulation of 300,000 to 3 million and making it one of the largest-selling women's magazines in the world.

Among the people who wrote for *Woman's Own* in those days were some who went on to even greater fame: Katherine Whitehorn, Correlli Barnett, who became a military historian and Keeper of the Churchill Archives, and author James Leasor. The Rev David Sheppard, later Bishop of Liverpool, was a popular columnist. One other person I remember, with good reason, was Philip Harben, a well-known stage and television chef, whose recipes were said to be eagerly awaited each week by countless breathless housewives.

Within days of my installation at *Woman's Own* I realised I had made a terrible mistake. I had been a hard-bitten Glasgow newsman and was

36

expected to edit stories and articles that appealed to girls whose intellectual horizons were limited, to say the least. Although hundreds of letters came in each week for Mary Grant, the magazine's agony aunt, the themes of many of the letters were monotonously repetitive, 'Should I let my boyfriend do this and that? ... Should I go on holiday with him? ... What do I do about my pimples? ... ', and members of the staff, including myself, often had to think up something different for Mary Grant to pontificate on. I have to admit I was not good at thinking up problems for young girls.

Besides, I had enough problems of my own. By this time I was married and missed my wife Jacqueline and our two sons Harvie and Michael who were still in Glasgow. All the free time I had was occupied with looking for somewhere for us to live.

Some of the intricate page designs in the magazine made editing very difficult. Items had to be fitted into the most awkward little spaces. On one occasion I had to cut a few words out of a Philip Harben recipe to make it fit the space allocated to it by a designer who knew very little about cooking, or anything else relating to the printed word. Cutting a recipe by Philip Harben was a crime akin at the very least to the cutting job visited upon Mr John Bobbitt's vitals many years later by his wife Loretta. I went to the page designer and told him the Harben recipe wouldn't fit the space he had allowed for it and his reponse was to the effect that the problem was mine, not his.

No sooner had the magazine hit the streets when an irate Mr Harben phoned to talk to the 'stupid fucking idiot' who had ruthlessly reduced his recipe to unintelligible rubbish. My defence that I had cut only three or four completely superfluous words did not placate the celebrated juggler of pots and pans. Jimmy Drawbell called me into his office and implied that Mr Harben was of more value to the world of women's magazines than I was and please would I stay away from his recipes in future.

One afternoon I happened to leave the office at the same time as two very beautiful girls who had been in to be photographed. I walked between them in the Strand wishing like hell that some of my old colleagues in Glasgow could have seen me. I was swinging an umbrella nonchalantly when the point of the brolly went into a hole in the pavement and I fell flat on my face. The two visions of loveliness glanced disdainfully down and walked on, twittering brightly.

The crunch came one day when I was editing a story about a girl who had come into the office complaining that she could do nothing with her hair, which resembled the stuffing in an old sofa. The magazine called in a fashionable London hairdresser who transformed the scraggy cockney waif into a beautifully-coiffeured cockney waif. Halfway through editing this I murmured, 'Why the hell am I doing this? This is not what I came to London for.'

I dropped my pencil on the desk, put on my coat, and walked out the door. I spent the next few days being thrown out of various Fleet Street newspaper offices and at the end of the week I took a train home to Glasgow. I went into the *Bulletin* office and was hailed by my old colleagues as the conquering hero from the big city. Comyn Webster, the Editor, wandered into the room and called me into his office.

'Did you jump or were you pushed?' he enquired. Bad news travels fast in the newspaper business.

'I jumped.'

'Have you got a job?'

'No.'

'Do you want to come back here?'

Relief flooded over me.

'Yes please.'

'Start on Sunday.'

I went back to the sub-editors' room and that was the last time I tried to break into the London big time. Eventually I became Chief Sub-editor, a very important job on a newspaper but one about which the public know very little. My salary was £1,200 a year. About the same time a pupil barrister in London named Robin Day was making 200 guineas a year and another young man named Michael Heseltine was an undergraduate at Pembroke College, Oxford.

The job of Chief Sub-editor varies slightly from paper to paper but my job was to decide the page and position of stories that poured in all day and night. Sometimes the editor and I liaised on what the page-one lead story should be if it wasn't blindingly obvious.

One night I gave one of my sub-editors a story from a news agency to edit about a doctor who had appeared before a disciplinary committee for some transgression of his profession's ethics. Asked by the tribunal about his qualifications he said he couldn't produce them because his dog had chewed them up.

The first edition of the paper came up while everyone else was at supper and I was turning over the pages to check that everything was in order when I came to a headline across eight columns which read 'DOG CHEWED DOCTOR'S TESTIMONIALS'. I'm the only one I've ever known outside Hollywood who ever picked up the phone and shouted 'Stop the presses!'

In the report of a youth club meeting one of our reporters wrote: 'The secretary said she hoped all the boys appreciated how lucky they were to have got so many lovely girls in the club.'

The *Bulletin* ceased publication on 2 July, 1960 after a life of 45 years during which it created an affectionate place for itself in Scottish journalism. A few weeks earlier Comyn Webster, the Editor, told me that David Keir, his deputy, was retiring and asked me if I would like his job. This put me in a quandary. John Blackwood, a former colleague in Outram and Deputy Editor of the *Scottish Daily Mail* in Edinburgh had offered me the job of Deputy Chief Sub-editor. Although I was Chief Sub-editor of the *Bulletin* the *Mail* job was a much bigger one. I had agonised for weeks over Blackwood's offer and couldn't make up my mind.

When Comyn Webster made his offer I told him about the one from John Blackwood and said, 'You know there have been a lot of rumours about the fate of the *Bulletin*. Will there be any paper for me to be Deputy Editor of this time next year?'

Comyn stared out the window for a minute or two and said, 'Take John's offer.'

Although many people looked on the *Bulletin* as a rather genteel picture paper more suitable to the tastes of elderly ladies, analysis of its pages will reveal that the men who ran it had a first-class news sense, not only for what was news at the time but for what was likely to develop into stories of significance.

Mind you, the paper did give prominence to some real trivia, which helped to generate its rather twee reputation. Page leads told its readers the best way to make tea, the correct way to carry a handbag, and what sex of budgerigar to buy.

Much of the credit for the more authoritative side of the paper must go to John Downie, Chief Sub-editor and later Night Editor, whom I've already described as one of the best journalists I ever had the good fortune to work with. He was chief sub-editor when I joined the sub-editors' table. Unmarried, he lived only for the job, and expected everyone else to do the same. One night I mentioned to a colleague that I was tired because I had been hanging wallpaper before I came in. John went off the deep end. 'You should get someone else to do that kind of thing. You are supposed to keep your energies for the job that gives you a living. This job requires concentration, not people coming in tired from hanging wallpaper!'

None of us took any notice of that kind of thing, for all the obvious reasons and because John had rather weird ideas about a number of things, women being one of them. That didn't prevent him from getting married in, I think, his forties. Understandably his attitude changed then.

The other daily newspapers were watching the situation closely and were determined to take advantage of the closure of the *Bulletin*. Donald Todhunter, Editor of the *Scottish Daily Mail*, sent the following note to all his senior editorial staff:

'This time it really looks as if the *Bulletin* is going under. I am drafting this memo so that you are all in the picture on what this move could mean to the *Scottish Daily Mail*.

Circulationwise out of its sale of roughly 100,000 the *Bulletin* appears to sell to 40,000 people who read no other paper. Therefore allowing for normal evaporation there could be at least 30,000 sales to be gained in the dogfight between the rest of the papers.

Apart from a publicity campaign to be accompanied by features and competitions extra effort is clearly needed on the news and sports pages in order to appeal to the kind of reader who for years has bought the *Bulletin*.

Primarily this appeal lies in the wider use of pictures, particularly the expressive, non-newsy kind, pretty girls, weddings, etc, women's sport, what is going on in the women's organisations and local society gossip. If the speculative closure date of 2 July proves correct we need to start slanting our appearance slightly towards the *Bulletin* reader right away. Obviously this does not mean losing our own character in the process, but with an event of this size in the offing I would like you all to think along these lines and make your own contribution towards winning as much as we can of the extra sales which will become available.'

From what I remember the *Mail* didn't make a very good job of catering for *Bulletin* readers and in the fulness of time its printing operation in Edinburgh closed down. Donald Todhunter was right on target on the *Bulletin*'s closure date. The company said it had been losing money, which was probably quite true, but the way I heard it certain *Herald* and *Evening Times* costs were unfairly charged to the *Bulletin* making it uneconomic to sustain. Some of my contemporaries felt it could have competed successfully, at least for another few years, with the popular papers like the *Express*, *Record* and *Mail* if resources had been devoted to it but I don't think the Outram board cared about the *Bulletin* and a newspaper needs a certain attitude of mind, not just money, to make it successful in a highly-competitive business.

The fact that the *Bulletin* had a special place in the affections of the Scottish public was more than proved 20 years later when I brought back the title, with of course the permission of a totally different Outram board, as the newspaper of Glasgow City Council, but more of that later.

My father's war-time identity card which he had to carry as a Russian alien.

My mother a long time ago.

THE EVENING TIMES
SCOTLAND'S GREATEST EVENING NEWSPAPER.

65 Buchanan Street.

Telephone:
CENTRAL 9200.

GLASGOW, C.1.   March 8, 1944.

Mr. Henry Diamond,
130, Abbotsford Place,
G L A S G O W.

Dear Sir,

     Following your interview here yesterday we offer you a temporary appointment as telephone clerk and editorial messenger at a wage of 25/. a week.   Perhaps you would be good enough to let me know if you accept this offer.

     If so could you report for duty to Miss Anderson in the Telephone Room at 9 a.m. on Monday 13th inst?

Yours faithfully,

J. P. Ingli   EDITOR.

I got a raise before I left 16 years later!

LEFT: As a young soldier in 1945 with my mother and young sister Sheila.
ABOVE: Egypt, 1947.

Among the crowd on the left waiting for news of the 129 men trapped underground at Knockshinnoch Castle Colliery disaster in 1950. All but 13 were rescued.

Writing furiously while interviewing students Gavin Vernon, Ian Hamilton and Allan Stewart who took the Stone of Destiny from Westminster Abbey in 1950.

At the home of Lord Provost Victor Warren who was not popular with Scottish Nationalists in 1951, or at any other time.

With Honor Blackman when we were both a lot younger.

My friend Phillip Seltzer's story is told in the Sunday Mirror *under the rather lurid title of 'Hell is My Surgery'.*

My young sister Sheila insisted on coming with me when I interviewed American singer Johnny Ray.

With a young Rolf Harris.

Hollywood star Telly Savalas and friend in the City Chambers.

One way to get rid of a car that's giving you trouble.

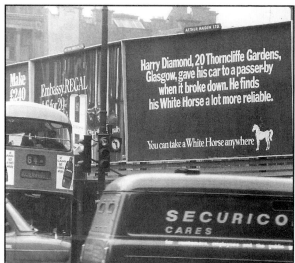

Make £240

Embassy REGAL 14 for 20p

Harry Diamond, 20 Thorncliffe Gardens, Glasgow, gave his car to a passer-by when it broke down. He finds his White Horse a lot more reliable.

You can take a White Horse anywhere

SECURICO CARES

Mary Marquis interviews me on BBC television about the growth of Chinese restaurants in Scotland.

The Jewish and Church of Scotland members of the committee whose deliberations brought about the Common Statement on the evils of anti-semitism.

Archbishop (now Cardinal) Winning, right, signs a letter of support at the biggest write-in for Soviet Jewry ever held in Britain.

With Lord Provost Michael Kelly and Opposition Leader Neil Kinnock.

LEFT: *A special edition of the* Glasgow Herald *which I masterminded for a 'Glasgow Week in Hamburg' promotion in 1974.*
BELOW: *American banker Norman Eckersley tells a press conference, 'I'll help to promote Glasgow in California.'*

I was with the *Mail* in Edinburgh about six months when I decided I had had enough. We had five editions a night in an effort to compete with the *Express* and *Record* in Glasgow, and our five editions were produced in an unnerving atmosphere of frenzy. The Chief Sub-editor was a man named Jack Sutherland, a real eccentric, but a very clever technician. As his deputy I sat beside him and watched him design page after page at the speed of light. He worked so fast I couldn't even follow what he was doing. One night he didn't come in and I almost had a fit when John Blackwood told me to take over. One of my first acts was to put a fairly large picture story on two pages in the same edition, an easy thing to do if you're not careful.

One night I shouted across the crowded newsroom to a reporter, 'Hurry up with that robbery story.'

'Another few minutes, Harry. I haven't got all the facts yet.'

'Never mind the fucking facts, just give me the story,' I shouted back, a remark that is quoted back at me to this day.

One afternoon a telephone call from London asked me to book a room for a member of the board of Associated Newspapers, the company that owned the *Mail,* who was coming to Glasgow for a couple of days. I was in no mood for this kind of thing as I considered my job harassing enough, but it was my own fault as I was the one who happened to pick up the phone.

I booked a room in the Central Hotel, one of the few half-decent hotels in the city at the time and, in a mischievous moment, told the London caller, 'Tell Mr Thing to go to the Great Eastern Hotel.'

The next evening our immaculate, bowler-hatted director came out of the railway station, swanned elegantly into a taxi, and told the driver loftily, 'The Great Eastern Hotel, please.'

'Eh?' said the driver.

'Great Eastern Hotel,' repeated the director.

'Ur ye sure?' said the taxi driver.

'Of course I'm sure,' said Mr Thing.

'Aye right, Jimmy,' said the driver, and took Mr Thing to the Great Eastern Hotel, a model lodging house in the East End of the city.

Mr Thing took one look at the building, which looked like a prison, and said plaintively, 'There must be some mistake.' He phoned our office and after a few minutes of confusion was told he should have gone to the Central Hotel. Later I managed to persuade a secretary in London that she had misheard me.

During my months in Edinburgh I got home to see my wife Jackie and our two boys only at week-ends. I had an uncomfortable ride in a delivery van early on Saturday morning and another uncomfortable ride back on

Sunday evening. I was living in a room in a large house in Bruntsfield. In the room through the wall there were two girl students whose record player started up at 7am. As I got back to my digs about 4am I didn't get much sleep. Appeals to their better nature went unheeded.

Eventually I wrote to Roger Wood, Editor of the *Scottish Daily Express* in Glasgow to ask for a job. Roger was a tough Londoner who had been brought north to liven up the paper. He certainly did that. His interviewing technique was novel.

'Why should I give you a job?'

'Because I need it and because even the *Scottish Daily Express* can use another good sub-editor,' I said.

'Start on Monday,' said Roger.

One night in the caseroom I was inspecting a rather uninteresting page when Roger looked over my shoulder and said in a voice that reverberated round the busy room, 'I can get a fucking clerk to do that,' meaning design a dull-looking page. As it had been designed by one of Roger's own bright boys he had brought from London with him I got a bit annoyed at the implication that it was me.

I crumpled the page, thrust it at Roger's clean white shirt, and said in my best cockney voice, 'Then get a fucking clerk to do it,' and strode off to the cheers of the caseroom staff. People just didn't talk to Roger like that and for the rest of the night I really expected to be fired at any moment, but nothing happened.

Another night I was editing a very lengthy story about a woman who was sent to a lunatic asylum by the High Court for dropping children out of a tenement building. It was hard going because I had to cut quite a lot of the copy to make it fit the space allocated to the story. I was getting very nervy because the edition deadline was fast approaching when Roger tapped me imperiously on the shoulder and said, 'Are you nearly finished?' Before I could stop myself I swung round and said 'Beat it, I'm busy.' As soon as it was out I expected the ceiling to fall on me but again nothing happened.

A few nights later I was given a story to edit about a primary school where every pupil had failed an English examination. I put a headline across six columns reading 'NOT WUN PAPER WOS RITE'. Roger went pale when he saw the headline but after thinking about it he had a dramatic change of mind and gave me a £10 bonus at the end of the week.

It was during this period in my newspaper career that I could easily have become an alcoholic. Every evening when the first edition of the paper was being put to bed I went down to the pub next door to the office with some colleagues in what was supposed to be our supper break and put away several rum and cokes before going back to the strains and stresses of another three or four editions of the paper. Some wonderful editing took place as the rum and cokes took effect.

Most of the editors I've known liked to write memos to underlings telling them what a great job they were doing or that they had botched something. This is a sample from Ian McColl, who succeeded Roger Wood as Editor of the *Scottish Daily Express* and later became Editor of the *Daily Express* in London. It was dated 14 November, 1962 and addressed to reporters and sub-editors.

'I call your attention to a disturbing trend in the preparation of stories and headlines. While our main competitor the *Daily Record* is emphasising the human element whenever possible we are subordinating it. I want to see the trend reversed, promptly. I do not believe that readers are primarily interested in the fifth accident having taken place in six years on a stretch of road rather than in the fact that a mother was out shopping when she was told her toddler son had been killed on the way to nursery school.

On this basis, too, we should have re-shaped our story of the man who died four hours after starting a new job. We should have angled it on the wife. I wanted to know how long he had been unemployed, how difficult things had been for her and the family, whether she had been overjoyed to find that he had work again, how her happiness was shattered … '

The memo ended, 'This newspaper has always had a reputation of maintaining a warm, friendly, kindly bond with its readers. When its approach to the news, whether in writing or headline seems metallic or clinical, it loosens that bond.'

Thus are formed the policies and philosophies of our great organs of public opinion. Having said all that I enjoyed my two years with the *Express* and made many friends, including Ian McColl.

Letters to the editor are useful in that they tell a newspaper what its readers think about its contents and whatever else interests them. A full list of letters and their contents was compiled for the daily editor's conference which is attended by the news editor and other members of the editorial and circulation hierarchy to determine a rough outline of what the following morning's paper will contain.

This is a sample of the list of letters in my day:

Malcolm Sinclair, James Nesbit Street, Glasgow, feels the translation of the New Testament is of no importance.

G Easson, Ullapool, wants the press to campaign for development of the

Highlands.

Mrs Isla Nicoll, Craigie Road, Perth, dislikes sticking to the rules of grammar.

Mr Adie, Kirkintilloch, says his wife felt cheated because the Paterson-Johannsson fight did not go 15 rounds.

Ellenor Lynch, Stepps Garage, is sure the Russians will beat America and the world into space.

D Campbell, Bruce Street, Greenock, does not trust Dr Adenauer.

Perhaps the most dramatic moment of my life in journalism occurred early on the morning of Thursday, 25 October, 1962. A couple of days earlier President John F Kennedy had imposed a blockade on Cuba to prevent any more Soviet ships taking arms and missiles to the island from which they could have struck at the heart of America.

About three or four o'clock that Thursday morning I was in a little room with Ian McColl and one or two others listening intently to a small short-wave radio on which an American commentator was giving a minute-by-minute account of the progress of Soviet arms-carrying ships sailing towards Cuba.

I had pencil poised over a wad of copy paper ready to write a front-page story for a special edition we would put out if the Soviet ships tried to get past the American destroyers. All of us in that room knew that if the Soviets tried to defy the blockade there was every possibility of a nuclear war.

Eventually the commentator announced that the Soviet ships were turning back and we all sat back with a sigh of relief. I vividly recall sitting on the night bus home thinking how little the few other passengers knew of the night's events and how their lives could have been dramatically changed if we had been plunged into another global conflict. This was the kind of thing that journalism meant for me: the drama, excitement and suspense that few other jobs could offer.

But moments like these were few and far between and although I enjoyed my two years with the *Express* I decided that 20 years of unsocial hours, hurried meals, and fighting deadlines was enough. The fervour with which I had started in the glamorous world of newspapers had worn off. I wasn't spending enough time with Jackie and the boys and to get any farther in the editorial hierarchy of the *Scottish Daily Express* I would have had to spend even more time on the job to demonstrate my commitment to the paper. I wasn't prepared to do this.

Chapter 6

DOCTOR IN THE GORBALS

DURING my two years with the *Express* I wrote a book in collaboration with a friend, Phillip Seltzer, whose medical practice was in Gorbals. Phillip was also my own general practitioner. Once when I was subjected to a lot of pressure at work and was feeling some anxiety he said, 'Go for a drive in the country and watch the cows grazing. They don't have any anxieties. Would you like to be one of them?' Not a very scientific observation on my condition but I went away cured!

Phillip was a burly, good-humoured, dedicated man with a big black moustache like the Hollywood version of a Mexican bandit. He used to tell me the most bizarre stories about his patients.

'Gorbals was a wonderful place to practise medicine,' he said. 'It contained every medical condition from the common cold to rare nervous diseases and was so overcrowded that disease spread quickly from person to person. It was a challenge to any doctor to see what he could do to ease the terrible plight of the people who lived there.'

One day I suggested we collaborate on a book about his adventures, which we did, but Phillip's epic struggle against disease in Gorbals did not appeal to a number of London publishers to whom it was submitted. They said it was too localized in scope. Six years later Dr Gladstone Robertson had a book published called *Gorbals Doctor*, a poor thing compared with ours.

For several months I carried a heavy Grundig tape recorder by tramcar to Phillip's house most afternoons and taped his stories. I slept for a few hours when I came home from the *Express* about 4am, went to Phillip's for a two-hour session in the afternoon, went home for a quick meal, and then went into the office for another demanding night of tension working against deadlines. Jackie put up with all this without a word of complaint. She accepted that this was the kind of idiotic life that made me happy.

Eventually we had a manuscript called *Not For Their Hurt*, a rather pretentious phrase from the Hippocratic Oath that doctors agree to observe.

45

The author's name was given as Michael Harvie, the names of my two sons.

After the publishers rejected our manuscript I sent a couple of chapters to the editor of the *Sunday Mirror* and almost before I got back from the postbox there was a *Sunday Mirror* man at the door wanting more. The newspaper paid us £600 and Phillip's story appeared as a four-part series under the lurid title 'Hell is my Surgery'.

I didn't offer the story to the *Express* as I knew they wouldn't pay us as much as one of the more sensational London newspapers who were trying to work up their circulation in Scotland.

Sandy Webster, editor of the *Sunday Mail* at the time, bawled me out on an underground train, 'I would have given you £100 for the story,' he shouted across a crowded carriage. Sandy didn't give money away lightly.

Mrs Alice Cullen, Member of Parliament for Gorbals went berserk at the 'totally unjustified slur on the good people of Gorbals' as she described it to the General Medical Council, the doctors' disciplinary body.

'Is any of it untrue?' she was asked.

'It's all lies,' said the faithful Mrs Cullen, a statement she was unable to substantiate. In view of the fact that Phillip wasn't identified and we didn't use any real names Mrs Cullen's complaint was thrown out.

I've read a lot over the years of the warmth, generosity and compassion of the Gorbalonians of those days; sentimental, nostalgic drivel. There were many respectable, hard-working people there but there were many others who would cut your throat for the price of a packet of cigarettes.

Phillip Seltzer cared for them all. His own compassion knew no bounds. Sometimes he saw such shocking conditions in a house where someone just could not be helped for one reason or another that he punched the wall of the close in frustration when he came out.

The year he started to practise there, about 18 months after he came out of the Royal Air Force, Gorbals covered 252 acres and had a population of 36,000 people. In the same year the town of Falkirk, only a few miles away, had 37,500 people living in 4,035 acres. The Lanarkshire town of Airdrie, which was even nearer, had 30,500 in 2,068 acres.

The plight of many young mothers and babies gave Phillip Seltzer a lot of worry. Many of the girls weren't married. In an area where so many people lived so closely together it was not surprising that the propagation of the species was such a popular diversion. Early one morning a woman phoned to say, 'Wull ye come doon and see Moira Kelly, doctor.'

'Yes, what's wrong?'

'Ah don't know,' said the caller. 'She just gave me a shout when ah wis goin' tae ma work. She just said she waanted ye to come doon.'

Phillip climbed the winding, damp-smelling stairway to the third-storey tenement flat. A lodger opened the door and he went to Moira's room. The pale morning light struggled through the grimy window. The furniture consisted of a bed, a wooden kitchen chair, and a small chest of drawers. A bare, 40-watt bulb hung from the dejected grey ceiling.

Moira was on the bed covered by a single grimy blanket. Her face was pale and her lank brown hair lay lifeless on the pillow. She was about 19.

'Oi t'ink oi've had a baby,' she said. Her accent was as thick as the bog in her native Ireland.

'What do you mean you think you've had a baby?' asked Phillip. 'Don't you know?'

He pulled back the blanket and found a new-born baby, kicking brightly in a pool of half-dried blood between the girl's legs. His skin was light brown.

'When did this happen?' asked Phillip.

'In the middle of the noight doctor.'

'Why didn't you call for help? There are other people in the house.'

'Och, oi didn't loike to make a fuss so oi just waited until the mornin'.'

Mother and baby miraculously survived.

Despite the poverty of Gorbals, gambling was endemic. For years Glasgow was one of heaviest betting areas in Britain. The number of bookmakers was drastically cut by the legalising of betting shops on 1 May, 1961. On that day there were 409 licensed betting shops in Glasgow. London, with nine times the population, had about 200 shops.

Not far from Phillip's surgery was a tenement flat that served as a bookie's headquarters. Two tall, tough-looking men guarded the entrance to the close. They wore hard-wearing brown suits and just stood there hour after hour with jacket collars turned up, caps well down over their foreheads, rubbing and blowing their big, raw-boned hands. They never wore coats, even in the most severe weather. If it rained or snowed they stood inside the close gazing mutely out.

One day Phillip's wife Rhoda took a telephone call from the bookie's house.

'The doactor's waantit doon here urgent,' said a hoarse voice. 'It's no' a health service call. It's private and we waant the doactor tae come hissel.'

Phillip later described the incident:

'I climbed out of my car and walked to the close. As I entered the two watchdogs looked me up and down with cold, expressionless eyes and fell in behind me. Wordlessly they followed me up the stairs. I felt like someone in an American gangster movie about to be taken for a ride.

The flat had two rooms and a kitchen. The rooms had been stripped bare except for some long tables on which rested several telephones. In a bed recess in the kitchen a man lay drenched in blood.

A fairly well-dressed wee man at the bedside said, "Will ye jist fix him up doctor. Nae questions, eh?"

The injured man was an obvious hospital case. The wee man smiled apologetically. "Er, ah'm afraid ye'll huv tae fix him up here doctor. Jist wan of them things ye know. Kinda awkward like. Don't worry about the expense doc. It's no a health service job. Jist fix him up nice."

I argued a bit more but there were mysterious reasons why the man couldn't go hospital. Eventually I rolled up my sleeves and stitched up a very deep head wound. A sewing machine would have been very handy. As I worked an occasional knock came at the kitchen door and a head poked round to enquire, "How's it goin'?"

The job took some time but the man didn't bat an eyelid even though I was stitching away without an anaesthetic. He was so drunk he didn't feel a twinge. By the time I was finished with him he had more bandages than King Tutenkhamen.

"That's fine," said the wee man. "We'll just get him hame noo."

"What!" I exploded. "You can't move him. He's in a bad way."

"That's awright doc. Don't worry about it. We'll see him awright."

A taxi and bodyguards were summoned and the man was trundled downstairs and bundled into the cab. Someone put a soft hat on his head in an effort to cover the bandages. He looked like the invisible man. As the taxi drove away into the night I expected to hear the director shout "Cut" in the best Hollywood tradition.

I never saw the man again but I was told he lived to fight again. His assailant was dealt with privately, without the assistance of the police. It was not the done thing to call the police into these private disagreements. They were settled quietly and without juridical delay but the settlements always meant a lot of work for hospital casualty surgeons.'

For some time Phillip was physician to a Glasgow theatre, looking after the medical needs of the various showpeople who came to play there. He didn't find much glamour in the job.

'Show business people can have a great nuisance value,' he told me. 'They make constant demands for special injections and treatments, for tranquillisers to calm them down and energisers to pep them up again.'

One famous singer haunted him all the time he was in Glasgow. His particular obsession was for throat sprays. He had only to hear about something that was supposed to be good for keeping his voice in trim and he was down to the surgery in a flash.

Among the people who came to the theatre was a troupe of famous dancing girls. Most of them were well-developed children not long out of dancing school. Whenever Phillip went into the theatre during rehearsals every one of them would come to him with some little complaint or other. All they wanted was a little bit of sympathy and they looked on Phillip as a father figure.

One girl phoned him at 3am. Weeping bitterly she said he had had a tooth out and it was hurting her. She was only 16 and this was her first job away from home and she was lonely. There was another 16-year-old girl in the lodgings with her, but as she was also lonely they weren't much comfort to each other.

One girl went onstage while she was having a miscarriage, despite Phillip's strict instruction to go to bed. How she got through the show was a mystery as she had lost a lot of blood. She couldn't tell the troupe leader as she would have lost her job and there were always a lot of girls desperate to get into the troupe.

Glaswegians are rarely stuck for a word to describe their symptoms. Their vocabularies may not be extensive but they are certainly imaginative.

One word that cropped up early in Phillip's career fascinated him.

'It sounded so authentic I thought I had somehow missed it during my medical training,' he said. 'I went to the length of searching for it in several medical dictionaries, but of course it didn't exist.' The word was 'defluction,' which was used to describe phlegm.

'I don't know how it came to be coined but it should certainly be absorbed into the language,' said Phillip. 'It sounds too onomatopoeic. People who suffered from brown kittles (bronchitis) are always having difficulty in getting rid of their defluction.'

Children were often described as 'towtie.' They took a towt of this or a towt of that; in other words they were susceptible to bouts of minor illnesses. Almost every day anxious mothers phoned Phillip to say 'the wean's hingin'. The literal translation of this was 'the child is hanging' but it really meant that he (she) was listless, not that he was suspended from the ceiling.

If a mother wanted Phillip to regard the call as really urgent she would say, 'the wean's nose is going in an oot' or 'it's drawing up its legs.' These were really serious symptoms but Phillip was never able to find out what they meant.

In Phillip's day there were apparently a large number of people in Gorbals who regurgitated rings of various kinds. Many callers said their children or spouses were 'vomiting rings' round them. 'Sometimes I was tempted to tell the callers to collect the rings so that I could count them when I got there to determine how serious the attack was.'

Women patients often came into his surgery to report on their operations. Some accounts verged on the sensational.

'I've had everything taken away, doctor,' they told him in hushed tones.

'I had visions of an abdominal wall, a backbone, and a hollow space between!' he said.

Phillip Seltzer died of a heart attack in his car one evening as he drove to his surgery. He was 43 and had been in practice about 16 years. Gorbals had claimed another victim.

Chapter 7

THE GAS MAN COMETH

'WHAT do you think of the visit of King Olav to Edinburgh, Mr Diamond?' I was asked.

'Oh, is that what the flags are for? I thought they were for me!' I said.

A few weak smiles appeared momentarily among the seven or eight members of the Scottish Gas Board who were interviewing me. Then the chairman leaned back, made a steeple with his hands, and said, 'You didn't mention in your application if you were married, Mr Diamond.'

'Oh, very much so,' I said. 'As a matter of fact my wife and two sons are walking along Princes Street right now asking each other, "I wonder how dad is getting on." '

I waited a few seconds and added, 'How IS dad getting on?'

the chairman threw caution to the winds and gave a short bark which I took to be a manifestation of amusement.

'Quite well. Quite well.'

One member of the board asked me why I wanted to leave newspapers and I said, 'Most days I feel we are entertaining our readers rather than informing them of what is important in their lives. If I wanted to be an entertainer I would buy a guitar and bawl into a microphone and make a fortune.'

When I got back to Glasgow a telegram lay on the hall floor asking me to return for another interview the following day. This was taken by Harry Hart, the board's Deputy Chairman who hadn't been present during my interview but whose approval for my appointment was apparently vital.

Harry prattled on for 20 minutes about the great job the gas industry was doing and what a great honour it was to work for it. I never said a word. Eventually he jumped up, thrust out his hand, and said, 'Welcome to the Gas Board, Mr Diamond.' I muttered my thanks and left.

It was 1962, the year tramcars stopped running in Glasgow and the Americans orbited the earth six times. It was playing a tape recorder early one morning after the last edition of the *Daily Express* had gone to press that launched me on my public relations career. I was trying out a new recorder I had bought by reading bits from the *Glasgow Herald*. I wasn't being disloyal. It was our job to read other newspapers to see if they had anything of importance we didn't have. Mind you, the *Express*'s opinion of what was important didn't very often coincide with the *Herald*'s sense of news values.

Next morning I was listening to the items I had recorded and suddenly heard myself reading an advertisement for a senior public relations assistant for the Scottish Gas Board. I didn't know anything at all about public relations except that it had something to do with creating images or good impressions but the job looked quite attractive, with sensible hours, so I wrote an application and eventually got an interview at the board's headquarters in Edinburgh. It was a nice day so I took Jackie and the boys to Edinburgh by car. The city was festooned with bunting and flags in honour of the royal couple from Norway.

A couple of weeks or so after the interview I was given a couple of small but comfortable rooms overlooking George Square, a secretary, and no instructions about what I was supposed to do. I spent a few weeks walking about talking to people and very quickly realised that the gas industry did a lot more than cause explosions in old ladies' kitchens.

It was helping industry and commerce in all kinds of ways; by advising on myriad technical problems, by producing more efficient boilers and other equipment, and by converting solid fuel and electric boilers to the use of the cheaper gas.

In the domestic market, too, there were giant strides in the production of new and better heating and cooking appliances. Everyone in the industry was anxious to make their work known as widely as possible and I received magnificent co-operation from everyone. All this helped me to make considerable impact on the public consciousness, even if I do say it myself. In the 1960s, too, the search for gas and oil off the northeast coast of Scotland provided many stories.

Our own flat was all-electric but as I had just become a spokesman for the gas industry in Scotland I thought it was appropriate that I should replace the electric appliances with gas ones. I bought a gas cooker and several modern, efficient gas fires and a squad of men took two or three days to fit them in.

Then one lunch-time we gathered at the cooker for the big switch-on. The gas fitter struck a match, held it to the gas ring, but nothing happened. The flame flickered out sadly. We tried another ring and again nothing. Then we tried the beautiful, chrome and timber gas fires I had bought. Still nothing.

The fitter looked at me and came away with the remarkable deduction, 'They're no' working. There must be something wrong.'

The appliances were disconnected and after some tests it was found that the pipes were filled with mud and dirt. When the lengths of piping were being pulled from the fitters' van one end fell into the gutter and scooped up the rubbish, clogging them completely. I was later able to amuse a number of gas industry dinners with this story.

Among the many interesting developments in the industry while I was there was the construction of a £2.4 million plant, a lot of money in those days, at Provan to produce virtually non-toxic gas from light distillate, a product of oil refining. I wrote a story about this which got a lot of publicity. Sydney Smith, the Board Chairman, came to Glasgow to be interviewed on BBC television by my friend John Hossack, their industrial correspondent.

After the interview I asked Mr Smith if he would be kind enough to give me a lift in his taxi back to George Square as he had to catch a train at Queen Street station nearby. On the way he said, 'Whose idea was it to publicise Provan?'

'Mine.'

'Really. Do you do a lot of this kind of thing?'

I thought this was rather an odd question in view of the fact that I had been telling Britain for a year about the great things the gas industry in Scotland was doing. I had also founded the newspaper *Scottish Gas* which quickly became one of the most quoted newspapers in the industry.

Another story which got a great deal of coverage was the installing in the sailing ship *Carrick* of gas boilers for central heating, cooking, and hot water for the galley, bathrooms, washrooms, and cabins. It was the first time in Britain that a gas-service had been laid from a busy city street, Broomielaw, to a ship floating on the water nearby, in this case the river Clyde.

The 103-year-old former *City of Adelaide* was at that time the headquarters of the Royal Naval Volunteer Reserve Club (Scotland). Many years later when the *Carrick* became derelict a friend of mine, John MacLaughlin, caused a minor sensation by sculpting a bust of me from a piece of the *Carrick*'s mast.

Among the former's most famous masters, when she carried Australian wool and passengers 13,800 miles from Adelaide round tempestuous Cape Horn to London, was Captain David Bruce, who had a wooden leg and wore a straw hat. He was succeeded in turn by each of his three sons.

I was the first journalist to write about the growth of Chinese restaurants in Scotland because they all used gas for cooking. The story appeared under a 3½ inch deep headline in Chinese, written by one of the restaurateurs, on the front page of *Scottish Gas*. I took the precaution of showing it to a couple of other Chinese people to confirm that it said 'Gas is best for cooking Chinese food because it is convenient and makes a very strong fire!' After all, a Chinese restaurant owner with a sense of humour could have ended my career.

Most of the other restaurants in Glasgow had gas kitchens and I wrote a great many articles for *Scottish Gas* and the catering press about them. Naturally it was necessary to sample the meals in the various restaurants, which I did regularly at their expense. One of my favourite restaurants was The Courtyard, owned by former footballer Billy McPhail, but I had to stop going there because Billy wouldn't let me pay the bill.

My Gas Board employers almost choked over their rice crispies one Saturday morning when they saw the headlines on the front page of my old paper the *Daily Express* and several other newspapers, 'FED UP HARRY GIVES HIS CAR AWAY'.

The previous evening I was driving home in the dark, rain-swept streets when the car conked out and glided gently to a halt. It was about the fourth time in a couple of months. I kicked and swore at it but it wouldn't budge. A figure bent against the driving rain approached and I said, 'Want a car, mac?' and held out the keys. The man instinctively held out his hand and I dropped the keys in it and walked away.

When I got home I told Jackie what happened and she said, 'Not before time.'

I knew it was a good story so I scribbled down a few sentences and phoned them round to the newspapers. The story even appeared in the Soviet newspaper *Pravda* a few days later. This one said we were so poor in Britain we couldn't afford to run cars so we gave them away. It didn't say how we could afford to buy the cars in the first place.

I went to the motor taxation office with the car's documents and told a clerk I no longer had the car, was no longer responsible for it, and wanted this fact noted.

'Did you sell it?' he wanted to know.

'No, I gave it away in the street.'

'Ohhhh, so it was yoooou,' said the clerk. 'We have to talk to you. You can't just give your car away.'

He told me I had committed numerous transgressions against various Road Traffic Acts and whatnot and I was liable to prosecution.

'Listen, son,' I said indignantly. 'I carried a rifle for three years for the privilege of giving my fully paid and owned property to anyone I damn well like and if you don't concede that the car is no longer my responsibility I'll make you famous, too!'

The clerk disappeared into the back shop for a few minutes and when he came back he said, 'Alright, leave it with us.'

I never heard any more from them. I did hear about the car, though. A friendly police traffic department tracked it down and told me later that it had conked out because of a wee electrical fault which a threepenny fuse had put right!

The story doesn't end there either. I bought another cheap car and was driving with Harvie and Michael in the back when we saw a big poster advertising White Horse whisky. The poster said some guy was a magician and could make a glass of whisky disappear and added, rather irrelevantly I thought, 'You can take a White Horse anywhere.'

'I could do better than that,' I remarked to the boys, who of course immediately challenged me. When I got into the office I scribed a few sentences on paper and finally arrived at 'Harry Diamond, 20 Thorncliffe Gardens, Glasgow, gave his car to a passer-by when it broke down. He finds his White Horse a lot more reliable.' Then came the campaign line, 'You can take a White Horse anywhere.'

I phoned White Horse in Glasgow for the name of their advertising agents and got a phone number in London. The guy in London said they didn't take suggestions from the public. Besides, they had hundreds of ideas in stock.

'But you haven't even heard my idea, how do you know whether it's good enough or not?' I said.

'Write to us and we'll think about it,' the voice at the other end said placatingly, so I did that and also sent them a cutting of the story from the *Express* to emphasise the topicality of the story. A few days later I got a letter saying the White Horse account director liked the copy and please would I sign the accompanying form allowing them to use it in any way they pleased. The upshot was that the poster with my name and address appeared all over the country and I got at least a couple of dozen phone calls offering me new cars and holidays in the Caribbean if I allowed the callers to use my name in advertising campaigns. They all turned out to be hoax calls of course.

For years afterwards all my friends were convinced I got a vast sum of money and unlimited cases of whisky for my brilliant few words. The truth is I got a cheque for £10 and one bottle of the water of life.

One day I was invited to the press office of White Horse for a drink. The press officer asked me what I did for a living and I told him I worked in a jeweller's shop in Govan. I think my mind tortuously worked out that it was not a good idea to tell them I was a public relations man in case they thought I was trying to upstage them or something.

I was politely asked a lot of questions about jewellery and who bought it when the editor of a drinks magazine came in and said to me,

'Hi, how's the gas industry's hot-shot public relations man?' The White Horse people took it well and we were friends for a long time afterwards. I even got another bottle of whisky one Christmas. I was told later that one or two rather stuffy members of the Gas Board expressed some concern about what the hell I was going to do for my next trick.

Walking through the showroom to my office one day I saw a girl of six or seven in a once-white dress, grubby face and wet nose, climbing onto a display float carrying a very expensive group of appliances. Suddenly her mother's voice rent the air from across the room, 'Haw, Natasha, get tae fuck affa therr … '

Natasha!

Another day one of our managers phoned to ask me rather excitedly to come down to a house in Monteith Row, overlooking Glasgow Green, where some of the tobacco barons of a bygone age had had their elegant establishments. They were anything but elegant by the 1960s.

'There's a couple dead in bed from gas poisoning and a crowd of reporters and photographers outside,' said the gas manager. 'Can you handle them, Harry?'

I rushed down to the house and I was led into a room where a blanket covered a man and woman in an iron-legged bed in a recess. The manager explained that underneath the blanket lay the bodies of a prostitute and a sailor she had picked up the previous evening. A gas pipe ran round the skirting board in the recess to a gas fire in the room. Apparently during the frolicking in the bed an iron leg had banged against the gas pipe and fractured it. The couple on the bed were too preoccupied even to notice the very distinctive smell of tetrahydrothiophene, which is put into the gas to give the familiar, characteristic smell.

'What can we tell the mob of reporters?' asked the gas manager.

'Come with me.'

I went outside, stood at the top of the few steps leading to the door of the house like the Prime Minister outside No 10, and told the reporters exactly what happened. The gas manager almost had a cardiac arrest.

'Trust me,' I told him.

'How the hell can we put that in the paper, Harry?' the reporters complained.

'That's your problem. You wanted to know what happened and I've told you.'

The photographers couldn't do anything either of course.

Next day all that appeared in one or two newspapers was the information that a man and woman had been found gassed in a house in Monteith Row. These were in the days when most newspapers, in Scotland anyway, did not go into details about sexual adventures. I doubt if they would bother to publish that kind of story now either.

I wouldn't want to seem callous but an extraordinary number of elderly ladies embedded themselves in kitchen walls in my day. They used to put a casserole or whatever in the oven, turn on the gas and discover they didn't have a match so they went round the house looking for the matchbox, came back, struck a match and ... booooom!

I was always asked by the newspapers for a comment and always told them what happened, adding 'The appliance was in proper working order.' The comment seemed a bit bland considering what had happened to the old dears.

Understandably I received a lot of complaints of one kind or another about the Gas Board which I didn't mind so much during office hours but I did resent having to listen to long tales of woe from friends and acquaintances wherever I went outside my job.

The matter came to a head one day at the burial of a friend. I was standing tearfully at his graveside when I felt someone behind me tugging my coat. I ignored the first couple of tugs but at the third tug I pulled my coat roughly away. The man behind me whispered, 'Your Gas Board is giving me a tough time,' to which I responded rather more loudly than I intended, 'I'll give you a lot more tough time if you don't leave me alone.' That didn't prevent the man from approaching me after the funeral. I don't remember all I said but even if I did I couldn't put it down here.

Once I helped the blood transfusion service to set up a ward in the basement of the Gas Board building in George Square so that members of the staff could donate blood. The event got a lot of coverage in the news media, mainly I think because of the heading on my press release, 'BLOOD-LETTING AT THE GAS BOARD!'

I commissioned a photographer to take a picture of me giving away my life-sustaining fluid for the benefit of the journalism and public relations trade press, but my brilliant idea backfired when a nurse told me after taking a sample of my blood, 'I don't think we should take your blood, Mr Diamond. Your need is greater than ours!'

That night I rushed to the doctor in a panic and was told, 'Don't worry, you're not dying. You're just a wee bit anaemic.'

The editor of a technical reference book phoned me one day to say that all the hierarchy in the 12 Area Gas Boards in Britain had alphabet soup after their names, degrees, technical qualifications, honours and so on but there was nothing after the name Harry Diamond and it looked odd.

'Can we put anything after your name?'

'I'm an MLHC,' I said.

The phone went dead at that moment so I wasn't asked what the initials stood for but for years they appeared after my name in the directory. Came the night when I had to speak at an industry dinner in London. After my speech a voice asked, 'What does MLHC, stand for, Mr Diamond?'

There was absolute silence as I said into the microphone, 'It stands for Member of Langside Hebrew Congregation.'

Uproar!

At another dinner in London attended by anyone who was of any importance in the industry in Britain I was scheduled to be the seventh speaker. By the time it came to my turn the audience was catatonic. The red-breasted master of ceremonies announced in a stentorian voice that Mr Diamond would now give his address. I stood up and said, 'My address is 9 George Square, Glasgow,' and sat down to tumultuous applause. People crowded round me afterwards and said, 'Congratulations, Harry, best speech of the night!'

Among the people we recruited to help us promote the use of gas for cooking was the celebrated writer and television chef Fanny Cradock and her long-suffering husband Johnny, whose role was mainly to absorb abuse, run errands, and fetch the eggs for the irascible Fanny. On one of her visits to Glasgow I had the job of meeting her at Central Station on her arrival from London.

The train stopped, Fanny finally alighted regally and said to me imperiously when I introduced myself, 'Get my luggage.' I ignored her instruction and started to walk along the platform with her.

'Get my luggage, I told you,' she repeated. 'I expect your co-operation while I'm here and if I don't get it I'll report you to the chairman.' She said this loud enough for everyone on the platform to hear.

'Listen, hen,' I said in my best Glaswegian, 'you can report me to the Pope and the Chief Rabbi but if you want my help don't bloody well talk to me like that or I'll leave you right now.'

To my considerable surprise and her eternal credit Fanny smiled broadly and said in her sergeant-major voice, 'We'll get along fine' and took my arm. The long-suffering Johnny attended to the luggage.

Another celebrated artist with the frying pan gave me a tip which came in useful many years later when I had to do my own cooking: put anything at all in the pan and if it turns out OK take the credit for inventing it and the public will think you're a culinary genius. If it doesn't work, fling something else in the pan. I have since amazed and astonished many of my friends with the inventiveness of my cooking.

Speedway racing had a very large and enthusiastic following in Scotland so I decided to cash in on its popularity with the help of Ian Hoskins, a fast-talking Australian-born speedway promoter. I persuaded the Gas Board to buy a 500cc machine with a JAP engine of the type that had won every major speedway event and world championship since it was introduced in 1930 and offered the Superbike as first prize in a speedway competition. Spectators who forecast the first three riders past the post were offered £200 worth of gas appliances.

The event attracted an enormous number of spectators to the final at the White City in Glasgow and brought the gas industry a great deal of publicity for its imagination and enterprise.

Gas Board social occasions were always enjoyable, especially lunches and dinners with local authority people, commercial and industrial customers, and other big gas users. Our own internal social occasions also tended towards the indulgent. One group whose gatherings I always attended was the Service and Sales Circle, whose name is self-explanatory, and one year I was very gratified to be elected Chairman.

This was quite an honour for someone who had not spent much of his life in the industry. I always thought there was an interesting camaraderie among gas industry people, more than in some of the other organisations I had worked for where the bonhomie had a brittle edge. There was a time when the gas manager in a town or village ranked in importance with the provost. Often they were the same person.

A speaker from the oil industry at one of our monthly meetings of the Service and Sales Circle responded in superior, sneering tones when I asked him if the exploration for gas and oil in the North Sea would have an adverse effect on the fishing grounds. I forget his exact words but I do recall the laughter at my expense when he implied that my question was the silliest he had ever been asked.

The reality of the situation is that the oilmen's hardware in the North Sea, 18,000 kilometres of pipeline, 430 platforms, 180 subsea installations and templates, 400 suspended wellheads, drilling rigs, pipelay vessels, trenching boats, supply boats and tankers and abandoned installations all disrupt the work of the 8,000 fishermen with their 2,200 fishing boats who contribute almost £1 billion a year to the British economy.

It becomes a matter of life and death when a fisherman has to decide in extreme weather conditions whether to stay and try to free thousands of pounds worth of nets caught on some abandoned oil equipment or get away before his ship and all aboard it go down.

In the gas industry, like anywhere else, there are schemers and men of ambition. One Glasgow Area Manager in my time, a burly, no-nonsense type, took me to a very expensive restaurant soon after he was appointed, bought me a number of drinks, and asked me a series of questions about all the local managers in the area: How good did I think they were at their jobs? How were they regarded by the people around them, what families they had, did they drink, how were they with the female staff?

Mr Brandon obviously believed that knowledge was power and that as I had free access to everyone I would know all about them. I did know one or two interesting things as it happened but I gave Mr Brandon a string of naive, ingenuous answers and he quickly gave me up as a bad job. I don't think he spoke to me again for the rest of the two or three years he was Area Manager.

Chapter 8

I ONLY PROMOTED THE SAUSAGES

I SPENT seven happy years with the Gas Board and was then persuaded by a friend in the advertising business to join his small agency to head a public relations department. A couple of years after I joined the company it was bought over by the Rex Stewart advertising group, which in its time was an important part of the advertising industry in Scotland, but which has gone now.

Rex Stewart had a public relations company with the rather pretentious name of International Image Consultants, which was where I met an enterprising, energetic young man named Tony Meehan. One day Tony was handling the publicity for a Soviet dance company who had come to Glasgow and was wondering how to attract some attention to their performance that evening. Eventually he dreamed up the idea of having them give a wee dance in Buchanan Street, one of Glasgow's smarter shopping areas.

I was busy at that time devising ways of bringing attention to the plight of Soviet Jewry in the course of communal work for the Jewish community so I suggested I should get some of my co-religionists to stage a protest near the dancers and send out a press release to alert the news media. The Russians arrived to do their dance and some of my protesters appeared with posters reading 'LET MY PEOPLE GO'. The stunt turned out even better than we had hoped when the protesters joined in the dancing. Tony later founded the public relations firm of TMA Communications and became a Visiting Professor at Glasgow Caledonian University.

I enjoyed consultancy work but it tended to be a bit precarious. There was pressure to acquire as many clients as possible in order to build up the company's fee income and Rex Stewart certainly knew how to get the most out of a client. The company had several divisions: advertising, public relations, design, photography, printing, and each one charged the client for its work. I don't know how many fees it got out of each client but I felt uneasy about the whole thing.

I may have been extraordinarily lucky but I had a good relationship with all my clients and formed genuine friendships with some of them. One of them was Eric McKellar Watt, Chairman and founder of McKellar Watt Limited, which at that time was Britain's largest privately-owned sausage and pie-making company. Before my rabbi bars me from synagogue I should say there is nothing, as far as I know, in the Five Books of Moses to prevent me from promoting non-kosher sausages as long as I don't eat them! I doubt, however, if that will get me off the hook!

Eric McKellar Watt was badly injured in the army in the 1939-45 war and while he was in hospital doctors told him he would never drive a car again, so one of the first things he did when he started in business was to buy a semi-automatic Lanchester and drive himself round local butchers to sell his sausages.

The day he came home on sick leave from the army hospital both legs were in plaster from hip to toe. The transport arrangements the army had made to get him home from the railway station seemed to be him to be too slow and ponderous, so he tipped a porter to get him a battery-operated luggage truck which he clambered onto and drove himself along the long crowded platform to a taxi rank.

After he was demobbed and before he got his car he had difficulty in getting round the city because of his war wounds, so he developed the habit of stopping tramcars by standing in their path. When the driver stopped he clambered aboard, explained he had a bad leg and rode on the driving platform until he reached his destination.

I was recommended to Eric by Murray Ward, his managing director, who was a friend of mine. I had been doing a lot of work for another sausage manufacturer, Adams of Dalkeith, and was beginning to irritate McKellar Watt with the amount of publicity I was getting for a major rival.

Murray made an appointment for me to see Eric, a well-built, square-jawed man with dark horn-rimmed glasses, and we had a longish talk which started off rather badly. He told me, 'Right, this is what I want. I want a mention in the *Financial Times* at least once a month and regular features in the food trade press and the Scottish business pages.' I listened to this for a few minutes and without saying a word got up and walked to the door.

'Where the hell are you going?' said Eric.

'Back to my office. I've never heard such rubbish in my life.'

'Really?' said Eric. 'Then what are you going to do for me?'

'I don't know yet. Right now the only thing I know about your company is that you make sausages and pies. When I know a bit more maybe I'll be able to answer your questions.'

Eric and I had a long talk and I went away. A couple of weeks later I went back with an article I had written about him. Eric worked quietly for some minutes on the pages, scoring out chunks here and there and rewriting bits. Eventually he handed it back and without looking at it I tore it to shreds, leaned over his desk and dropped it into his wastepaper basket.

'What the hell are you doing?' said Eric.

'I gave you a perfectly marketable product and you ruined it,' I said. 'I don't tell you how to make sausages and pies so don't you tell me how to write for newspapers.'

Eric looked nonplussed for a few seconds.

'Aye, that's all very well but look at some of the things you said about me.'

'Were they untrue?'

'No.'

'Then leave the damn thing alone.'

'Well, what do we do now? You've torn it up.'

I reached into the inside pocket of my jacket and produced another copy of the article. 'I've met people like you before,' I said. 'That's why I came prepared. Let's start again only this time I want you to correct only matters of fact.'

Eric smiled wryly, flipped a knob on his intercom and said to Murray Ward, 'That's a cheeky bastard you sent me.'

'Yes, Eric,' said Murray and switched off his intercom.

A few weeks later my secretary came on the phone to say Mr McKellar Watt was on the phone in a state of great excitement.

'Come for lunch,' said Eric.

'Not today, I've got too much on.'

'Come for lunch, it's important.'

Eventually Eric persuaded me to drop everything and go to the factory for lunch. At the end of the board room table was a pile of magazines containing my article about him. He said he had been bombarded all morning with calls from other food companies congratulating him. Eric McKellar Watt and I were firm friends from that day.

I had started off the article about Eric:

'Beneath the tough, unyielding exterior of Eric McKellar Watt beats an even tougher, unyielding interior. Other men known for their strength, poise and confidence have emerged from sessions with Eric McKellar Watt white, trembling, and sapped of all vitality. Ena Simons, his secretary, regularly dispenses hot black coffee to the victims as they reel out of his line of fire.

Eric Watt works hard to maintain this man-of-granite image. He does it mostly by alighting on an inconsistency and probing it, worrying it, hammering it, and going back to it until it is either explained to his satisfaction or is made to vanish in a verbal cloud of sulphurous contempt.

His attitude stems solely from his uncompromising insistence on the highest possible standards and because his people know this there is an atmosphere of buoyancy and confidence among the team of young executives who work for him.

They know that behind the steely glare is a shrewd, hard-working, highly efficient, generous man who knows how to achieve commercial success and is prepared to share the fruits of that success with anyone who is willing to work with him.'

One of his directors told me Eric asked him to come to his office to collect a Christmas gift. Instead of the bottle of whisky or piece of glassware he was expecting he got the keys for a new Ford Consul.

During a conversation with Murray Ward one day he said there was absolutely nothing happening in the company at that moment that I could write about. On the way out of the factory I passed a man putting drops from a test tube into a sausage-mixing bowl. He explained they were experimenting with whisky-flavoured sausages! The story went round the world.

Several months later I asked Murray, 'What happened to the whisky-flavoured sausages?'

Murray jumped up, closed the door of his office, and said in a hushed voice, 'Oh, for God's sake don't say anything about that. It was a disaster!'

'Wait a minute,' I said. 'Let me tell everyone it was a disaster. A lot of people will want to know what happened, especially in the food trade. I want to tell it in such a way that people will say this is an enterprising company with a sense of humour and confident enough to admit they tried something which failed.'

'OK' said Murray.

So I wrote another story which again went round the world. It ended with the quote from Eric, 'After all, who wants to drink their whisky out of a sausage!'

Another favourite client was Alfred Littman, an Englishman, whose factory in East Kilbride made shirts for Marks and Spencer. Alfred was a first-rate artist and always carried a small tin box of water colours, a pill bottle filled with water, a tiny brush and a waterproof black pen with which he produced beautiful paintings in seconds. Some of his paintings were done in taxis between business appointments and he even claimed to have done one while driving, although he admitted he was stuck in a traffic jam at the time. I still have two of Alfred's paintings in my home.

Students of Glasgow School of Art were commissioned to paint pictures round the walls of his factory to make it congenial for his staff, mostly women, to work in and he cordoned off a section of the factory where workers could go for a smoke as they obviously couldn't smoke while they were sewing shirts.

At the end of our contract period he wrote to the managing director of my company, 'Mr Diamond has had many remarkable successes and the job has been well and thoroughly done. We now have more staff than we need and a long waiting list, due to the work done by Mr Diamond … '

Another client was Clark Hunter, a marvellous, kindly man who ran a metal drum factory in Paisley and was an authority on Robert Burns. He was also a director of Bydand Distillers, owners of Fettercairn Distillery in the Howe (valley) of the Mearns, near Laurencekirk in Kincardineshire, for which I did some work. Fettercairn is deep in the heart of an area where illicit distillers in ye days of yore waged a constant war against the government gaugers (excisemen).

The man in charge of operations at Fettercairn was John Scott Livie, a big man in every sense of the word, for whom I developed great respect. It was Livie who inspired a piece of promotional literature I wrote in 1983 for another whisky company (see Chapter 15).

Chapter 9

NO TIME FOR JEWISH FUNERALS

CLIENTS leave agencies for the oddest reasons. Two or three of mine dispensed with our services because I had done too good a job for them. They had had a considerable amount of publicity, were doing well, and thought they didn't need us any more. I also put two companies out of business by giving them so much publicity they were bought over by rivals. Not that they minded, but there was little profit in that for us as their buyers didn't want us.

I began to feel as if the things I was doing had little significance in the great scheme of things; that I was passing my time interestingly enough, but was not adding much to the sum total of the world's good or knowledge. I think I felt like the comic actor who yearned to play Shakespeare.

Then Harry Dutch, Public Relations Officer of Glasgow Corporation, advertised for an assistant and I felt this was the kind of job I should really be doing rather than selling sausages and shirts. Some of my friends and colleagues had a jaundiced view of the politicians who ran the city and told me I couldn't do much for their image or that of the city, which was regarded by many people outside it as 'Siberia in a kilt'.

I had for long felt strongly, however, that ordinary working people did not take enough interest in the things and people who influenced their lives. Local authorities exert quite a lot of influence over our lives one way or another and in those days I could hardly find anyone who had the slightest idea what their local authority was doing and why. I'm not convinced the situation is greatly different now.

I wrote to Harry, who had been the Corporation correspondent of the

Herald in bygone days, and asked him if there was any point in my applying for the job as his assistant. He said yes, so I applied and got the job. My first major triumph was in a Glasgow Week in Hamburg promotion. I had nothing to do with the organising of it but I did get the public relations bit to handle. I wrote a lot of stories leading up to the event and eventually a large party went to Hamburg for a week to promote Glasgow. Among the events were trade displays in 76 Hamburg department stores and shops, performances of *The Taming of the Shrew* by the Citizens Theatre Company, a challenge match between Rangers and Hamburg SV, an exhibition of Scottish paintings, a tourism exhibition, industrial conference, fashion shows, demonstrations of Scottish country dancing, and piping, and quite a number of civic receptions and dinners.

About 120 people went to Hamburg from Glasgow; businessmen, councillors, representatives from Glasgow Chamber of Commerce and the Clyde Tourist Authority. Our aim was to sell to Germany in a big way everything that Glasgow and the West of Scotland had to offer. Whether we did that or not I don't know but I do know we all had a good time.

Before we went to Hamburg I produced, with the help of the *Glasgow Herald*, a special edition of the paper to take to Germany. After the final edition had been printed about 3am on a Saturday morning, the front and back pages were re-plated with stories, headlines and captions in German and the presses restarted. Five thousand copies were taken to a waiting aircraft at Glasgow airport and flown to Germany. My stories were translated by Rosemarie Rey, a German-born member of the Corporation's public relations staff.

The night we arrived in Hamburg the entire Glasgow contingent were guests at a state banquet given in our honour. I spent much of the evening autographing copies of the *Glasgow Herald* because my name was on the lead story on page one.

During the promotion I sat each morning in an elegant room in the Hamburg Plaza Hotel churning out speeches for Lord Provost Sir William Gray to deliver. It was a hard grind but I enjoyed listening to the applause as Sir William uttered my golden words.

The reform of local government in Scotland was almost complete by then and the new authorities, including Strathclyde Regional Council, were busy recruiting staff. Strathclyde was to become the largest local authority in Britain and Harry Dutch understandably wanted to be its Head of Public Relations. He eventually got the job and I was left on my own in the City Chambers.

I didn't get the job of Head of Public Relations of Glasgow City Council automatically. I had to apply like everyone else. My application was one of 113. Twelve of us were interviewed one Sunday in a hotel in George Square. I did get the job eventually but it was a near thing. I only beat by a hair's breadth one man who interviewed rather better than me. At one point in the interview I picked up a pile of papers in a plastic folder which slipped out of my hands and dozens of sheets of paper flew all over the floor. At the end of the interview the Chairman, Ellen McCulloch, a lady I got to know and like, asked me if there was anything else I wanted to say.

'Yes, there is. I want this job because I know it better than anyone else and I've been doing it for several months.'

The man I beat by a very narrow margin subsequently had five jobs in as many years.

It didn't take long to find out the character of some of the people I would be working for in the City Chambers, as the Town Hall is known in Scottish cities. My interviewers were four Conservative and four Labour members of the General Purposes Committee. All the Labour members voted for my appointment and all the Conservatives voted against. Luckily the Chairman had the casting vote and I got the job.

A few days after I started work one of the Conservative members who had interviewed me and who had known about me for some time put his arm round my shoulder and said, 'I knew you were the best man for the job Harry but I couldn't vote for you if the Labour side voted for you.' This was in direct contravention of all the council's rules of employment as all appointments were non-political.

A story went round the City Chambers that Pat Lally, a senior councillor at the time, stopped Dick Dynes, the council leader, in the corridor and said, 'You're not really going to give Diamond the job, are you?'

Dick replied, 'He'll die if we don't and I don't have the time to go to Jewish funerals cos they last all day!' They don't, but why spoil a good story!

The day I started I had a secretary and a young man, Willie McGarva, who I inherited from Harry Dutch. Willie had orginally come from the health department, I think, but turned out to be a valuable colleague. My secretary, Sandra Short, also turned out to be worth her weight in gold. Working for the local authority was dramatically different from anything I had experienced before. I was 47 when I joined the Corporation so I wasn't an innocent at large.

One thing that struck me with some force was the total lack of a sense of urgency in many of the people around me. There were times when I phoned senior officers for information about something and got the response, 'Well, let me see, I'm busy this week and next week I'm having a few days off, then

I have to go to a conference in Harrogate and … Can you give me a ring in a couple of weeks?

With uncharacteristic restraint I said, 'I think you misunderstand. I need the information now.' I didn't always get it now but gradually my colleagues realised I was working in their interests too and they began to co-operate.

One man who proved a valuable friend was Theo Crombie, a town clerk depute and gifted administrator who could separate substance from hyperbole in a flash. He came into my office one morning and said, 'I think I have a good story for you,' which turned out to be the understatement of the decade.

Dorothy Henderson, a well-rounded, good-humoured but determined lady, started something which dramatically changed the face of Glasgow, won her a number of environmental awards, and helped me immeasurably to tell the world about the 'new Glasgow'.

One evening in 1974 she went to a meeting to hear about environmental improvement grants available from Glasgow City Council. She went home and told a friend, Mrs Angela Petrie, another owner-occupier in their grim, soot-blackened, unattractive block of tenement flats in the west end of the city.

The two women rounded up all the other 109 owner-occupiers in the block and formed Woodlands' Residents' Association. They applied for, and were granted, an improvement grant of £36,000. Then they went to work. They had the building stone-cleaned and to their surprise it came up a gleaming, honey colour.

They also had doors made for the closes, cleaned up gardens and back courts, and when they were finished they found they had created an architectural and environmental jewel. People in nearby tenement blocks and from property for miles around came to see what Dorothy and Angela had achieved, and embarked on similar improvements on their own properties.

In the years that followed most of Glasgow's tenement buildings were stone-cleaned and refurbished. When the city's business houses saw what the householders had done they did the same with their own buildings. The city council also cleaned its many properties, including the City Chambers, and Glasgow was no longer the depressing, soot-blackened city of yesteryear.

When new hotels, office blocks, sports centres, walkways alongside the river Clyde, shopping centres, an extension to the Mitchell Library (making it the largest civic-owned reference library in Europe), a new transport museum, and other projects were built, the stories of how they all came about were written up for the news media at home and abroad. Gradually it dawned on the world that something interesting was happening to Glasgow.

Public relations and professionally-written press releases did not change the image of Glasgow, even if they were written by an enthusiastic, tolerant team led by an idiosyncratic leader. Behind the press releases were an army of people who had been working for years to enhance the quality of life in the city, politicians, administrators, developers, architects, builders, designers, artists, musicians, dreamers, people with ideas and no money, people with money and no ideas, and people who just wanted to get their names in the papers.

Out of this bubbling cauldron of endeavour and determination and enthusiasm and self-interest and arrogance emerged a product that was worth projecting to the world.

Chapter 10

THE TOUGHEST JOB IN SCOTLAND

THE headlines said: 'IMAGE BUILDER SLAMMED ... GLASGOW'S P.R.O. ACCUSED OF EMPIRE BUILDING ... DIAMOND HAS DELUSIONS OF GRANDEUR.'

They appeared the day after I appealed to a council committee for more staff to enable me to do something about Glasgow's poor image. My written report to the committee laid it on a bit thick because I knew I had to make an impact on the none-too-receptive members. It was in the early days of the new district council's life in 1975 and many councillors had no idea at all what public relations was or what I was there for.

I told the councillors that 'an opportunity exists as never before for a major effort to be made to balance the effect of the many attacks, often uninformed, which are launched against the city, and influence radically what people throughout Britain and the rest of the world think about the City of Glasgow'.

It was Jack Richmond, leader of the Conservative group, who provided the headlines by commenting that it would be wrong to expand my staff because it would be seen as empire building. Then he added, 'I think you have delusions of grandeur, Mr Diamond,' a comment that was reported throughout Britain.

A leader in the *Scottish Daily Express* said:

'Our hearts go out today to the man with the toughest job in Scotland, Mr Harry Diamond, Public Relations Officer of Glasgow District Council. He represents "one of the least understood cities in Britain," he tells the general purposes committee as he seeks an extra £21,000 a year to increase his staff from seven to 12. He is told sharply by Tory Bailie Jack Richmond that his department has delusions of grandeur and that this is the wrong time to make such a proposal.

The wrong time was indeed a kindly understatement, looking at all the newspaper headlines yesterday proclaiming how Glasgow had thrown away £12.3 million on housing money by deciding on a rents freeze just as it was asking the Government for £3.7 million to improve some of its houses.

Poor Harry Diamond. This £12.3 million could have brought him 2,900 assistants for a year to improve Glasgow's good name. But a whole army of PROs could do nothing for the city while it has some of its present councillors'.

That day when I went into the dining room for lunch there were smiles all round as councillors taunted me with, 'Poor Harry. He can't get 2,900 assistants!'

I didn't get the additional staff but the handful of us who were there in 1975, mostly secretarial and administrative staff, struggled on. We took on rather more jobs than we could comfortably handle because we adopted a campaigning role rather than the passive one of merely defending the council's whimsicalities.

Over the years I made repeated requests for more staff. My fellow officials and councillors looked forward to my flights of rhetoric as I pleaded for the resources to tell the world what a great job we were all doing.

On one occasion I told my committee, 'News media throughout the world are constantly telling readers, listeners and viewers about Glasgow's deprivation, poor housing, vandalism, and the mindlessness of some of its football supporters.

I believe it is essential for us to do something now to demonstrate to the world that Glasgow is a good place to work, bring up one's children, establish new commercial and industrial enterprises, and to visit on holiday'.

Michael Kelly, a young Labour councillor, who years later had good reason to be grateful to the Public Relations Department when he became Lord Provost, said the department should be merged with the Information Bureau, a hut in George Square which gave out tourism pamphlets.

A columnist in the *Sunday Mail* wrote, 'Harry Diamond, the fortunate City of Glasgow's winsome public relations officer, has six of a staff to help him cope with the outpourings of the bampots' convention in George Square. Not, I gather, enough for Harry. He is so convinced that he needs twice as many hirelings that he is busily trotting round the various council groups drumming up support.'

Latest in line for the sales talk was the SNP group, better known as The Wombles.

After listening to 20 minutes' powerful persuasion from the silver-tongued spokesperson, a motion was proposed, 'That the department be disbanded!' All good knockabout stuff.

Eventually when it was realised what I was doing I was given the staff and money but it was hard work. Not every councillor thought my propaganda efforts on behalf of the city were all that useful. One came into my office one day when I was drooling over a full page about Glasgow in the *New York Times*.

'What about than then?' I said proudly.

'That's no use to me Harry, I've got no punters (constituents) in New York,' he said.

Appeals for staff were by no means the only time my journalist colleagues had fun at my expense. A *Herald* story in 1978 revealed that after the sound and fury of the day's work I liked to wind down by playing a recorder for a little while before I went home. My musical talents, said the *Herald* writer, also encouraged my staff to leave the building on the very stroke their conditions of employment allowed!

A couple of days later the newspaper revealed that John Boyle, Director of External Relations of the Scottish Council, Development and Industry, had a clarinet concealed in an office drawer. There was some talk about John and myself joining that marvellous entertainer Roy Castle, who played innumerable instruments, in a concert for charity but John and I decided it would be more charitable on our part if we didn't bother.

Just before a couple of by-elections in 1976, in which one of the candidates was young Michael Kelly, I wrote an article for the *Glasgow Herald* telling candidates what would be expected of them if they were elected. My real purpose was to give the public an idea of how demanding a councillor's life could be. I pointed out that as councillors they would have to serve on about six committees, hold regular surgeries, be available to constituents day and night and observe a strict code of conduct. For this they would receive £10 a day for attending duties approved by the council. They would also get a telephone allowance of £14.50 a quarter to pay a telephone account which always exceeded that amount, often by more than 100 per cent.

Then came the bit that caused a minor uproar. I wrote that councillors also got lunch free in the City Chambers dining room and free travel on buses. Next day a *Daily Record* headline screamed, 'COUNCIL CHOKES ON PR MAN'S "FREE" LUNCHES'. One or two mischief-making councillors had gone to my journalist friends and complained that I had libelled them. The lunches weren't free, they said. They sacrificed a subsistence allowance so that they could stay in the chambers and work. The exact nature of the work was unspecified.

The rewards that councillors receive has always been a subject of much speculation. The average man in the street, whatever that means, tends to think they are all grossly overpaid for whatever they do. My own view is that some of them are worth the money they receive and some of them are not, which is hardly a profound judgment, but makes them not much differerent from people in many other jobs.

Nowadays, Glasgow's 83 councillors receive allowances on a scale suggested by the Convention of Scottish Local Authorities (Cosla). Each councillor receives a basic allowance of £6,000 a year. The Leader of the Council gets an additional £18,540 Special Responsibility Allowance. His deputy gets an additional SRA of £13,905. The chairmen of important committees like Education, Social Work and Housing also receive the basic £6,000 plus £13,905 SRA.

The convenor of the Labour Group, a post specially created in the new administration for Councillor Jean McFadden for a reason known only to a select few but which is the subject of myriad theories, is not paid beyond the basic £6,000 for this post but she does get an allowance of £7,416 as Chairman of Social Strategy, whatever that means. In previous administrations the leader of the council always took the chair at Labour Group meetings.

The Lord Provost gets the same as the council leader. Both, however, get many opportunities to travel and be entertained lavishly both abroad and at home. According to the council's budget estimates for 1995-96, which may be seen in any library, the Lord Provost gets an allowance of £100,000 to cover travel, entertaining important visitors to the city, gifts to charities, and a variety of other things. That figure could be a great deal more now.

The Leader of the Opposition, whose frustration at being powerless to achieve anything in a Labour-dominated city like Glasgow is considerable, gets the basic £6,000 plus a SRA of £5,562. All the councillors also receive a telephone allowance of £75 a quarter but most of their business calls are made from the City Chambers which are also paid for by the council, or more accurately the tax payer. And they still get a very good free lunch although they will continue to argue the point, and an excellent selection of cream cakes with tea in the afternoon. Elected members of towns with smaller populations than Glasgow receive smaller allowances.

One friendly councillor who tried to do me a good turn one day was rewarded with a *Daily Record* headline reading 'JOHN TALKS HIS WAY TO A RED FACE'. The previous day John McQueenie had come at my request to a manpower committee meeting to support a proposal of mine. He was in full flood when the chairman of the committee stopped him with the words, 'You are not a member of this committee, John. You are not entitled to speak!' John and I slunk out sheepishly.

Just before the local elections in 1986 I achieved nationwide headlines by signing a nomination form for a candidate certifying that she was a fit and proper person to be a councillor. Jean Hamilton had already been my local councillor and was standing for re-election and although senior officials were supposed to keep their political allegiances to themselves I thought it would be churlish to refuse to sign. Besides, I was half asleep in front of the television set when she came to the door of my house that night and my wife brought her in. She mumbled something to me about needing my signature and I scribbled it on the form she gave me. I wasn't all that sure what I was signing.

Unfortunately Mrs Hamilton was a Tory councillor and the Labour-controlled council was not amused. Jean McFadden, the council leader, with whom I had many run-ins over the years, told reporters, 'I think Mr Diamond has done irreparable damage to his relationship with all members of the council. I do not expect our officials to be political eunuchs but I think it is inappropriate for a senior official to come out publicly in support of a candidate. I would say the same if it involved a member of my own party. Relations between Mr Diamond and councillors will never be the same'.

I don't know what she meant by that last comment because my relations with Jean were never the same at any time. One day she could be friendly and reasonable and the next she could be impossible to talk to. I was by no means the only one who thought the best way to cope with Jean was to keep out of her way.

Throughout the years each political party was convinced I was an adherent of their opposition and I told every group leader I was an anarchist.

'You'll all be put to the sword when we take over,' I told them. They regarded this as another of my many idiosyncracies.

It wouldn't be fair, though, not to mention two occasions when Jean McFadden was at her most human. In 1990 when I came out of hospital after a very unpleasant operation she sent me a very warmly-worded letter. She also spoke stoutly in my defence after Ian Jack, a friend for many years, came into my office one day to interview me for an article on Glasgow for the *Sunday Times Magazine*. During the course of conversation I got a bit carried away and expressed myself with some emphasis. When Ian's article appeared he quoted me as saying, 'Look, son. Ah've seen Nice, Cannes, the Costa del

Sol, Italy. Take away the sunshine and you're left with fuck all.'

My friend John MacCalman of the *Herald* followed up the magazine piece and sought comments from Jean McFadden and others. The *Herald* headline read 'CITY FATHERS DEFEND THEIR ROUGH DIAMOND'.

Jean told him, 'Ian Jack has done the dirty on Harry Diamond. The article doesn't reflect the Harry Diamond I speak to.'

The Lord Provost, Bob Gray, with whom I had also had differences of opinion over the years, said, 'If Mr Diamond used these expressions it only goes to show the enthusiasm he has developed for the city. It was his enthusiasm that carried him away.'

Even the Tory group leader Iain Dyer told MacCalman, 'I just do not recognise the language attributed to him.'

My response quoted in the *Herald* was rather pompous, 'My vocabulary is of sufficient range, power and subtlety to obviate the necesssity to communicate my thoughts in the type of language that is unacceptable in polite society.'

Ian later wrote to me apologising for the offending paragraph and I told him I wasn't really worried about an occasional colourful quote.

Interestingly, while the controversy raged over my language a surgeon phoned to congratulate me on my defence of Glasgow and added, 'I'm glad there are no reporters in operating theatres. Some of the language we use when things are not going too well would strip the paint off the walls!'

Chapter 11

YOU'RE BONKERS, DIAMOND

JOHN CABLE-ROBBIE was an imaginative headmaster of Durrington Middle School in Worthing, Sussex, who named 14 of the 25 classrooms in his school after British cities, including Liverpool, Cardiff, Edinburgh, Aberdeen and Glasgow, instead of giving them the conventional numbers.

The children were asked to write projects about their cities and the 35 pupils in the Glasgow class, aged nine and ten, each sent me a letter asking for information about the city. I stayed behind in the office one night and made up 35 packs of information and sent them off. Not long afterwards I got 35 letters of thanks. Many of the children said they would like to visit Glasgow one day. Some of them touchingly showed the innocence and trustfulness of youth by ending their letters with love and good wishes. It was obvious the letters had been composed by the children themselves and not by a teacher because they told me things the teacher wouldn't have thought of.

Then I had a brainwave, or a brainstorm, whichever way you look at it. If my job was to persuade everyone that Glasgow was a good place, here was a great opportunity. Why didn't I invite the children to Glasgow and let them see for themselves what we had to offer? As a journalist I knew that a story like this would be picked up eagerly by the news media.

With the help of my assistant Willie McGarva I researched the cost of transporting 35 children and a handful of teachers from Worthing to Glasgow, putting them all up in a hotel for two nights, taking them on bus tours round the city and entertaining them. British Rail and the New Glasgow Centre Hotel gave us special rates and the whole bill came to £900, which seemed

77

a very reasonable expenditure for the kind of favourable publicity the city would get.

I took my proposal to the Labour-controlled Policy and Resources Committee, to whom I was answerable for my department, and the resultant discussion was reported throughout Britain.

Tory leader Jack Richmond, who had earlier got me nation-wide headlines by telling me I had delusions of grandeur, weighed in again with, 'There is something distasteful in this project which is admittedly to try to influence children of nine and ten years and through them their parents about the good qualities of Glasgow'. I thought this was a particularly inane remark as the whole purpose of the exercise was to influence people in favour of Glasgow.

John Young, Jack's deputy, exploded, 'Anyone who extends this type of invitation in the present economic climate must be stark raving bonkers. A local authority like Glasgow, in creating a precedent like this, could find itself playing host to many other groups of schoolchildren. Supposing children in Peking, Melbourne, or Auckland have a classroom project on Glasgow, are they (the Labour administration) also going to send them an invitation to visit the city at our expense?'

Dick Dynes, Leader of the Council and Chairman of the Policy and Resources committee, told John Young, 'Your language is unnecessarily explosive and uncharitable. I am sure it will not reflect the attitude of the council or the people of Glasgow.' The committee, which of course had a majority of Labour members, then approved the proposal.

All this was great stuff for my journalist colleagues. Next day's headlines read 'STORM OVER PLAN TO INVITE PUPILS ... ROW LOOMS OVER FREE SCHOOL TRIP ... SCHOOL TRIP STARTS FREE-FOR-ALL'.

The *Daily Record* said of the Tories, 'How mean can you get? We only wish that ALL civic public relations officers used a budged so shrewdly'.

Two readers of the *Glasgow Herald* did not approve of the visit. Mr David Tomlinson wrote, 'At a time when mentally-handicapped and deprived children's schools have been closed, youth clubs and summer camps cancelled, and subsidies removed from educational trips for our own children, for the district council to host a visit by schoolchildren to our city is at best reckless and at worst a further monument to the maladministration of our city.'

Ms Elizabeth Wardrop wrote on the same lines. Neither writer apparently knew that the cuts they complained about were not the responsibility of Glasgow City Council.

The *Brighton Argus* commented, 'By opening their sporrans and showering money on a group of Sassenach children the Glasgow council has dispelled the myth that the Scots are mean', but then added rather churlishly, 'The children of Durrington could set their Northern benefactors an example of good housekeeping if, instead of accepting the jaunt, they asked for the cash. They could then spend the money on one of the sections of their own community hardest hit by cuts in social services'.

The ratepayers of Worthing, however, did not think we were bonkers. They were delighted by our gesture although I learned later that members of the borough council were very worried indeed at the thought of having to return our hospitality.

On a Thursday afternoon in April 1976 the children, their headmaster, and five teachers eventually arrived in Glasgow and were met at the Central railway station by a large contingent of councillors and press. Jack Richmond and John Young stayed away, pleading pressure of business. The visitors were taken to the City Chambers for a civic reception and then to their hotel, in which their rooms had their own television, radio, telephone, and bathroom. The bathroom was important because we didn't want children wandering about hotel corridors in the middle of the night. The visitors were overwhelmed.

In the next two days the children were taken to Glasgow's famous Art Gallery and Museum at Kelvingrove, the Thomson Foundation Television College (where they operated cameras, went into control rooms, and saw themselves on televison), the offices of the *Daily Record*, a pop concert, and various other places. All this was reported by newspapers, radio and television throughout the country, including of course the *Worthing Gazette* (the editor's son was one of our visitors), the *West Sussex Gazette*, the *Evening Argus*, and Radio Brighton. Mr R A Syderif, Manager of the Marine and General Mutual Life Assurance Society office in Glasgow, told his head office in Worthing about the visit and they sent me a cheque for £100 towards the expenses with a letter saying, 'We feel the goodwill engendered by your invitation is most worthy of support', and John Menzies, the bookshops chain, gave each of the children a £1 voucher to spend in their main city centre store. During their tour of the city a woman bought all the children ice cream.

As I predicted the visit was an enormous success. Newspaper readers from all over the country wrote to me congratulating me on the idea and even the Tories on my council had to admit that the city had received a great deal of favourable publicity. Mr Frederick G Bagshaw wrote from London, 'Mr Keir Hardie would undoubteldy have approved your action.' I wasn't too sure of the relevance of this comment but I was grateful for it just the same.

After the visit the children of course wrote letters of thanks to the Lord Provost, councillors, department officials and almost everyone else they met. I estimate they must have written about 500 letters altogether.

Typical of the letters was the one from nine-year-old Timothy Hughes: 'Thank you for the wonderful time you gave us in Glasgow. I enjoyed myself very much. Thank you for the food which was very nice indeed. Thank you for the places you took us to. My mum liked the heather very much. I learned quite a bit in the city of Glasgow.'

One little girl couldn't come to Glasgow because she had chickenpox so I sent her a Glasgow tartan scarf. She wrote back, 'I will always think of the scarf as a kind gift from you and the people of Glasgow. I only wish I could have come with the other children. I hope you are keeping well. Love from Susan Jenkins.'

A boy wrote to say he hoped the hotel bill wasn't too expensive.

John Cable-Robbie wrote a letter of thanks to the Lord Provost, who really had had very little to do with the exercise. His only function was to get his picture in the papers with the children. The letter said, 'Everyone was so kind and generous to us and the greatest credit must reflect upon your Public Relations Officer for his organisation which could not be improved. We were all sorry to leave.'

I can only say thank you on behalf of 35 children who are absolutely certain that Glasgow is a wonderful, friendly city, 70 delighted parents, and 750 children who are envious of their companions' good fortune'.

This particular Lord Provost, who was determined during his term of office not to give me credit for anything, did not tell me about the letter, but his secretary Eric Hamilton thought I should see it. As a human interest story it was probably one of the most successful public relations exercises I ever carried out.

The children who came to Glasgow were:

Kim Dowell	Marion Churcher	Alan Ifould
Alan Olieff	Peter Barnard	Richard Pearce
Joanne Giles	Christopher Pullen	Robert Morley
Nicholas Smith	Karen Sherrell	Timothy Hughes
Andrew Sinsbury	Debra Lloyd	Anthony O'Connor
AmandaHarding	Philip White	Lyndsey Clarke
Richard Cork	Andrea Simpkins	Allison Stiles
Mark Sinsbury	Melanie Haylock	Shirley Naftel
Nicholas Brown	Sally Howell	Sheila Crump

Stella Smith   Christina Hull   Simon Hart
Elaine Smith   Vanessa Mitchell   Andrew Roas
Alison Alcock

The visit had one result that no-one could foresee. Valerie Coward, one of the teachers, wrote to me about three months later to say, 'We thought you would like to know that as a direct result of your brainstorm, Bob Johnson (another teacher who came with the party) and I got engaged a couple of weeks ago. Now see what you've done!'

This story also received considerable press coverage under headlines like 'THE CITY OF ROMANCE' and 'THE CITY OF LOVE'. One of the comments attributed to me was, 'It's all part of our service. We are always trying to bring some joy into people's lives!'

Valery and Bob's son Jamie is now 18.

Chapter 12

BACK TO THE FOLD

UNTIL a telephone call late one night in 1968 I had taken very little interest in Jewish communal affairs, partly because I hadn't had time and partly because no-one asked me. That night Dr Jack E Miller phoned as I was preparing some paperwork for the following day.

'I want you to join my executive committee,' he said. 'There's a lot to be done and you can help.'

Jack Miller was an icon of Scottish Jewry and had just become President of Glasgow Jewish Representative Council, an elected body which exists to represent the myriad interests and views of the Jewish community of Glasgow locally, nationally and even internationally, although I have serious reservations about the last named.

Jack proved to be an inspired president. He looked and sounded the part too, with his distinguished appearance, thin moustache, and slow measured speaking voice. There was hardly an aspect of Jewish activity in which he had not been involved. He was a general medical practitioner by profession and an important figure in medical politics, a Fellow of the British Medical Association and the Royal Society of Medicine, and a Fellow and founder member of the Royal College of General Practitioners. Later he was to become national treasurer of the BMA and a recipient of the Association's gold medal for distinguished service. He was awarded the OBE in 1983.

Jack took over the leadership of the Representative Council with a number of laudable aspirations, to give the local community a greater self-awareness and confidence and to improve the image of the council and the community among the wider community of Britain. He told me that although I was a member of the Jewish community I was not identified with it and as I seemed to be working very effectively for the city he decided to recruit me as the Council's first public relations man.

I took up Jack's offer to join him and became the Representative Council's honorary propagandist. During his three years in office Jack was involved in bringing to Glasgow many prominent speakers on Jewish and Israeli affairs. He also initiated courses for local people to enable them to give authoritative talks to Jewish and non-Jewish audiences on the myriad aspects of Jewish affairs and life.

Among the things the Representative Council had always taken great interest in was the plight of Jews in the Soviet Union who suffered every kind of oppression and deprivation. Jack Miller promoted a number of events to draw the problem to the attention of the British public and, perhaps even more importantly, to make the Soviet government aware of the strength of feeling world-wide about their treatment of Jews.

In the Representative Council's report for 1970-71 its joint honorary secretaries, The Rev Dr I K Cosgrove, Garnethill Synagogue's dynamic minister, and Mr Kenneth Davidson, a Glasgow business man, reported, 'The situation of the Jews in the Soviet Union continues to be more and more fully exposed, to the obvious displeasure of the Soviet authorities, who give the impression of being exceedingly perplexed and confused by the whole thing. They are unaccustomed to great masses of courageous and intelligent people publicly demanding no more than their rights according to the law of the land.'

The secretaries also reported that, 'Dr Golombok, editor of the *Jewish Echo*, and Mr Diamond continue active in characteristic style and indeed are currently engaged in ensuring that the General Assembly of the Church of Scotland pass a motion deploring the plight of Jews in the Soviet Union.'

I don't remember what happened to the motion but 14 years later, in May 1984, after a series of meetings lasting two and a half years between ministers of the Church of Scotland and leaders of the Jewish community, the Church and the Glasgow Jewish Representative Council issued a Common Statement on the evils of anti-Semitism.

A week later I sat in on a session of the General Assembly in Edinburgh along with a number of colleagues from the Representative Council to see Mr Henry Tankel, a Glasgow surgeon, president of the United Synagogue Council of Scotland, and a past president of Glasgow Jewish Representative Council, become the first Jew to address the supreme court of the Church in its 424 years. His speech was received with enthusiasm and acclaim.

Tankel told the fathers and brethren:

'The Deliverance (resolution) which initiated our discussions was a brave and noble sentiment and you placed its execution into the hands of far-seeing and upright men and women.

It is not in our hands to speak on behalf of the millions of our martyrs who have died for their faith, but it was and is in our hands to grasp firmly the hand of genuine friendship and co-operation, and this we have done. We have learned much from the meetings we have held together. Mutual respect and understanding have taken deep root and flowered into friendship.'

The meetings between the two groups started in 1981 when a Deliverance of the General Assembly stated that its Overseas Council should initiate talks with the Jewish community with a view to finding ways to strengthen the bonds of friendship and understanding between Christians and Jews.

Several people from each side took part in the talks. The leaders were the Rev Alastair Lamont, former convener of the Kirk's Church and Israel Committee, and Mr Kenneth Davidson, President of Glasgow Jewish Representative Council. Henry Tankel was another member of the Jewish group. A close observer of the talks was the then Sir (now Lord) Immanuel Jakobovits, Chief Rabbi of Britain and the Commonwealth.

My part in the operation, with the agreement and co-operation of Bruce Cannon, the Church's Director of Publicity, was to translate the very formal Common Statement into a form which would be easily digestible by the nation's news media and to organise a press conference.

I obtained permission to mount the press conference in a committee room of the City Chambers and it was attended by a large number of newspaper, radio and television people. The Statement was reported throughout Britain. Later the Rev John M Spiers, minister of Orchardhill Parish Church, Glasgow, wrote to me, 'Last Tuesday will be long remembered by all of us and I do believe it marks a new depth of understanding between our two communities.'

The Common Statement ended with the proposal that a continuing framework of liaison should be established to maintain relationships and to facilitate co-operation in matters of mutual concern and in fact this liaison is still very active.

Henry Tankel and his wife Judith have both had the distinction of serving as presidents of the Representative Council, Henry from 1974 to 1977 and Judith, the only woman to hold the post, from 1989 to 1992.

On Christmas Eve, 1970, Jack Miller was one of a party of Jews who held a 24-hour vigil in George Square in support of two Russian Jews sentenced to death by firing squad after they were found guilty at a secret trial in Leningrad of the attempted hijacking to Sweden of an airliner. If you look closely at the protesters carrying placards you can see yours truly.

Protest meetings were also held about the treatment of Jews in Arab countries. In January 1969 Iraq hanged nine of its Jewish citizens for allegedly spying for Israel. A three-hour protest vigil by Glasgow Jews in George Square attracted more than 1,200 people to the scene, including a large number of prominent churchmen.

The churchmen also turned out in force to a shop in fashionable Buchanan Street to sample the type of breakfast given to Jewish prisoners of conscience in the Soviet Union: two slices of black bread, an ounce of herring, and a cup of unsweetened hot water. My job was to ensure national press coverage for the events.

Some years later, with the co-operation of another imaginative president, Bernard Sakol, a furniture manufacturer, I devised a public write-in to our co-religionists in Russia to encourage them in their struggle for civil liberties and human rights, including the right to leave the country to live somewhere else, preferably Israel.

The write-in turned out to be the biggest event of its kind ever staged in Britain. A thousand leaders of religious groups, writers, trade unionists, politicians, academics, and many others came to the Representative Council offices in Glasgow one Sunday afternoon to write letters to people in the Soviet Union whose names and addresses we had compiled. We even supplied the notepaper and pens.

Actually the supporters didn't have to write more than their own names and addresses because members of the council's executive supplied drafts of various types of letters. The event was reported internationally by newspapers, radio and television.

Later I sent a comprehensive report about the project to every other Jewish Representative Council in Britain suggesting they mount a similar operation, but not one responded, a fact which disappointed us greatly in Glasgow. That was the kind of response that, unjustly, earned representative councils a reputation for being mere 'talking shops' where people liked to sound off about everything but didn't want actually to do anything.

I served under seven Representative Council presidents until 1994 when I lost my place on the executive committee, although I am still a delegate to the Council on behalf of the Association of Jewish Ex-servicemen. My departure from the executive committee did not upset me very much as it meant I would no longer have to sit through lengthy, boring meetings, although as a delegate I still attend the council's plenary sessions which last hours and are often even more boring.

Successive presidents have been far too democratic in allowing council members and delegates who really have nothing to add to discussions to pollute the air with the dullest of thoughts at extraordinary length, and on a disconcerting number of occasions I have said to colleagues after meetings,

'What did we decide?' to receive the answer, 'I don't know.'

One of the most excruciatingly boring subjects was the Council's constitution, to which an incredible amount of time was devoted. Over the decades council members had initiated countless useful, effective projects without even being aware that the Council *had* a constitution. This unhealthy preoccupation with, and manipulation of, constitutions is exactly the kind of thing that damages the credibility of political parties, too.

The council is currently involved in a nationwide project, Jewish Continuity, designed to persuade Jews generally to take a greater interest in their religious heritage. In Glasgow's case an enormous amount of time and money is being devoted to an attempt to bring many of its largely indifferent sons and daughters of Abraham, Isaac and Jacob back into the fold. Regular reports of the progress of Jewish Continuity contain a very high fog factor.

It is the Council's misfortune that whatever it does the Jewish community at large is still cynically ignorant of its work. One of the main reasons is that a lot of useful work is done outwith committees and the public meetings are not the stuff of newspaper headlines, even in the very few Jewish newspapers which cater for our community in Britain. Another reason is that the hierarchy of the community have little skill in communicating with their public in a way that is intelligible to them.

The last president I served with on the executive committee was Harvey Livingston, managing director of a furniture manufacturing company, a conscientious, hard-working man and the only Scottish Jew to be introduced to the Pope. Thomas Winning, Archbishop of Glasgow, invited him to Rome, along with others, to see him installed as a cardinal in November 1994. This was an acknowledgement of the Representative Councils' role in Jewish affairs rather than a personal recognition of Livingston's undoubted worth. Livingston is not the only Jew to attend a Mass, though. I have attended quite a number of them over the years for one official reason or another.

Every Representative Council president wants to be remembered for some achievement or innovation during his term of office. Some have done very valuable work for the community. Others have left behind them only relief that they have gone.

Livingston introduced the idea of 'key topic' discussions which enabled delegates and members of the community to air their views on things like education, welfare, defence, youth affairs, and the role of the Council itself.

He also conceived the admirable idea of inviting the London-based Board of Deputies of British Jews to have one of their meetings in Glasgow in March 1994 to mark the 80th anniversary of the Representative Council. It was the Board's first meeting in Scotland since it was established 234 years earlier. Some of the Londoners seemed to be surprised we northerners did not run about smeared in woad and clad in loincloths.

The guest speaker was Mr Malcolm Rifkind, Secretary of State for Defence, who was personally known to many of the delegates and of course to us in Scotland as he came from a well-known Edinburgh family and was a former Secretary of State for Scotland. He's now Foreign Secretary.

Mr Rifkind was having a pleasant Sunday among us when his day was clouded by the resignation of Sir Peter Harding, Chief of the Defence Staff, who had been revealed by the *News of the World* to have had a torrid romance with Lady Bienvenida Buck, the ex-wife of Sir Anthony Buck, a former Defence Minister.

Like Lord Provosts some Representative Council presidents have more to offer than others. One or two gave me the impression they just liked to sit at the top table in the centre of their executive officers and be looked at by an admiring audience. Their contributions certainly did not add much to the sum total of the world's knowledge.

Many years ago it was suggested I become honorary secretary of the Representative Council and work my way up the hierarchical ladder to the presidency but there are certain conventions one must obey to be lay leader of the Glasgow Jewish community and I was never very good at obeying rules.

Among them are strict adherence to religious observance, going to synagogue on every Jewish festival, eating only food prepared in accordance with Jewish dietary laws, and taking certain courses of action, not necessarily because they are productive, or even sensible, but because the president of the Representative Council is expected to be seen to be doing something about a given situation whether there is any point in his efforts or not.

On many occasions there isn't. Time after time over the more recent years the president of the Representative Council has been persuaded to issue pronouncements about international events because our community thought this was the right thing to do or because they thought their tiny voices should be heard. I really cannot see that anyone in the international corridors of power gives two hoots about the opinions of even a vociferous ethnic minority in Glasgow. I don't know how anyone can be so naive, or arrogant, to believe otherwise. The campaign for Soviet Jewry was entirely different as it was part of a world-wide campaign which went on for years.

For a time I was Chairman of the Council's Public Relations Committee but I gave up the post when I quickly discovered that I was the only one actually doing anything while everyone else just talked. The same thing applied to the Media Committee, whose function was to monitor the

Scottish news media and respond to anything which we thought misrepresented any aspect of Judaism or the policies and activities of our co-religionists in Israel. No-one on the committee was prepared to buy a large number of newspapers and listen to every radio or television news broadcast, so the only thing the committee could decide, after lengthy deliberation, was when to hold the next meeting.

The Jewish community is not an easy one to serve. Golda Meir, a former prime minister of Israel, once told a visitor that Israel had three million prime ministers, all of whom thought they could do the job better than she. The Glasgow Jewish community also has experts on every subject, a failing shared with every other Jewish community I have ever known. The less they know about a subject the more expert they are. It is no secret that I am sometimes not a patient man and I don't like to do things merely for the sake of appearances, nor do I like to be told how to do my job by people who know nothing about it.

It was an event in Russia which brought the Representative Council into existence. A Jew named Mendel Beiliss was put on trial in Kiev in October 1913 for allegedly killing a small boy, Andrew Yushinksy, for the purpose of obtaining from his body blood to be used in Jewish sacrificial rites. The charge was so ludicrous that Jews, and Christians, throughout the world protested to their own political leaders and to the Russian government.

In Glasgow the Lord Provost and a number of other local politicians signed a protest which was sent by leaders of the Jewish community to the Russian ambassador in London. Beiliss was eventually cleared of the charge against him and as a direct result of the 'blood libel' against Beiliss the Glasgow Jewish Representative Council was formed in February 1914.

It's ironic to note that in April 1981 when I was working 12 or more hours a day to promote the city of Glasgow I also helped to get Dundee some of the worst publicity in its history. The Labour-controlled city council had caused considerable anguish to Jews and non-Jews alike by twinning with the Israeli-occupied West Bank town of Nablus, flying the flag of the Palestine Liberation Organisation in the City Chambers, and sending Lord Provost James Gowans and councillors Colin Rennie, Ken Fagan, and Ian Mortimer on a 'courtesy visit' to Nablus.

A leader in the *Scotsman* commented, 'To take part in a well publicised love-in with the Palestine Liberation Organisation is a strange way for any group of Scottish politicians to behave, even if they all come from Dundee'.

The Lord Provost and his colleagues demonstrated their razor-sharp intellect and awareness of the rightness of things by presenting the mayor of Nablus, Mr Bassam al-Shaka, with a bottle of whisky he could not drink because he was a Muslim and a kilt he could not wear because his legs had been amputated after an extremist bomb attack on his car.

One of the prime movers in the 'love-in' with the PLO was the young Secretary of Dundee Labour Party, Mr George Galloway, who 13 years later as Member of Parliament for Hillhead, Glasgow, created considerable anguish in the Labour Party by going to Baghdad and appearing on Iraqi state television with the butcher of Iraq, Saddam Hussein, to salute his 'courage, power, and indefatigability.' Mr Galloway was understandably severely reprimanded by Chief Whip Mr Derek Foster and warned to behave in future.

The flagrant disregard by the city council of the feelings of most of the people of Dundee, and a great many outside it, prompted Glasgow Jewish Representative Council to stage a protest meeting in Dundee. Among the people invited to join the meeting was Mr Greville Janner, QC, MP, who was also President of the Board of Deputies of British Jews. I wrote a story about the impending visit and sent it to all the major news media.

Mindless vandals chose the day of the visit to cover the walls of Dundee Synagogue with swastikas and other anti-Semitic and anti-Zionist slogans, escalating what might have been an ordinary news story into an event of international interest. In the weeks that followed the news media gave wide coverage to Dundee's indiscretions. Among the milder comments about the city was one by Tom Brown in the *Daily Express* who wrote that Dundee was now the city of 'jute, journalism and jackasses'.

Greville Janner wrote to me later to tell me, 'Thanks for all you have done and are doing to ensure that the Dundee episode will provide a sufficiently nasty shock to the people concerned, at least to minimise the chance of a repetition elsewhere'. I'm glad my Labour masters in Glasgow didn't know what I was doing otherwise my local government career might have been cut dramatically short.

Another event for which I managed to achieve a great deal of publicity was the 50th anniversary, in November 1988, of *Kristallnacht*, night of the broken glass, when the Nazis ran amok in Germany and Austria and murdered and arrested thousands of Jews. Reporters flocked to a commemorative service organised by Glasgow Jewish Youth Council and hundreds of Jewish homes in the city had lighted candles in memory of their co-religionists who suffered the night of mindless violence and terror when 36 Jews were killed, 40 seriously injured, and 30,000 arrested and sent to concentration camps, 191 synagogues were set ablaze, 76 demolished and more than 800 Jewish shops and 170 homes were destroyed. I supplied the press with the names and address of several Glasgow people who had survived that terrible night, 9 November, 1938.

Although I try not to be obtrusive about it I am one of those people who think that people living in comfort and safety, including my fellow Jews, should not be allowed to forget the things that have happened to our co-religionists over the decades, and even centuries. My own community was by no means the only ethnic community for whom I handled publicity projects. I took the view that it would do my community no harm if a Jew was known to be willing to help others, too, and over the years I helped the Chinese, French and Muslim communities with publicity projects. In November 1986 Bashir Maan, a leader of Glasgow's Muslim community and at the time a district councillor (he is again now), asked me for help in publicising a feat achieved by eight-year-old Jamil Moghul.

Jamil had memorised the 86,430 words of the Koran, the sacred book of Muslims, and had successfully passed a test of random passages. My story of his achievement went round the world. Bashir told me later that my story appeared in the newspapers of most Islamic countries, in America, and even in Japan.

The book, written in Arabic, is regarded as the word of God as revealed to the prophet Mohammed through the angel Gabriel. Its various parts were written down from the prophet's lips on dried leaves, bits of leather and whatever else came to hand. Those who could not write memorised the words, which consist of history, legends, prophecies, moral precepts and laws. Only about one per cent of the world's Muslims (the faithful) memorise the Koran these days, Bashir told me.

The histories are chiefly about Old Testament characters and many of the doctrines and laws are the same as those of Judaism or of Christianity. Moses, Jesus, and Mohammed are named as the greatest of the line of prophets sent by God to lead mankind in the path of truth. All of which makes me wonder why there is such hostility between many of the devotees of three of the world's leading religions.

There was one occasion in which I had to turn down a request for my help. In May 1984 the Central Mosque was opened in Glasgow at a cost of £2,750,000, in what was the old Gorbals area and Bashir Maan asked me if I would do some public relations work for it.

At that time I was what the news media described as 'a leading member of the Jewish community', and as Muslim countries, including Pakistan, did not, and still don't, recognise the State of Israel which means so much to people like me I had to decline the invitation.

It's interesting that an ethnic community other than my own had to come to me at all. The reason was that although they had spokesmen these were

BACK TO THE FOLD

only called upon by the news media when 'something bad' happened in their communities.

'Very little of the positive things that happen among us, in cultural, social, communal activities appear in print,' said Bashir.

Some years ago I was one of several members of the executive of the Jewish Representative Council who met, at their request, with a number of Asian leaders who were interested in forming a representative council. After the formal talks were over one of our visitors told me, 'We can't form an organisation like yours. We would start a war between ourselves over who would be the president.'

Nowadays there are a number of Asian journalists among their 150,000-strong community in the West of Scotland, but apparently still no-one who can supply the news media with the more positive type of material about the community's activities, a lack which I think is rather sad.

Chapter 13

THE *EXODUS* SAILS AGAIN

ISRAEL has a number of *shlichim*, emissaries, stationed in various parts of the world whose job ostensibly is to strengthen ties between Israel and local Jewish communities, but whose real job is to persuade people, especially young people, to make *Aliyah*, emigrate to Israel. All the emissaries are volunteers employed by the Jewish Agency. In addition to doing something useful for their country it gives them the opportunity to work abroad for two or three years and experience life elsewhere.

In 1986 the emissary in Glasgow was Uzi Shilon, a Tel Aviv lawyer. One day he came to me and said he had an idea to commemorate *Yom Ha'atzmaut*, the anniversary of the declaration of the State of Israel in 1948. As honorary Public Relations Officer of the Jewish Representative Council I was often called upon by a variety of Jewish organisations and groups to do some publicity work for them. I didn't mind because most of the publicity jobs were interesting and enabled me, too, to do something useful for my co-religionists.

Shilon had the idea of hiring the Clyde pleasure steamer *Waverley* and re-enacting the voyage of the *Exodus*, whose exploits in 1947 made headlines throughout the world. We were sitting in his office discussing how we could make the re-enactment really newsworthy when he mentioned casually that he knew the whereabouts of Ike Aranne, the man who captained *Exodus* 39 years earlier. Now 62, he was living in Tel Aviv and understandably was in the shipping business.

'Get him on the phone,' I said. 'Tell him what we are doing and ask him to come and join us.'

Aranne wasn't all that enthusiastic about the idea but Uzi was very persuasive and he finally agreed. The next obvious step was to get another man who played a major role in the 1947 adventure, Captain Tony Bailey, who commanded *HMS Childers*, one of the six British destroyers which prevented the Exodus from entering Haifa with its human cargo of 4,554 refugees from all over Europe.

Bailey, now 70, had long retired from the Navy and was living in Bridgewater, Somerset. He, too, agreed to come to Glasgow and join the 600 Scottish Jews who took part in the re-enactment, which was reported throughout Britain and in Israel.

The 1986 'emigrants' aboard the *Waverley*, renamed *Exodus* for the day, sailed from Anderston Quay on their three-hour voyage on a chilly May morning. They were more fortunate than their predecessors four decades earlier who spent two months at sea in conditions which shocked the world.

The modern-day voyagers reported to an 'emigration' registration desk on the quayside although there was no time for such formalities in 1947. Five areas of the ship were named after Israeli cities, Jerusalem, Haifa, Tel Aviv, Ashkelon and Eilat.

Various activities were organised for each area, some relating to the massive outpouring of Jews from Europe and some more appropriate to a summer's evening sail on the Clyde. Among the activities was a showing of the film *Exodus* with Paul Newman.

As we sailed down the quiet river Captain Bailey told me, 'There is no bitterness between Ike Aranne and me. We are good friends. This is not our first meeting since 1947. We had a very enjoyable dinner with our wives in Jaffa one night in 1980. As a naval officer in 1947 I considered it my duty to obey my orders to prevent the Jews from landing in Palestine. If we had failed there would have been another Arab rebellion causing chaos in the Middle East and perhaps even preventing the establishment of a state of Israel at all. We had a lot of sympathy for the immigrants, herded as they were like cattle in overcrowded, insanitary and often unseaworthy craft. It was the most distasteful as well as the most difficult assignment ever given to the Royal Navy, certainly in peacetime.'

Ike Aranne said, 'All of us at that time of turmoil were reluctant players in a macabre drama. British politicians of the period had a lot to answer for but the servicemen were generally not unkind in an impossible situation.'

The original *Exodus*, real name the *President Warfield*, was a former pleasure steamer which had been used for sailing in Chesapeake Bay, Maryland, when she was bought by the Jewish Agency from an American scrap dealer and taken to France to be fitted out as a refugee ship. It had also been a British training ship during the war.

The *President Warfield* had been christened by the owner's niece Wallis Warfield, later to become Duchess of Windsor. Despite strict orders from the French government, in response to British representations prohibiting the ship's departure, Captain Aranne, a 23-year-old former wartime seaman in

Britain's merchant navy, quietly sailed the *President Warfield* out of the tiny port of Sète at 0600 hours on 12 July, 1947 carrying 1,600 men, 1,282 women, 1,017 teenagers, and 655 children on a ship that was built to hold 600 people.

Once in the open Mediterranean on route to Haifa a huge banner bearing the words 'HAGANAH SHIP EXODUS 1947' was unfolded. The Haganah was the Jewish defence force which in 1945 began organising the emigration of displaced European Jews to Palestine in defiance of the British blockade.

Twenty miles from Haifa the 1,800-ton *Exodus* was buffeted by the destroyers *Childers, Ajax, Cheviot, Chequers, Chieftain* and *Charity* and boarded. Among the weapons used by the boarders were Chinese crackers to create noise and confusion. The refugees fought back with cans of food, iron bars, steam and oil jets, metal buckets and bottles. Three of the refugees were killed and more than 200 injured in the battle.

The battered *Exodus* was towed into Haifa on 18 July and the embittered passengers transferred to three caged transport ships *Runnymede Park, Ocean Vigour* and *Empire Rival* which sailed back to Port-de-Bouc, near Marseilles. The French government, however, would not allow the refugees to be forcibly landed in France and they were taken to Hamburg, back to the country in which they had for many years suffered unspeakable horrors.

Most of the *Exodus* refugees later sailed in other illegal immigrant ships to Cyprus and then to Israel when the new state was born on 14 May, 1948. The *Exodus* was the largest of the 34-strong armada of illegal ships. One of them, the *Struma*, sank in the Black Sea after being refused entry to Palestine. Not one of the 769 people aboard survived.

Every move of the *Exodus* and the plight of its passengers was reported worldwide to the embarassment of the British and French governments. The episode and the relentless Arab hostility towards the Jews finally led Britain to relinquish its rule over Palestine, which had begun in December 1917 when British troops marched into Jerusalem to wrest the country from Turkish control.

The last British commander in Palestine was General Sir Gordon MacMillan of MacMillan under whom I served in the 1940s and again decades later in a very different capacity when he became chairman of Erskine Hospital for disabled ex-servicemen and women at Bishopton, near Glasgow.

General MacMillan's contacts with the Jewish Agency during his command in Palestine were through a young liaison officer named Chaim Herzog who later became President of Israel.

The historian Netaniel Lorch wrote of General MacMillan, 'Although he was often at loggerheads with the Haganah he did his best to carry out his responsibilities as an officer and a gentleman. He personally intervened on occasion to safeguard the lives of the Jewish population under his charge.'

Chapter 14

THE SCULPTOR WHO NEFFER HEARD OF ME

WORK started at the end of 1995 on a restoration programme of Garnethill Synagogue, the first purpose-built synagogue in Scotland, at a cost of almost half a million pounds. Such is the regard in which this great institution is held that considerable contributions to the restoration fund were made by bodies like Historic Scotland, Glasgow City Council, the Heritage Lottery Fund, the Wolfson Foundation, and the Scottish Churches Architectural Heritage Trust, in addition to the synagogue's own capital fund and individual members.

Several members of the synagogue were involved in the fund-raising process but two men did more than anyone else to achieve what many people thought was impossible: Mr Gerald Levin, the congregation's president, and Mr Trevor Schuster Davis, its honorary solicitor.

Not everyone approved of the expenditure of such a large sum of money on the synagogue's restoration, least of all the other synagogues and their members, because Garnethill, in the West End of Glasgow, does not have the volume of attendances it once had. Most of Glasgow's Jewry belong to congregations in Giffnock and Newton Mearns, on the south side of the city where they live. Some of my co-religionists have fallen by the wayside and don't belong to any synagogue and efforts are made from time to time to attract them back to the fold.

Garnethill, with the role it has played in the history of the Jewish community of Glasgow, does however attract many visitors and in the past few years it has been visited by hundreds of schoolchildren, students, and church groups. Open Doors Day can attract more than 500 visitors.

Another justification for refurbishing the synagogue at such great cost is that it has housed the ever-growing Scottish Jewish Archives Centre since it was established in April 1987. The centre is visited by almost 1,000 people a year, including Jews, non-Jews interested in Judaism, students doing research, youth groups, and, like the synagogue, many church groups and schoolchildren. Coincidentally, the archives came into being a year after I wrote a proposal to establish a Museum of Judaism at Garnethill to ensure the building's survival.

Garnethill Synagogue is considered by many to be Scotland's premier Jewish house of worship. Although it was the first synagogue to be built in Scotland a number of premises were used as synagogues a long time before that.

Its members also founded a considerable number of communal organisatons: the Glasgow Hebrew Philanthropic Society, the Hebrew Boot and Clothing Guild, the Ladies' Benevolent Society, the Dorcas Welfare Clinic, the Jewish Lads Brigade, Lodge Montefiore and Glasgow Jewish Choral Society. The last three are still flourishing, although the Lads Brigade now has lassies, too.

Members of the synagogue have played important roles in Glasgow's political and professional life over the decades. Mr Michael Simons, one of its founders, served on the town council for many years and became a magistrate and Deputy Lieutenant of the city after turning down the post of Lord Provost.

Half a century later in 1958 another Jewish councillor, Myer Galpern, became the city's first Jewish Lord Provost and later a knight, Member of Parliament for Shettleston, Deputy Speaker of the House of Commons, and in 1979 a life peer.

Another councillor, Ernest Greenhill, became City Treasurer and in 1950 a peer. Horace Phillips became a distinguished diplomat, a knight, and Britain's ambassador to Turkey from 1973 to 1977. Eight of Garnethill's members became university professors: Ian Heilbron distinguished himself in chemistry; Noah Morris and Abraham Goldberg in medicine; Otto Hutter, physiology; Michael Samuels, English language; Frederick Stone, psychiatry; Daiches Raphael, politics; and Israel Levine in mathematics.

Sir Ian Heilbron, a son of David Heilbron, another of the synagogue's founders, was scientific adviser to the government in the 1914-1918 war. Asher Asher, Glasgow University's first Jewish student, graduated in medicine in 1856. In 1926 the synagogue's newly-appointed cantor, the Rev Issac Hirshow, graduated in arts and in October 1939 he became the university's first Bachelor of Music and was given the privilege of choosing the academic colours of the new degree, blue and white.

The day Garnethill Synagogue opened Queen Victoria still had two more decades to reign, the telephone and the gramophone were grating infants, Tchaikovsky's masterpiece *Eugene Onegin* was given its first performance in Moscow, and in Glasgow Mr McTear of St Rollox Chemical Works claimed to have made artificial diamonds.

The year was 1879 and on an overcast Tuesday afternoon crowds of people, mostly on foot but some in hired broughams and landaus, made their way up several steep cobbled streets in the West End of Glasgow to attend what the *Glasgow Herald* called 'a unique and attractive ceremony', the dedication of the synagogue.

One hundred years to the day later, 9 September, 1979, with a flair that would have impressed that old master interpreter of the Bible himself, Cecil B De Mille, a group of Glasgow Jews, myself among them, produced a spectacular of our own in celebration of the centenary.

Jack Miller, a member of the synagogue's ruling council of laymen, and his friend Dr Sidney Naftalin had a few months earlier conceived the idea of staging a series of celebratory events appropriate to an institution of such importance in the history of Scottish Jewry.

I had no connection with the synagogue but Jack recruited me to the organising committee anyway. As Head of Public Relations for the city it was not difficult for me to negotiate venues for all the events with my colleagues in the Council and to publicise them widely. The result was that a local event was made of interest to news media in Israel, Europe and America, as well as of course the rest of Britain.

The Israeli newspaper *Ma'ariv* (Evening) described Glasgow as a noisy industrial city, the Tel Aviv of Scotland just as Edinburgh is the Jerusalem. The paper went on, 'Many people who wanted to make a name for themselves in business went to Glasgow. One of the most famous is Sir Isaac Wolfson who still has a faint Glasgow accent although he left the city many years ago in his youth.'

The curtain went up on the main celebratory event on 9 September when a cast of 400 gathered in the old synagogue-on-the-hill for a thanksgiving ceremony. This was followed by a banquet in the Victorian splendour of the City Chambers.

A galaxy of stars from a variety of firmaments, including politics, the church, medicine, law, science, diplomacy, the halls of academe, and industry and commerce, joined in the celebrations.

Among them were Mr George Younger, Secretary of State for Scotland, Lord Provost David Hodge, Roman Catholic Bishop Joseph Devine, Lord Galpern (a former Lord Provost), Dr Alwyn Williams, and Sir Samuel Curran, principals of Glasgow and Strathclyde Universities, and retired diplomat Sir Horace Phillips.

The thanksgiving ceremony was conducted by Dr (later Lord) Immanuel Jacobovits, the Chief Rabbi, Rabbi Leon Benarroch, minister of Garnethill, and the Rev Ernest Levy.

At the banquet my wife and I had no sooner sat down when a council usher tapped me quietly on the shoulder and said, 'Would you go along to the Lord Provost's room, please, Harry?'

There I found the Secretary of State, the Lord Provost, and one or two others trying to sort out some difficulty which had arisen with the arrangements for the Chief Rabbi's return to London later that night. By the time I got back to the dinner table the meal was almost over. I was not amused as I had been looking forward to the occasion for months.

Among other events were a 'Jewish Way of Life Exhibition' in Hillhead Library, with which we were given great help by Andrew Miller, Director of Libraries, an exhibition of Jewish art in Glasgow's flagship museum at Kelvingrove, and two quizzes, one for schoolchildren and the other for adults. The two exhibitions were a great success and attracted 38,300 visitors.

The Exhibition of Jewish Art had its own organising committee to assist the City Council's very experienced Director of Museums and Art Galleries, Alasdair Auld. The members of our committee included my friends Miller and Naftalin, and Mr Benno Schotz, the Queen's Sculptor in Ordinary in Scotland, whom we elected Honorary President. The Chairman was Mr Michael Goldberg, an arts graduate of Glasgow University, a director of the Scottish National Orchestra, a former chairman of the Citizens Theatre, a lover of painting and sculpture, playwright, and joint managing director of the department store group A Goldberg and Sons. A formidable collection.

At one meeting at the home of Michael Goldberg the subject of publicity was brought up by Benno Schotz. I was sitting next to him and said quietly, 'I don't think you need worry about publicity, I'm looking after that.'

Benno leaned back, stared at me with raised eyebrows as if I had suddenly been beamed down from the Starship *Enterprise*, and said imperiously, 'Vot iss your name?'

'Henry Diamond.'

'I haf neffer heard of you!' said the Queen's Sculptor in Ordinary.

'I don't think you're alone in that,' I told Benno, 'but I'm taking care of the publicity anyway.'

A slight edge had entered my voice as I perhaps arrogantly considered myself quite good at what I did, including convenership of the one-man Centenary Publicity Committee. Benno made no further comment.

In the weeks that followed I organised messages of goodwill from the Queen, Prime Minister Margaret Thatcher, and Menachem Begin, Prime Minister of Israel. In my letter to Begin I told him I had heard him speak at the Methodist Hall in London the previous year and I was taking the advice he had given to the audience, 'When you are trying to achieve something worthwhile never take no for an answer'.

I learned later that Begin wrote a lengthy message and told an aide, 'See that Henry Diamond gets this message in Glasgow as soon as possible. He never takes no for an answer!'

Naturally I publicised the messages widely, not forgetting my own part in the operation.

Not long after the celebrations my wife and I were delighted to be awarded honorary membership of the synagogue, which I have attended regularly ever since. For some years now I have also been a member of the Synagogue Council.

A year after the centenary celebrations Sidney Naftalin, a close friend of Benno Schotz and his general practitioner, asked me if I could do anything to obtain the Freedom of the City of Glasgow for Benno. I have to admit I was not filled with enthusiasm at the idea. Maybe I was being small-minded about Benno's comment about neffer having heard of me, but Sidney was a man of great charm and persuasiveness for whom I had affection so I finally succumbed and wrote a nomination for Benno, who generated affection and loyalty from his friends despite a tendency to identify himself with Epstein and Rodin in the Mount Rushmore of sculptors.

I couldn't put my own name to the nomination as I felt I made enough demands on my political masters without that kind of thing so I gave it back to Sidney who had it signed by a number of influential figures including the then president of the Representative Council, Dr Gerald Jesner, Lord Galpern, Harry Barnes, Director of Glasgow School of Art and Sir Robin Philipson, President of the Royal Scottish Academy.

I then got it back and slipped it furtively under the door of the Town Clerk and Chief Executive Steve Hamilton who in turn gave it to the Leader of the Council for consideration by the ruling Labour group. I don't know if Steve knew where it really came from because he never said anything but there weren't many people in the City Chambers who didn't know I was active in Jewish affairs. Besides, I think many people also had come to recognise my flights of rhetoric. I had a few chuckles as I indulged in one or two of them in Benno's nomination:

'The accompanying biography will give you the highlights in the career of this distinguished Glaswegian whose work is recognised worldwide and who has brought such credit to the city in which he has lived and worked so long. Conferment of the Freedom of the City would be regarded by this great artist as the ultimate honour.

It would be difficult in a letter of this kind to list the famous and not-so-famous who have been immortalised in the work of Benno Schotz or the cities and institutions of the world in which his work is proudly displayed. In Glasgow itself his artistry can be seen in many churches and schools and in private institutions, including the Art Galllery and Museum in Kelvingrove. We hope this submission will be given the earnest consideration of your council.'

A few days later a senior member of the Labour group asked me, 'Did you write the nomination for Benno Schotz?'

'Me!' I exclaimed in feigned surprise. 'Nothing to do with me. I'm just an innocent bystander.'

Benno was later awarded the Freedom along with world champion lightweight boxer Jim Watt, Sir Samuel Curran, and Nelson Mandela, the black African nationalist leader, who was still confined on Robben Island. Dr Alex Ekwuene, Vice-President of Nigeria, accepted the Burgess Ticket Freedom on his behalf.

I'm rather ashamed to admit that when I first heard the name Nelson Mandela I didn't know who he was, but I wasn't alone. When I hesitatingly asked a friend in the City Chambers he said, 'Isn't he a pop group leader!'

Some years later Benno Schotz's daughter Cherna Crome, a trustee of his estate, phoned to say she wanted to present one of her father's works to the City Council and could I do something to bring that about. She told me it had been his intention to present the work to the Lord Provost as a gesture of gratitude for his Freedom but a combination of circumstances interfered with this plan and he died in 1984 without making the gift.

I wrote to the Lord Provost explaining Mrs Crome's request and a presentation was organised for Wednesday, 28 August, 1991, the 100th anniversary of his birth.

The presentation of the work, 'Dedication', a 5ft 6in welded bronze, valued at £20,000, was made by 14-year-old Avigail Schotz, the sculptor's granddaughter, who flew from her home in Los Angeles for the event. Her father Amiel flew from the biblical town of Beersheba in the Negev desert of Israel.

'Dedication' is considered to be one of the sculptor's finest pieces of its kind and is still prominently displayed in the City Chambers.

Cherna very kindly gave me one of the many drawings of stones done by her father but unfortunately it is not signed, which rather diminishes its value.

Chapter 15

I'M SUED FOR £7 MILLION

TOURISM and conferences are big business for Scotland, although I am consistently astonished at the attitude of many hotels and restaurants in so-called tourist areas where it is impossible to get a meal outside the traditional lunch and dinner hours. In some places which should know better the staff will give you a cup of tea, but no biscuit, if you make a fuss. I think our problem in Scotland is that we equate service with servility. The sooner this attitude changes the better.

In the area covered by the Greater Glasgow Tourist Board tourism and conferences mean an annual income of £600 million and employment for 47,500 people. For the city of Glasgow alone the conference market is worth more than £33 million a year.

These figures may well be considerably increased by events like the Festival of Visual Arts in 1996, the Rotary International Conference in 1997, and the city's role as City of Architecture and Design in 1999.

In May 1978 a writer in the magazine *Conferences and Exhibitions* wrote, 'If Glasgow becomes one of Britain's major conference cities ... thanks will be due to six people. The first is Harry Diamond, Public Relations Officer of Glasgow District Council, the person responsible for convincing several committees and individuals that the city should have a full-time conference officer.'

I had long been interested in conferences as a source of revenue for the city. I had spent a great deal of time the previous year doing a survey on the subject which revealed that not many people in the city appeared to know much about this very fruitful source of revenue.

There were exceptions like Hamish Taylor and his colleagues in the Round Table movement who had successfully negotiated Glasgow as the venue in 1978 for the annual conference of the National Association of Round Tables in Great Britain and Ireland, when something like 6,000 Round Tablers came to Glasgow. Hamish was generous enough to thank me in some of their promotional literature for my 'forward-looking' help with the conference.

During my survey I was surprised at the attitude of the city's big hotels, even the ones that belonged to international groups. Their idea of promotion was to produce expensive colour brochures with pictures of empty rooms and hotel managers and guests wearing funny hats. The hotel people didn't seem to understand that a hotel cannot effectively be promoted in isolation. People also want to know what the location, town or city, has to offer after the day's talking is over.

I decided that another way to publicise the city far and wide was to appoint someone whose specific function would be to persuade conference organisers and tourist agents throughout the world that Glasgow was the place to come to.

One of the people who encouraged me into doing something about conferences was John McGhee, Chairman of the Scottish Conference Association, who was quoted in the *Glasgow Herald* as saying, 'Glasgow has exceptionally good conference facilities but there is no-one there with the sole responsibility of spreading the word among conference organisers.'

Although John was also Conference Manager of Edinburgh District Council and a rival, he took the sensible view that there was enough business for us both, and that we should both go after it. In the *Daily Express* a writer said, 'Glasgow may be losing millions of pounds a year by failing to cash in adequately on the conference business.'

I gathered a lot of information about the industry and eventually submitted a proposal to my council to let me employ a conference promotions manager in my department. A member of the council, Dr Michael Kelly, an economics lecturer at the University of Strathclyde, told the General Purposes Committee, 'This is the best proposal we have had for a long time.' The proposal was approved.

The following day a leader in the Glasgow *Evening Times* said my proposal was an excellent scheme which would have many spin-off benefits:

'Most important is that it will bring people from other cities and other countries to Glasgow to see what we have to offer.

Business will get a chance to see the city's potential and individuals who enjoy their stay may come back and bring their families. There are major cities in America and Europe which are known almost exclusively as conference centres — and there's no reason why Glasgow shouldn't cash in. The council has no choice but to give it the go-ahead. It could give Glasgow a new lease of life — and a new image.'

A number of candidates applied for the Conference Manager's job and I appointed a young man named Chris Day from another department of the Council. Chris worked very hard, travelled widely, and created quite an impact on the conference scene. I also encouraged him to stir up interest in the tourist business and we formed GLASGOW ACTS, the Glasgow Association for Conference and Tourism Services. The council had a tourist information hut in George Square from the early 1960s but it catered only for passers-by or people who wrote asking for information.

The real trick was to go out to the big wide world and tell everyone what Glasgow had to offer and persuade them it was in their interest to go there. We produced brochures containing information about conference facilities, hotels, function suites, and exhibition areas and sent them all over the world. And of course we continued to write news stories about the city's attractions which also went far and wide.

Our efforts did bring a lot of people to Glasgow to find out what all the noise was about. Among them was a young lady named Yoko Hasegawa, Senior Information Officer of the British Tourist Authority in New York, who wanted to gather information for a BTA guidebook being published in Japan.

Yoko spent three days in Glasgow seeing the sights. She also went for a ride in the underground which she said the Japanese were asking about. At the end of her stay in the city she dutifully commented with a smile, 'Glasgow is very interesting!'

There was one exhibition in which I played the major role in bringing it to Glasgow through my friendship with John Whiffen, Director of Public Relations in the Japan External Trade Organisation (JETRO) in London. The Japan Today exhibition came to Glasgow for nine days in October 1981. It was the first exhibition of its kind in Britain and was devised to explain the Japanese way of life in the 1980s.

Mr Tadao Iguchi, director of JETRO, was widely quoted as saying they had chosen Glasgow because it was Scotland's largest and most important city, a statement which I was told later generated some indignation in the office of my opposite number in Edinburgh. The exhibition was held in the banqueting hall of the City Chambers and was a great success. Later it went to Manchester and Cardiff.

Officials from JETRO visited Glasgow a number of times in the following years. After one visit in 1988 John Whiffen wrote to me to thank me for arranging for his Director General Mr Tsuneo Osumi to meet the Lord Provost and for driving him around the city. 'Your excellent driving technique left Mr Osumi in a state of shock. It took him a week to recover!'

John told me recently that Mr Osumi, who retired to Japan some time ago, still asks after my health and welfare. He is far too polite to say so but I get the impression he is surprised I am still alive!

Six months after Chris's appointment we were able to announce that he had brought 11 conferences to the city, bringing in £500,000 in revenue. His enthusiasm reached fever pitch when I sent him to an International Police Association conference in America. He made an enthusiastic and impressive presentation to the conference and later sent me a telex to say the organisers had decided to hold their 1984 conference in Glasgow. I spread widely the information that 1,000 policemen from 50 countries would meet in the city, which would benefit from an income of about £200,000.

Unfortunately Chris had misunderstood a statement by the conference organisers who had decided on a different venue. The newspapers gave him a hard time because of something that wasn't altogether his fault and he resigned, quite unnecessarily in my opinion as he may have got some ragging from politicians and officials but they wouldn't have demanded his execution. They were more likely to have demanded mine. I certainly wasn't prepared to fire him as he was doing a good job.

The conference and tourist business went from strength to strength. In 1982 preparations began for Welcome Home to Glasgow 1983, the biggest tourism promotion ever mounted by the city, sponsored by the City Council, Scottish Tourist Board, and the British Tourist Authority at a cost of about £130,000.

Lord Provost Michael Kelly told 25 million listeners to the Overseas Service of the BBC about the promotion. He also went to America and Canada to spread the word. News stories and advertisements appeared in most English-speaking countries, including America, Canada and Australasia, where there were said to be 10 million people with family connections with Glasgow and the West of Scotland.

Newspapers, airlines, travel agents, and individuals all helped us to collect many thousands of names and addresses of people abroad who had any connections with Glasgow and the West of Scotland. Fifty thousand booklets were produced, listing nearly 600 events spread out through 1983: exhibitions, concerts, anniversaries, displays, and sports events among them.

At a launch in the City Chambers attended by about 1,000 people a specially-produced brochure containing 70 holiday ideas featuring Glasgow and the West of Scotland was given to everyone. The brochure was produced by Harry Steven, UK Marketing Manager of the British Tourist Authority who had been seconded to Glasgow to help to promote the Welcome Home promotion. Steven also went to America and France with news of the promotion. Groups of travel agents from America and Canada arrived in Glasgow weekly. At the end of 1983 it was estimated that an extra 10,000 people had visited the city.

Among the business organisations in the city which used the promotion to help sell their own products was a whisky company who produced an attractively-boxed flagon of 'Old Glasgow' blended whisky. The managing director of the company asked the Lord Provost to write a personal message to go into a presentation box and of course I got the job of writing the message. I have to admit I was rather pleased with the magnificent bit of hyperbole I conjured up:

'Few potions devised by man have contained the magical properties of Scotch whisky. Throughout the centuries it has been immortalised in poetry, song and prose. Two centuries ago in the turbulent times that followed the union of Scotland and England the English tried to impose a tax on whisky, a circumstance which led to smuggling and illicit distilling on a heroic scale in the Highlands of Scotland.

It also prompted Robert Burns, Scotland's greatest poet, to write "whisky and freedom gang thegither." Round about the same time James Hogg wrote that if whisky were taken in the right proportions every day a body "might leeve for ever without dying at a' and doctors and kirkyards would go oot o' fashion." A fanciful notion but obviously written with deep sympathy and reverence. Perhaps that's why whisky is known to Gaelic speakers as *uisgebeatha*, "water of life".

In 1969 John Scott Livie, a formidable but knowledgeable figure in the Scotch whisky industry, was quoted throughout the world as claiming that even the animal feed which is a by-product of whisky-making has a magic of its own — "It cures cows of rickets and makes blind hens see again."

This flagon carrying the city's Coat of Arms and its contents have been specially produced for Welcome Home to Glasgow 1983, the most ambitious holiday promotion in the 808-year history of our great city, aimed principally at the estimated 10 million people in the world said to have family connections with Glasgow and its immediate environs.

I hope that when you taste the warmth of Old Glasgow it will remind you of the warmth of your welcome home, of the renewal of old friendships and the making of new ones, of the fascinating changes you have seen in old Glasgow, which have transformed it from a one-time grimy but bustling heart of a great industrial empire into the famous commercial and administrative centre, holiday base, and acknowledged

European city of culture it has become.

And I hope you will be persuaded to come back again and bring others with you.'

At the height of the Welcome Home promotion Mr Raymond Gillies, a Glasgow businessman, came into my office one day and asked me to let him have a copy of the list of names we had collected from the various sources because he had a scheme to promote the city overseas. I wasn't at all happy about the idea as I didn't really see how a small businessman could do anything that we weren't doing a great deal better. Mr Gillies pleaded commercial confidentiality when I asked him what the scheme was but he insisted it was a good scheme from which the city would benefit, and he was willing to pay for our list of names.

I finally gave in and sold Mr Gillies the list for, I think, about £150, a purely nominal sum as the various sources which had helped us to compile the list had devoted considerable time and expense to collecting the many thousands of names on it.

A few months later the Scottish press revealed that Mr Gillies's scheme to raise £100 million by selling square-inch plots of Loch Lomondside had failed, leaving Mr Gillies with, he claimed, debts of £200,000. He had formed a charity called Mission Possible International and spent £35,000 on parchment certificates to give to buyers of square inches. The £100 million was to be devoted to sponsoring Highland gatherings round the world, Scottish music and art studies, folklore, Gaelic Mods, and a national park, among other things.

None of this was now possible, Mr Gillies told the newspapers, because the number of names sold to him by Harry Diamond had contained a lot less than the 85,000 names he had been told. Thousands of the certificates sent abroad had been returned 'address unknown'.

I felt rather sorry for Mr Gillies, who was also principal of the well-known House of Hearing, as I felt his scheme had one or two flaws, one of them being that he did not own the land he offered for sale.

About a couple of months later a Sheriff officer appeared at my office and handed me a writ issued by Mr Gillies for damages of £7 million. Lord Provost Michael Kelly, Mr Steven Hamilton, the Town Clerk, and Mr Theo Crombie, a town clerk depute, were also named as defenders.

This was the first time I had ever been sued, although I had been threatened often enough, and the 13-page writ in legal jargon looked extremely intimidating. The writ said, among a great many other things, that we had entirely decimated the pursuer's worldwide sales campaign at a stroke by communicating malicious, injurious falsehoods and imputations on the honour and on the validity of the pursuer's title to the aforesaid property which he had properly and correctly acquired from Glasgow District Council and paid for in full, thus severely hampering the pursuer's sales marketing promotion, leaving his entire sales campaign in utter ruin.

There were a number of hearings at which we were represented by our very able solicitor Mr Peter Balance, and eventually a Sheriff told Mr Gillies that he had no alternative but to dismiss the action on the present state of the pleadings, and in order to save himself further expenses Mr Gillies agreed to the dismissal.

None of this interfered with our promotion of conferences and tourism and the conference business was given an enormous boost by the Confederation of British Industry's annual conference which came to Glasgow in November 1983. It was the first time the event was held outside England. Sir James (now Lord) Goold, immediate past president of the CBI in Scotland, was quoted as saying, 'We chose Glasgow because it is the business capital of Scotland', a remark which I used to good effect in many press releases.

In 1983, too, the Greater Glasgow Tourist Board was opened. A couple of years later came the Scottish Exhibition and Conference Centre and in 1987 the Tourist Board added its Convention Bureau to its activities. A new auditorium costing £30 million, big enough to accommodate more than 3,000 people, will be built on to the SECC in time for the Rotary International conference in 1997. Incidentally, Edinburgh's International Conference Centre opened for business in September 1995.

The Glasgow Tourist Board's first chief executive, an Ulsterman named Eddie Friel, was appointed in the second half of 1983. He immediately demonstrated his perceptive observation of the world's news media by declaring on radio and television that Glasgow's merits as a tourist centre were 'the best kept secret in Europe.' Eddie later went to Belfast as Chief Executive of the Northern Ireland Tourist Board and generated headlines on both sides of the Irish Sea by mysteriously disappearing a few months after he got there. He eventually turned up back in Glasgow as a tourism consultant.

Ever mindful of the value of a headline-making phrase, Eddie, according to the *Sheffield Weekly Gazette*, told a press conference in Sheffield in July 1944, that their city was 'one of the best kept secrets on the globe.'

Chapter 16

CALIFORNIA ...
HERE WE COME

The attraction of investment and the creation of jobs was always in everyone's mind in the City Chambers, and still is. Politicians frequently made pious statements about what the Council was doing in these areas. In fact a local authority could do very little about either. Inward investment, which really meant from abroad, and the creation of jobs depended on many factors outside a district council's control: the value of the pound, the state of the country's economy, the state of European and world economy, interest rates, public confidence.

I really thought I had cracked it when a letter arrived in December 1978 from Mr Norman Eckersley, Chairman of the Chartered Bank of London's American operation in California.

Mr Eckersley said he had read about my plan to promote Glasgow to the world and attract more investment and offered to help me in the western states of America. His bank was in the final stages of completing the largest foreign cash investment in America by the purchase of the Union Bank of California for $400 million and they would then have 65 branches throughout the state. All of these would be at our disposal.

Understandably I got quite excited about Mr Eckersley's offer and immediately reported to it Steve Hamilton, the Town Clerk and Chief Executive, and the political hierarchy. This was attracting attention to the city at a time when it really needed it. Unemployment was very high and the city's economy was in the doldrums. Help to attract inward investment and create more jobs was just what we were looking for.

Mr Eckersley's letter told me he had personal connections with Glasgow and still had a house there. He said he was a regular visitor to Glasgow and would call in to see me next time he was there. It turned out that Mr Eckersley had once worked in Glasgow, his wife Ena was born there, and he had a strong affection for Scotland. He was also a keen football fan and used to phone Glasgow from America to get the result of Rangers' matches.

The banker later wrote to tell me when he would be in the city and with the agreement of the Council I arranged a press conference at which he would announce his offer to help us. He told the enormous number of news media people who turned up that he would give Glasgow free use of his bank's marketing, public relations, and promotions departments, an office, reference facilities, and support staff in Los Angeles and San Francisco.

All Glasgow had to do was appoint a 'super-salesman' to stay in California for a year or two and sell the city's merits to the influential and very wealthy American business community in 'Silicon Valley' and beyond.

The following day the headlines in local and national newspapers read, 'MR MONEYBAGS. Banker wants to pour money into Glasgow ... SCOTS HEAD OF U.S. BANKING GROUP HAS MASTER PLAN TO AID GLASGOW.'

The plan had the blessing of the Scottish Development Agency, the Scottish Economic Planning Department and Glasgow Chamber of Commerce. When Mr Eckersley went back to California he wrote to confirm that our main competitor in the race for inward investment was Ireland as it offered very considerable incentives and had virtually unrestricted powers to offer whatever was necessary to persuade the Americans. He added that it was worth looking at the incentives given to Texas Instruments to change their location from Irvine to Dublin.

A great many discussions between the various organisations took place and the Chamber of Commerce finally identified a suitable candidate to be our 'super-salesman' in California, Mr Hugh Laughland, a former director of Scottish and Universal Investments Limited. Unfortunately Mr Laughland wasn't interested in the job and the search began again.

Advertisements appeared in the *Financial Times* and several other newspapers in January 1980 seeking someone with 'an outstanding record of innovative business management coupled with marketing flair, administrative ability, and a thorough and up-to-date knowledge of Scottish industry.'

A hundred people applied and three months later the £22,000-a-year job, plus generous expenses, went to Mr Edward Brodie, Deputy Chairman and Managing Director of Insight Business Systems, a company in the Black and Edgington Group in Greenock. Eddie had an impressive professional background and confidence. I recall being mildly irritated at his interview when he leaned nonchalantly back in his chair and wedged his knee on the edge of the desk separating him from his interviewers.

Eddie didn't want to talk to the press about his appointment as he took the view that he had nothing to tell them until he had done something positive in the job, which was reasonable enough, but I pointed out that the whole of Scotland, and farther, was interested in what we were doing and there was no way he could avoid talking to the press. Besides, it was vital to us to have the press on our side.

Eddie finally agreed and this time we had headlines like 'SUPERMAN BRODIE ... OUR VOICE IN AMERICA ... THE PRIMING OF MR EDWARD BRODIE ... GLASGOW PICKS ITS SUPER-SALESMAN.'

A leader in the Glasgow *Evening Times* said, 'Glasgow gets a bargain in Edward Brodie, off to California to persuade Americans to invest here, buy from Scotland, and give us jobs. We have a distinguished representative. All we have to do now is show willing to deliver at this end and a gold rush in reverse is ours for the taking.'

Unfortunately the gold rush never materialised. Eddie duly went to America and shared an office with Mr Jim Reid of the Scottish Development Agency in the Chartered Bank building in San Francisco. Naturally we were anxious back at the ranch to know what he was doing and Eddie sent us regular reports. In his first three months he introduced himself to a great many business people and to nearly 20 Chambers of Commerce in the West Coast of America. He also joined golf clubs and various organisations where he could meet the Californian movers and shakers.

A few months later he suggested a Glasgow Week in San Fransisco at which we could show the Californians just what the city had to offer. I wrote to Steve Hamilton to say it was a good idea but would cost a great deal of money and suggested instead that a party headed by the Lord Provost and the leader of the Council should go to California and talk to people at first hand, demonstrating our serious commitment to the city's interests and showing the Americans that Brodie had full political support for what he was trying to do, although he was 6,000 miles away from his political masters.

More discussions followed and in January 1981 an impressive delegation flew to America. The members included Lord Provost Michael Kelly, Council leader Jean McFadden, Steve Hamilton, Remo Verrico, City Estates Surveyor, Mr Forbes Macpherson, President of Glasgow Chamber of Commerce, and Mr George Heaney, Deputy President of the Chamber and former head of General Motors in Scotland. Sir Samuel Curran, Principal and Vice-Chancellor of Strathclyde University and one of Scotland's leading scientists, joined the mission later at his own expense.

Sir William Gray, a former Lord Provost and the man who had worked hard to try to persuade the government to relocate Civil Service departments to Glasgow in the early 1970s, said in an article in the *Glasgow Herald* that our competitors (mainly Ireland) were prepared to invest 'to the extent of the cost of the visit (which turned out to be about £10,000) to get just one job.'

Before we set off Norman Eckersley told me, 'You won't come back immediately with briefcases bulging with contracts, but you will be able to bring home to the industrialists of California that Scotland is ready and able to give them the things they need to expand their operations in Europe any time they are ready.'

I devised a plan to publicise our expedition in Californian newspapers and radio and television stations and arranged for Lord Provost Kelly to give a regular report to Radio Clyde on how we were doing. Scottish Television gave me some film clips of Glasgow to show to the Americans.

We spent nine days in California, did a round trip of 14,000 miles and took in 16 cities in California, Washington State, Utah and Arizona in which different members of the party met about 250 people from 100 organisations and companies. We were given enthusiastic and courteous welcomes by everyone. Norman Eckersley described the mission as the most important of its kind ever carried out in America by a single Scottish city.

At a lunch hosted by San Francisco Chamber of Commerce we were all asked to make a brief speech introducing ourselves. I told the gathering in a mock American accent, 'I am very happy to be in your wunnerful country, Canada, home of your famous baseball team the Oakland Raiders.' The members of my party nearly had a fit. Apart from not being in Canada the Oakland Raiders is an American football team, not baseball, and they had recently beaten the Philadelphia Raiders in the Superbowl, America's equivalent of the Cup Final.

I went on in a normal voice to explain, 'I've been waiting 30 years to get my own back on an American audience. When I was a young reporter I used to interview your film and stage stars who came to Glasgow and most of them told me how happy they were to be in England!' The audience of business leaders applauded enthusiastically.

Most of our contacts in America were with people in electronics manufacturing but we also met people in the oil industry, tourism, real estate developers, investors and bankers. We answered questions about the availability of sites, labour relations, labour skills, education standards at schools, technical colleges, and universities, financial incentives, taxation, housing, transportation, communications, productivity, conference facilities, tourism and local government.

Although we could offer the Americans a skilled and experienced work force, high educational standards in colleges and universities, first class road, rail and air communications, we couldn't compete with the kind of financial incentives and tax concessions the Irish government and the Irish Development Agency were offering. Nor could the Americans get from us any concessions in rates or corporation tax. National government left it to the city to offer what we could and it just wasn't enough.

Ireland and other competitors were also able to offer greenfield sites, something else we didn't have. America's modern high-tech industries didn't want an old warehouse to convert or a derelict site to build on. They wanted the kind of environment that Compaq, one of the world's biggest computer companies, were later able to acquire at Bishopton, near Glasgow, a site surrounded by pleasant green fields and the gently flowing river Clyde.

When we came back the news media in Scotland were impatient at the fact that we could not list half a dozen American companies which had made a commitment to us to set up shop in Glasgow and its immediate environs as a result of our mission. In fact we were able to boast about nothing at all, apart from our exhaustive tour of the West Coast of America.

Eddie Brodie came back to Scotland at his own request after about 18 months because, he said, the campaign had been so successful he felt his place was back in Glasgow helping American firms as they arrived and providing a power base from which they could operate. Unfortunely no-one came. Councillor McFadden said the establishment of Locate in Scotland, an offshoot of the government-funded Scottish Development Agency, made it unnecessary for Eddie to stay in America. Brodie, now living in retirement in Spain, agrees that we were outmanoeuvred by the Irish.

It is interesting to note that Locate in Scotland, now part of the government-funded Scottish Enterprise, was involved in the decision in September 1994 of the Japanese electronics corporation, NEC, to build a second factory at Livingston at enormous cost.

Their decision was based on a favourable financial package from the British government and the skill and productivity of the Scottish workforce. Glasgow had that skilled and productive workforce in 1981, too, but not the support of the government.

Our California project cost the council almost £200,000. It began to sour when newspaper stories appeared about the £75,000 expenses Eddie Brodie had incurred. These seemed rather excessive to people like local newsmen and provincial politicians who didn't have the difficult task of impressing American entrepreneurs. They included items like £14,000 for entertaining contacts, £15,000 for domestic expenses, club membership fees of £7,500, and £850 for dictionaries. From what I saw of the Americans it would have taken a lot more than £75,000 to impress them.

The Controller of Audit, Local Authority Accounts, later criticised the Council's accounting procedures because there was no adequate supporting documentation for the expenditure of £52,000. The Controller emphasised that he was not criticising Mr Brodie himself. The Council's answer was that receipts were provided where available but in America receipts were not always issued by hotels, restaurants, and airlines where payments were made by cheque or credit card.

Forbes Macpherson, now Chairman of Glasgow Development Agency, told me in September 1994, 'I think the lesson I learned is that it takes a long time and constant contact to persuade international companies to make major investments. Our one-off visit generated goodwill but was not sustained enough to focus their decisions.'

All of which would seem to indicate that the mission was a failure, but who is to say that somewhere along the line we did not sow seeds which eventually resulted in companies like Compaq (Bishopton), Amphenol (Greenock), ATS Medical Limited (Glasgow), Methode Electronics (Dumbarton) and other American high-tech companies coming to the West of Scotland. One thing we did do was to enhance the city's image by demonstrating that we were imaginative and adventurous.

The visit to America was by no means the only move to attract investment and create jobs. At the end of 1980 Glasgow had almost 60,000 unemployed, the highest figure for a decade and more than 10,000 people had lost their jobs in the 12 months to May 1980 because of closures and redundancies in the city.

The City Council set up an Economic Development Bureau and a special sub-committee on employment to create jobs, stimulate business enterprises, and safeguard existing employment. Members of the sub-committee included representatives of Glasgow Chamber of Commerce and the Scottish Trades Union Congress. All this is now the province of the Economic Regeneration Unit.

The Local Government and Planning Act of 1982 forbade an individual city like Glasgow from promoting itself overseas or organising promotional missions abroad. Strathclyde Regional Council could do it with the permission of the Secretary of State for Scotland and the regional council could invite Glasgow to take part but the city would still have to have the permission of the Secretary of State. The only organisation that could do overseas promotion without the express permission of the Secretary of State was Locate in Scotland, which made it very difficult for Glasgow to promote itself and improve its economy.

In March 1982 more than 1,500 key industrialists and financiers at home and overseas were invited to a promotion 'Why Not Belong to Glasgow?' in London's Holiday Inn Hotel in Hyde Park. The promotion coincided with the monthly council meeting of the Confederation of British Industry and many representatives of Britain's major companies were invited to come and talk to us about opportunities in Glasgow. Regrettably none of them took advantage of these opportunities, whatever they were.

In an effort to help business in the city the Council resolved deliberately to discriminate where possible in favour of Glasgow companies in buying goods and services. This policy was killed by the Local Government Act of 1988 which decreed it was anti-competitive and in conflict with European Economic Commmunity policies.

In 1989 the Council spent £26,000 on a feature on Glasgow in *Forbes*, one of America's most influential business magazines, in collaboration with the Scottish Development Agency or its offshoot Glasgow Action. More than 700 enquiries were received from the presidents, vice-presidents and chairmen of major American companies but not a lot came of that either. Information packs on the city were sent to them all. A video film with sound tracks in German, Mandarin Chinese, Russian, Italian and French was also produced and widely distributed but it would be difficult to quantify the result of this either.

One way in which the Council gets round strangling government regulations is through twinnings with various cities abroad including Rostov-on-Don, Dalian in China, Turin and Nuremberg, although what effect these twinnings have on the economy of Glasgow is very difficult to determine. In my experience the foreigners invariably wanted to sell us their products but were not at all anxious to buy anything from us.

In the years since the city twinned with Dalian in 1987 I have read many stories about groups of Chinese coming to Glasgow with untold riches which they were prepared to spend here but if these delegations ever bought anything from us I have not seen much about it in the public prints. It is true that Weirs of Cathcart have been trading successfully with China for two decades but they didn't need a twinning arrangement to achieve this.

Sir Horace Phillips, who went to China as a business consultant for Taylor Woodrow after a distinguished career as a diplomat, refers in his autobiography *Envoy Extraordinary,* published in 1995, to the Chinese propensity for squeezing all they could out of their foreign partners in any joint venture while themselves putting in a minimum.

And as for the city's friendship link with Bethlehem, this was established at the instigation of the supporters in the City Chambers of the West of Scotland Friends of Palestine only to irritate Israel and its supporters and could not possibly be of any benefit to Glasgow.

Chapter 17

THE
AMBASSADORS

FOUR ambassadors of the State of Israel have been among the many friends I have made in the course of my communal work. All of them were men of great ability and astonishing good humour considering the difficulties of their job.

One of them was Mr Shlomo Argov, a man of immense intellect, who represented his country in Nigeria, Ghana, America, Mexico and the Netherlands before coming to Britain in 1979. In a talk I gave to a speakers' course on Jewish and Israeli affairs I told my audience, 'Mr Argov's comments on current affairs and Israel's attitude to its many and varied problems can be regularly read in the Jewish newspapers and sometimes in the non-Jewish press. Reading his speeches is as good as any course on Middle East affairs anyone is likely to get in this country.'

One of my voluntary jobs for many years has been to arrange meetings with local politicians and news media people in Glasgow for visiting Israeli ambassadors. Nowadays I do this in collaboration with Dr Ezra Golombok, Director of the Glasgow-based Israel Information Office.

On the morning of Shlomo Argov's visit to Glasgow with his wife Chava in March 1980 I took him to the BBC for a radio interview, to the Chamber of Commerce to see Forbes Macpherson, the President, and then to the *Glasgow Herald* to talk to Arnold Kemp, the Editor.

After lunch with Lord Provost David Hodge at the City Chambers Argov asked me, 'Can we get away from all this for a little while? I'd like to walk round the town.' Argov had spent a night in Glasgow in 1953 during a honeymoon visit to Scotland and wanted to have another look at the city. As we walked we were closely followed by a number of security men who were not at all happy.

I also arranged, at her request, for Margaret Milne, an *Evening Times* reporter, to interview Mrs Argov.

'How do you feel about the fact that your husband is a potential target for terrorists?' asked Margaret.

'It is something you have to live with,' said Mrs Argov. 'If you let your mind dwell on it too much you could not cope.'

Margaret's story was headlined 'A QUIET STROLL FOR TARGET NO 1.' Little did Mrs Argov know what the future held for her and her husband.

A couple of days after the Argovs went back to London the ambassador wrote to thank me for my help in arranging his Glasgow visit. His letter ended, 'I hope it won't be long before we have a chance to see each other again.'

To my great sorrow an Arab terrorist made it virtually impossible for us to meet again. On 3 June, 1982, Argov was coming out of the Dorchester Hotel in London after a diplomats' dinner when the terrorist fired a burst from a sub-machine gun at him, wounding the 52-year-old father of three in the head. The ambassador survived but was completely paralysed.

In immediate response the Israeli Air Force attacked two known terrorist bases in the Beirut area of Lebanon without loss of civilian life. The Palestine Liberation Organisation then began a 24-hour attack on civilian targets in Northern Galillee and on the Christian enclave in South Lebanon. More than 1,000 shells were fired at 23 settlements, including the towns of Kiryat Shemona and Nahariya, setting the whole of Northern Lebanon ablaze.

Only then was Operation Peace for Galilee launched not, as was often claimed by the news media, as a reprisal for the shooting of Shlomo Argov.

The Israel Defence Forces found in Southern Lebanon weapons supplied from virtually every arms-dealing country in the world: America, Britain, China, France, Germany, Japan, Libya, the Soviet Union, Sweden, and Vietnam. They included rocket-launchers, cannon, anti-aircraft guns, tanks, and thousands and thousands of light arms and ammunition, enough to equip seven brigades.

A report in the London *Times* of 19 June, 1982 said, ' "When the Israelis came," said one middle-aged Lebanese woman, "the Palestinian fighters took their guns and placed them next to our homes, next to apartment blocks, hospitals and schools. They thought this would protect them. We pleaded with them to take their guns away but they refused. So when they fired at the Israelis the planes came and bombed our homes." '

The director of one Sidon hospital still seemed to disbelieve his own words as he described how the terrorists deliberately set up their anti-aircraft guns around his clinic. At their own Ein Hilweh camp the Palestinians actually put their guns on the roof of the hospital.

Shlomo Argov is still completely paralysed and spends much of his time in hospital. The dedication and love of his family and the doctors and nurses who have looked after him over the years cannot easily be expressed in words.

Enthusiasm for my communal work for Israel once caused an international incident involving the Israeli Foreign Office in Jerusalem, an Israeli government-owned company which was somewhat coy about some of its products, the Israeli ambassador to Britain, Buckingham Palace, Scotland Yard, and the British security services.

The story started in 1982 when a man named Michael Fagan broke into Buckingham Palace and sat on the Queen's bed for an informal, if rather one-sided, chat.

Scotland Yard and the security agencies were understandably upset by this unthinkable breach of security and a worldwide search was undertaken to find a security system that did not allow such intrusions into the life of the Head of the United Kingdom and the Commonwealth. An appropriate security system was finally found in Israel and in the course of time was set up round the palace.

I learned about the security system during a holiday in Israel. When I went home I wrote a story about it for distribution to the British news media by my younger son Michael who at that time ran the Scottish-Israel Information Office in Glasgow, the function of which was to distribute material about political issues and news about cultural, scientific, industrial, commercial, and social developments in Israel.

The story appeared in a number of newspapers — including the London *Times*, *Daily Telegraph*, *Glasgow Herald*, and the *Scotsman* — and all hell broke out. The newspapers tried to follow up the story with Buckingham Palace, Scotland Yard, the Israeli Embassy, Israel Aircraft Industries, the manufacturers of the security fence, and anyone else they could get, but all these sources remained tight-lipped. Understandably the newspapers treated the story as some kind of sensational revelation.

I was quoted as saying, 'I took the view it was good public relations for Israel for it to be known that an Israeli-made product was guarding the Queen and her family. The story was meant to deter anyone else from camping in the palace grounds (as a group of Germans had earlier done) or sitting on the Queen's bed to have a chat with her.' Michael maintained a discreet silence.

Two tall raincoats from an unnamed government body appeared in my office in the City Chambers demanding to know where I got the story but under the journalist's prerogative of not revealing his source of information I declined to tell them. Later my phone rang and a voice told me to hang on for the Israeli ambassador.

'I would be grateful if you would tell me where you got this story,' said His Excellency Mr Yehuda Avner.

'I'm afraid I can't do that, sir,' I said.

'Henry,' said the ambassador, 'the wires between here and Jerusalem are in danger of melting. I have not been here long and if you don't tell me where you got that story I am liable to be directing the traffic in the Negev desert next week!'

I had tried to give the impression all along that I had got the story through brilliant investigative reporting but the truth was rather different.

'I got the story from a magazine published by the Israel Information Centre in Jerusalem,' I told the ambassador. 'The story was also in the *International Security Review* some months ago so it was hardly a secret.'

'Oh,' said a nonplussed ambassador. 'Er … thank you.'

The director of the Information Centre later told me the Israelis weren't really concerned about the story at all, only that the embassy in London hadn't been told that the office they were funding for Michael in Glasgow was sending it out and were unprepared for the subsequent bombardment by the press.

Ambassador Avner, who incidentally was born in Manchester, was indulging in a bit of journalistic hyperbole when he phoned and we later had a number of friendly meetings during projects in which we were involved.

When Ambassador Yoav Biran came to Glasgow in February 1993 he asked me to ride with him in his car but a security man led me gently aside and said, 'Give us a break, Harry. It's difficult enough guarding the Ambassador without having to look after you, too! Come in our car.'

British and Israeli security men weren't the only spooks for whom I caused some heartburn. During a visit to Glasgow of Mr Vasily Zakharov, Soviet Minister of Culture, I took him and his wife Irina for a walk in crowded Buchanan Street, followed by several of his minders. Mr Zakharov's programme was packed with visits to museums of all kinds from Madame Tussaud's to the Burrell Collection, operas, and theatres. Towards the end of lunch with Lord Provost Susan Baird his interpreter whispered in as diplomatic a way as possible that Mr Zakharov had just about had his fill of museums and formal lunches and dinners and had expressed an interest in seeing something of the famous Glasgow.

After lunch I suggested to Mr Zakharov's interpreter that we go for a walk round the elegant shops in Buchanan Street. His security men almost had a cardiac arrest when he and his wife split up and he walked down one side of the street while Mrs Zakharov inspected the other side. At one point when Mr Zakharov was trying on shoes in one of the shops we went into I bitterly

ABOVE:
Councillor Pat
Lally, kneeling
left, with the
children from the
'stockbroker' belt
of Sussex.
RIGHT:
Preparing 500
press packs on the
Burrell Collection
for distribution
worldwide.

U.K PRESS GAZETTE: WEEK BEGINNING 29 AUGUST 1983   60p

U.K PRESS GAZETTE

EVERY MONDAY: FOR JOURNALISTS AND ALL WHO WORK WITH THEM   No. 910

Express group sacks 290 in pay row

EXPRESS NEWSPAPERS sacked 293 journalists in the Manchester offices of the Daily and Sunday Express and the Daily Star after they refused to end a mandatory chapel meeting over a pay deal. Full story page 5.

VULCAN We admit we're not perfect!

PUTTING THINGS RIGHT: PAGES 3 AND 17

£4m BOOST FOR IPC MAGAZINES
page 11

PRESS COUNCIL ADJUDICATIONS
page 12

LOCAL PAPER WEEK MOVES
page 19

Harry Diamond is a writer's best friend

THIS IS A PICTURE of a man reaping the whirlwind he whipped up himself.

Harry Diamond, head of PR for Glasgow council, didn't do things by halves when he invited journalists to view the city's Burrell Collection of art. He asked the lot.

Hence the shot of Mr. Diamond amid a sea of Press releases, ready for the journalists he lured from, among many others, the New York Times, Sydney Morning Herald, La Stampe, the Geneva Tribune, all of Britain's quality Press and hordes of TV and radio teams.

The publicity exercise is reckoned to be the biggest ever mounted in Glasgow.

390 JOBS GO AS EVENING FACES CLOSURE: p.7

At the Burrell Collection.

יש חיים אחרי הכית

Henry Diamond

Israel reads all about Glasgow.

The Queen signs the visitors' book after opening the Burrell Collection watched by my wife Jacqueline and Alasdair Auld, Director of Museums and Art Galleries.

Lord Provost Bob Gray presents a case history of the Burrell Collection Public Relations exercise to Sir Alwyn Williams, Principal of Glasgow University. It is the only public relations case history in the university library.

LEWIS SEGAL PHOTOGRAPHY

LEWIS SEGAL PHOTOGRAPHY

Sharing reminiscences with Ike Aranne, who captained the refugee ship Exodus.

With Jacqueline at a council dinner.

LEWIS SEGAL PHOTOGRAPHY

Jacqueline and me with Israeli ambassador Yehuda Avner and Lord Provost Bob Gray.

Reggie Watts, President of the Institute of Public Relations, presents me with the Stephen Tallents medal for 'exceptional achievement' as Glasgow's PR chief.

Lord Provost Susan Baird and her husband George see a new-born baby at the Shaare Zedek Medical Centre in Jerusalem.

Japan reads all about Glasgow.

ケルヴィングローヴ美術・博物館

スゴーのあとすぐ東京へ行くという。"マハ
ブハラタ"というのはサンスクリット語で
書かれた世界一長い詩で、最も古いものは
紀元前5、6世紀に書かれている。"マハブ
ハラタ"とは"人間の叙事詩的物語"という
意味で、聖書の15倍にも匹敵する10万スタ
ンザの詩にはある一族の冒険とそれに続く
戦争などが描かれており、この詩から発展
した多くの思想、伝説、思考、教訓、性格な
どが今日もインドの信仰や生活の基盤をな
しているという。

この途方もないテキストを元にロイヤル・
シェイクスピア劇団の演出家で世界的に有
名なピーター・ブルックが作家ジャン・クロ
ード・キャリエールと共に13年かかって3
部作の芝居に仕立てあげたわけである。グ
ラスゴー公演は4月13日から5月17日まで
の間に3晩連続か1日又は1晩で3部通しで
計11公演行なう（公演日程参照）。出演者
は20カ国から集まった35人の俳優とミュー
ジシャン（音楽監督に日本名も見られる）と
いう国際的なもの、最新のシアター経験が
できるチャンスである。

このほかシティ・フェスティヴァルでは
オペラ、クラシック音楽コンサート、演劇が
夏の間もずっと続けられ、7月には第1回
国際ダンス・フェスティヴァルが催される。

また、モスクワ州立サーカス団の来英が決
まり、ベラハウストン・パークで6月24・26
日に公演することになっている。

恒例のフェスティヴァル

5月1日〜21日に開かれるメイフェス
ト"は今年4回目、子供のサーカスや路上行
事など多彩な催物が企画されている。6、7
月のグラスゴー国際ジャズ・フェスティヴ
ァルと7月のグラスゴー・フォーク・フェ
スティヴァルでは演劇、音楽、ダンスなどの
グループがブラジル、アメリカ、カナダ、ギ
リシャ、アフリカ、イタリー、チェコ、ドイ
ツ、ソ連、フランス、ノルウェイ、スウェー
デン、日本、中国などからやってきて各々の
芸術を披露してくれる。

8月13日には世界パイプ・バンド選手権
大会がある。これはスコットランドのバ
グ・パイプ競技会。また国際大道芸人フェス
ティヴァルも8月に予定されている。

グラスゴー市では毎年1,800万ポンド（約
43億円）を市の文化的行事の予算としてい
るが、今年は別予算のガーデン・フェスティ
ヴァルの他に6075万5千ポンド（約1億5千
万円）をつぎ込んでフェスティヴァルの成
功を期している。"ヨーロッパの文化都市"

はすでに手中にある。

Produced in collaboration with Harry Diamond, Head of Public Relations, City of Glasgow.

マハブハラタ演日程

公演（3部1連） 期日	時間
❶ 4月13、14、15日	各晩7.30pm
❷ 4月17日（3部通し）	1.00pm〜11.00pm
❸ 4月19、20、21日	各晩7.30pm
❹ 4月23日（3部通し）	1.00pm〜11.00pm
❺ 4月26、27、28日	各晩7.30pm
❻ 4月30日（3部通し）	1.00pm〜11.00pm
❼ 5月3・4・5日	各晩7.30pm
❽ 5月7／8日（オールナイト3部通し）	8.00pm〜7.00am
❾ 5月10・11・12日	各晩7.30pm
❿ 5月14日（3部通し）	1.00pm〜11.00pm
⓫ 5月17日（3部通し）	1.00pm〜11.00pm

〔チケット〕£15〜30（小人、学生割引あり）
〔予約〕The Ticket Centre,Candleriggs,Glasgow
G1（月〜土・10.30am〜6.30pm）
Tel. 041-227-5511

A chance encounter with Council leader Jean McFadden at a Burns Night dinner.

I'm on the left. The other one was made by my friend John McLaughlin.

The Glasgow gospel, according to Harry

JOHN MacCALMAN looks at how journalist and PR man Harry Diamond has helped put Glasgow on the world map

■ Glasgow public relations chief Harry Diamond who has sent the Glasgow's Miles Better message to every corner of the world.

The Glasgow Herald *reports my retirement.*

Some people keep press cuttings in a folder. I keep mine on my shirt.

JAMES MILLAR/THE GLASGOW HERALD

JAMES MILLAR

MAURICE OF GLASGOW

My older son Harvie with children Gideon and Tiffany and wife Rejane.

My younger son Michael and his wife Yaffa with their children Yuval and Ophir.

regretted not having a camera to record the Soviet Minister of Culture in his socks, balanced delicately on one leg as he manoeuvred into a highly-decorative, expensive pair of capitalist brogues.

Mr Zakharov came to Britain under the aegis of the British Council to 'familiarise himself with British culture.' I discovered that his programme included Edinburgh but not Glasgow. I pointed out indignantly to the British Council that the absence of Glasgow in the programme was ludicrous, especially as we were to be Cultural Capital of Europe the following year, 1990. In addition Robert Palmer, who had been appointed to mastermind our year of culture, had been in Moscow to talk to Mr Zakharov's ministry about the Soviet's involvement in our 1990 celebrations. Glasgow was quickly added to the Minister's itinerary.

An example of the pitfalls that attend the entertaining of VIPs was revealed in a letter I received from the British Council's Glasgow office asking me to ensure that the Zakharovs were not given smoked salmon, venison, or strawberries for lunch in the City Chambers as that what was on the menu for their lunch the following day with Mr Malcolm Rifkind, Secretary of State for Scotland

Once, at a City Chambers dinner for a group of diplomats from one of the emergent countries, we were munching at haggis and neeps which an inspired catering manageress decided to serve that night when one of the group asked me, 'Do you eat a lot of this Mr Diamond?'

My diplomatic skills not having been too finely honed, I replied before I had a chance to stop myself, 'You must be joking. We only bring this rubbish out for people like you.'

To my great relief my dinner companions were convulsed with merriment.

I once told that story at a dinner attended by the Secretary of State for Scotland which may account for the fact that my knighthood has been in the post for a helluva long time.

Chapter 18

TREASURE HUNT

ALTHOUGH I have no pretensions as an art lover, Jackie and I always visited art galleries and museums in our holiday travels and I always enjoyed writing about the various exhibitions mounted by our own museums. The museums' staff were always helpful in gathering information and the news media gave my stories a lot of coverage, particulary on television, because of their visual dimension.

I can't talk about a painting's aesthetic merits or how the painter deals with the problem of chiaroscuro, and I am unable to debate the claim that Leonardo da Vinci was probably the clearest thinker who ever worked with paint.

I belong to the I-know-what-I-like school, especially if I can tell what it is. On one occasion when I told Alasdair Auld, Director of Museums and Art Galleries, that some modern paintings were a confidence trick on the public he responded with the the the unanswerable question, 'What is art?'

I am still completely convinced that many artists bring out their gear and say to themselves, 'Right, let's see what we can get away with today.'

Anne Donald, Keeper of Fine Art, wrote to me in February 1981, 'I hope you will be able to help us with the publicity for the most important art exhibition we have had here for many years … We would be most grateful if you could give it the full treatment as you did for Jewish Art two years go.' The Jewish Art exhibition was one of the events held to celebrate the centenary of Garnethill Synagogue in 1979.

The exhibition referred to by Anne Donald was The Realist Tradition to be held at Glasgow's flagship museum at Kelvingrove for two months from November 1981. It was to be the first showing of the exhibition in Europe.

Realism was a 19th-century literary and artistic movement which sought to show people and objects as they really were. The Realist artists painted tinkers, labourers, craftsmen of all kinds, factory workers, street scenes, dockside scenes, and everything else that reflected the lives of ordinary people.

The exhibition was organised by Dr Gabriel P Weisberg, former Curator of Art History and Education at the Cleveland Museum of Art, and it took him more than five years to do it. I wrote to Dr Weisberg, who by that time was Andrew F Mellon, Professor of Art at University of Pittsburgh, for some colour transparencies and black-and-white photographs for the press pack I was preparing along with a story about the exhibition.

Professor Weisberg asked me if we could get some publicity in the London-based press and I said I would do what I could. As it turned out the exhibition received wide coverage throughout the British news media.

Among the angles that appealed to the press and television was, of course, the fact that the exhibition had never been seen in Europe before, that the paintings were to be secretly flown to Prestwick from America, that a 24-hour guard was to be put on them during the run of the exhibition, and that they were worth nearly £3,500,000.

The exhibition contained more than 200 works by about 70 French artists from 1830 to 1900. Among them were Jean François Millet, Gustave Courbet, Eugène Boudin, Honoré Daumier, Henri Fantin-Latour, Edgar Degas, and Camille Pissarro. One of the paintings, *The Reader (Le Liseur)* by Edouard Manet, owned by St Louis Art Museum, was said to be worth a million dollars. That was in 1981. Who knows what it could fetch now at an auction.

Two of Glasgow's own pictures were in the exhibition: *Oxen Ploughing* by Leon Lhermitte and *Village Scene, Barbazon*, by Adolphe Hervier, an oil-on-wood painting which measures only five inches by 12 inches and was one of the smallest works in the exhibition.

In the words of several newspaper reports, the Realist Exhibition was one of the most successful events held at Kelvingrove in its 81-year history. It attracted 119,000 visitors in its two-month run. Other record-breakers at Kelvingrove in which I was involved were the showing of the Queen's wedding dress in 1948 (when she was Princess Elizabeth) which drew 140,000 people and the 25 Glorious Years Exhibition in 1977 when 356,000 people went to see a large number of art treasures acquired over the years and put together to mark the Queen's Silver Jubilee.

I first read about the Treasures of the Holy Land Exhibition in Jerusalem in August 1987. A story in the Glasgow *Jewish Echo* said it could not go from America to Japan as scheduled because the Japanese government was unable to provide 'diplomatic immunity' for some of the exhibits. In other words someone might try to get them back because they came from another exhibition in East Jerusalem.

I thought it would be a terrific coup for Glasgow if we could have it for our culture year celebrations in 1990 as it was the only exhibition of its kind in the world and featured artifacts from 13,000 years before the Christian era to the 13th century. There were Old Stone Age hand tools, hoards of coins, gold and silver objects, household articles, jewellery, religious ritual objects, ossuaries (pottery containers for human bones), armour, glassware, pottery, statuettes, and a vast number of other objects which, in the words of one writer, 'bring the Bible to life.'

I wrote to Bob Palmer, Glasgow's Director of Festivals and the man who was to mastermind our year as Cultural Capital of Europe in 1990, and asked him if we should try to get the Treasures to Glasgow. Palmer had the same attitude as myself, nothing ventured, nothing gained.

I made a few tentative enquiries at the Israeli embassy in London and they were very polite but I did get the impression they thought I was crazy. The difficulties were numerous and complex. I left the subject for a while but a few months later I read that the exhibition, which had been compiled by the Israel Museum in Jerusalem, was at the Metropolitan Museum of Art in New York. The following year it was due to go to the Royal Ontario Museum in Toronto before going back to Israel.

My younger son Michael was living in Israel by this time and during a brief stay with him towards the end of 1987 I persuaded him to drive me for three hours through the heat of the Negev desert from his home in Dimona to Jerusalem, and after some tortuous explanations to security guards and officials we finally got to see Mrs Freda Rubel in the Cultural and Scientific Affairs Division of the Ministry of Foreign Affairs. Although the Israel Museum is an independent institution some of its exhibits, like the Treasures of the Holy Land, belong to the State, which is why the Foreign Ministry has to give its permission for any of the artefacts to be loaned out.

Mrs Rubel was friendly and sympathetic to my approach but really didn't think it likely that the Ministry could be persuaded to let the treasures go to Glasgow, wherever that was, especially as they had been away from Jerusalem for some time and would need careful renovation when they returned.

I had nothing to lose by trying so when I came back to Glasgow I perusaded Alasdair Auld to initiate official talks with the Israel Museum. The negotiations to get the treasures exhibition to Glasgow, involving transport, insurance guarantees and goodness know what else, would make a book by themselves, but we finally made it with the help of a considerable number of people, including Jimmy Thomson, Depute Keeper of The Burrell Collection, who played a major part in the negotiations.

The treasures went on display at Kelvingrove from 16 October to 16 December and attracted 164,000 visitors and worldwide attention from the news media. The treasures have not been out of Israel since their visit to Glasgow.

Lord Provost Susan Baird was given a preview of the exhibition when she visited Israel in June 1990. As I had engineered the invitation I went with her and her husband George. Mrs Baird said later that the exhibition was a fascinating insight into the lives of people of the Middle East so far back in time, reflecting as it did the lives of adherents of three of the world's leading religions, Christianity, Judaism, and Islam.

Mayor Teddy Kollek of Jerusalem paid a special visit to the Israel Museum, of which he was Chairman, to see Mrs Baird and told her, 'We are delighted that our unique exhibition will be staged in Glasgow during such an important year for you.'

Sixteen items from our own collections were added to the exhibition for the Glasgow showing, including a hoard of Islamic jewellery in a pottery jar possibly buried to escape the Crusader attack on Caesarea in the 12th century.

Another collection of jewellery dated back to when what is now Israel was ruled by the Egyptian Fatimid dynasty, about 1,000 years ago. A pottery stand from the 11th century depicted five musicians standing in rectangular windows cut into the pedestal. One strikes the cymbals, two play double pipes, a fourth performs on a stringed instrument, and a fifth shakes a tambourine.

The exhibition also represented one of the major events of the Festival of Jewish Culture organised as the Jewish community's contribution to culture year.

At the opening of the exhibition Mrs Malka Ben Joseph, Cultural Counsellor from the Israeli embassy, was kind enough to say it would not have come to Glasgow at all if it had not been for my efforts.

There was one exhibition which I would have given anything to see in Glasgow, but after months of negotiation, cajoling, letter-writing, and telephone calls I got nowhere at all. In 1985 I read a small item somewhere that an exhibition of the 2,000-year-old Dead Sea Scrolls had opened in Paris.

I immediately started enquiries to bring it to Glasgow but when all my efforts came to nothing I asked my friend Greville Janner, QC, MP, if he could help because he was President of the Board of Deputies of British Jews, President of the Commonwealth Jewish Council, and a friend of many Israeli politicians, including Teddy Kollek.

Greville wrote to his friend Kollek who wrote back, 'The fact is that a very small piece of the original scrolls (not even that, but a contemporary letter) was included in the Paris exhibition. The rest were facsimiles — and in fact was the major criticism of the exhibition. And thus, with all the goodwill in the world, our original decision concerning sending the scrolls abroad still stands. We find that with all the most modern equipment and the most up-to-date technology, we often have to remove scrolls or parts of scrolls from display because they are so fragile. Please do convey this to Mr Diamond with our sincerest regrets.'

I don't think it is likely that the Dead Sea Scrolls, which were stumbled on by a shepherd boy in a cave at Qumran overlooking the Dead Sea in 1947, will ever go out of Israel. They are housed in a specially-built division, The Shrine of the Book, of the Israel Museum.

About 20 years ago a painting of Alexander Reid, a Glasgow art dealer, by his friend Vincent Van Gogh, came on the market and Glasgow was given first option to buy it. An appeal fund was set up to raise the necessary £160,000 and I wrote a press release about it.

A few days later an envelope dropped on the desk of Trevor Walden, Director of Museums and Art Galleries, containing a cheque and a wee note to say the sender had seen the story in the *Financial Times* and 'here's a contribution.' The cheque was for £40,000.

Eventually the painting was acquired and Trevor arranged a reception for the Civic Amenities Committee, who had approved the purchase. The painting, 16 1/2 inches by 13 inches, was beautifully framed and placed on an easel in front of purple curtaining and lit by spotlights.

As the line of committee members, in whose hands Glasgow's cultural heritage lay, filed past, one of them pulled me aside and said, 'Didn't you have something to do with this?'

'Yes.'

Then came the imperishable comment 'Could we no' have got a bigger picture for that kind of money?'

Chapter 19

PUBLISH AND BE DAMNED

THE *Bulletin* is Glasgow City Council's main means of telling the people of Glasgow what the Council is doing. It also tells Scots emigrés all over the world what is happening in the city, and it even helps to keep the news media informed about Council activities and developments in the city which they may overlook, or not have time for, in the sound and fury of daily newsgathering.

It was in 1980 that I decided the time had come for the Council to have its own newspaper. The daily newspapers, television and radio had always given most of our stories a good show but these stories were heavily outweighed by political debate, petty squabbles between politicians and every other ill the news media could uncover.

The constructive decisions the Council took and the many things its departments did to make the city a better place in which to live and work and bring up one's children, did not get the coverage I thought they should.

I resolved our newspaper would not be a newsletter with items about bowls outings among the staff and pictures of happy brides but a newspaper with real news in it. Naturally the material had to be relevant to the work of the Council and its departments but I knew there was plenty of scope there. After all, we had been producing news stories about the Council's work for years.

David Bell, my deputy, had been Editor of the *Rutherglen Reformer*. Alan Redfern was a former *Daily Express* man like myself and Hugh Leishman had worked for the Aberdeen *Press and Journal*. All we had to do was to produce enough stories to fill eight pages.

Two years earlier we had produced a four-page paper over a week-end after Prince Charles had opened a new model ship gallery in our Museum of Transport. A week-end may seem a long time compared with what they do in the newspaper industry but we had to write every word and go outside the Council for setting, printing, and distribution. When the paper came out on the Monday everyone in my department was very pleased with our achievement but none of our political masters or anyone else said a word. I shouldn't have been surprised or hurt at this as no-one knew the work that went into the exercise.

In addition to being an editor David Bell was also a first-class sports reporter and his handling of major sporting events organised by the Parks and Recreation Department could not have been matched by anyone in the public relations industry, even in London where they delude themselves they can do everything better than anyone else. Producing a monthly newspaper should not be all that difficult.

I was determined to lay down certain ground rules for the newspaper: that it would not be used as a propaganda tract by the political hierarchy; that it would not be run by a committee of politicians; and that I would be the only one to decide what should go into it. All this was a colossal bluff on my part because the politicians could have dictated every move and there was nothing I could have done about it.

I lay awake night after night thinking how to achieve my objective. Then I cracked it. I would produce the paper without telling my political masters! I had the money in my budget for publicity projects and I could produce one issue and call it an experiment. I was sure they would let me carry on if it worked and if it didn't nothing would be lost. After all, we had produced one-off newspapers in the past about specific projects.

I knew that if I went to my committee with a proposal to publish a newspaper regularly I would have been asked innumerable unanswerable questions. Every councillor would have very definite ideas about how the paper should be run and what should go into it and there is not the slightest doubt that I would have ended up with an editorial board of councillors who would have interfered to an extent which would have made it impossible to produce anything worthwhile at all. The only solution was to Publish and be Damned, as Hugh Cudlipp of the *Daily Mirror* wrote so compellingly in 1953.

Then I had to find a name for the newspaper. I had a long debate with my staff and a whole lot of names were proposed but I didn't like any of them. One of them was *The Glaswegian* which coincidentally was the name of a freesheet launched some years later by the *Daily Record* group.

Finally, in the middle of the night, I came up with *The Bulletin*. My staff were agog with apathy at my suggestion. *The Bulletin*, one of the newspapers in the George Outram (*Glasgow Herald*) group, had died 20 years earlier and to the younger members of my staff the name meant nothing at all. But I knew something they didn't: that a great many Glaswegians had fond memories of the newspaper and that they would be delighted to see the name again.

I put my idea in a letter to John Crawford, Managing Director of George Outram and Company, and told him I would use the very efficient publicity machine under my control to tell the world about the return of *The Bulletin* in its new form and about the agreement with Outram. I knew we would achieve great coverage for a story of this kind which would reflect well on both our organisations and the skill, imagination, enterprise, daring and wit of the public relations people involved!

I also told John I would not solicit advertising to try to defray the cost of producing the paper because I didn't want to take revenue away from other newspapers who relied for their income on advertising. In reality I wasn't all that morally upright; I knew it would be difficult to persuade companies and their advertising agencies to subsidise a Labour council in this way. This was the case for quite a long time although we did eventually get quite a lot of advertising but never enough to make any significant contribution towards the cost of producing the paper. Besides, I looked on the paper as a valuable public service, like Libraries or Museums or Parks which weren't required to make a profit.

John Crawford agreed to ask his board if I could have the title *The Bulletin* on permanent loan, or at least as long as we needed it. The negotiations took only a couple of months and in September 1980 the first issue came out.

As I predicted the event was reported throughout Britain because the title had been brought back after 20 years in limbo, an event which couldn't possibly fail to appeal to the sentimental side of media people, and because it was the first time a commercial newspaper company had given one of its titles to a local authority.

John Crawford was quoted as saying, 'It is good to see the title *The Bulletin* again, a name which was so loved by the people of Scotland and by emigré Scots throughout the world. It was a first-class idea to bring the name back into use and I wish Harry Diamond and Glasgow City Council all success with their venture'. Even the *Scotsman*, the *Herald*'s main rival, reported the comeback at length.

Our first page-one story also got tremendous news media coverage. It was about eight librarians from Belfast who were coming to work in Glasgow's Mitchell Library for a couple of weeks to relearn how to work under normal conditions and cope with normal crowds of library traffic.

Mr Ivor Crawley, Belfast's chief librarian, was quoted as saying, 'After 12 years of terrorist activity the number of users of the Central Reference Library in the centre of Belfast has dropped dramatically. Many young people have never been in the centre of the city, let alone in the library.'

Mr Crawley added, 'More than 180 bombs have exploded near the library; all our windows have been blown out 12 times.'

I got this story from a four-line mention in the Library Committee minutes. No municipal correspondent, however conscientious, would have bothered to enquire why eight librarians from Belfast were coming to the Mitchell Library.

Another story was about the plan to build a £10 million hotel at Anderston, the Holiday Inn (now The Marriot) and the Skean Dhu (now the Hospitality Inn) in Cowcaddens. The justification for publishing these stories was that the Council had given them planning permission, thereby demonstrating its commitment to tourism and conference promotion.

We also reported on the continuing development of the Clydeside Walkway, replacing miles of derelict dockland, that the city had given the Queen Mother a silver medallion for her 80th birthday, that Councillor Jean McFadden had been appointed the first woman Vice-Lieutenant of the city, and that Mrs Susan Baird (later to become Lord Provost) had been appointed Chairman of the Manpower Committee. Altogether I think we had a good mix of stories.

A few issues later we had a picture of Debbie Peterson, a young lady from Fresno, California, who came into the City Chambers to tell me she had been following with interest the Council's efforts to attract investment from the West Coast of America. Debbie had arrived in Glasgow only a couple of months earlier to have a look around and after deciding it was a great place she got a job with an advertising firm so that she could stay a bit longer.

Later, in January 1984, after a business course at university, she started the California Cake and Cookie Company in Govan and has been going from strength to strength ever since. The company, of which she is chief executive, now employs 75 people, has a turnover of £2 million, and produces a wide range of products, some of which go to America, Paris and Amsterdam. And she still thinks Glasgow is a great place.

The result of all this was that I was allowed to continue to publish the paper, which soon began to win awards from the British Association of Industrial Editors. One of the judges commented, 'One of the very best newspapers of its kind. With this level of content you must generate a lot of interest in the city'.

A popular feature of the paper was a complete list every few months of councillors along with their pictures and surgery times because many people did not know who their councillors were or how to contact them. For years after the reform of local government in Scotland, to the despair of politicians and officials alike, many people still did not know which authority, Strathclyde Region or Glasgow City, was responsible for many public services. I confidently expect the public are similarly confused now that the new Glasgow authority has taken over the running of the city.

When I published a brochure about the Council's services and departments and who ran them it was hailed by the news media as a masterpiece of imaginative thinking.

My intention had been to publish the newspaper every six weeks but it caught on so quickly that we decided to bring it out every month. Within a short time Glaswegians started to send the newspaper to relatives and friends abroad and we got many letters from Scots and their descendants asking us to send them a copy each month. Eventually we had readers on all five continents.

In 1986 I decided to find out if *The Bulletin* was still popular and if the ratepayers of the city still wanted it. After all, it was a lot of work producing it and I didn't want to carry on if the public didn't really want the paper. We were producing 30,000 copies a month and distributing it through council offices, libraries and other outlets.

I wasn't all that surprised when the MORI (Market and Opinion Research International) poll revealed that 82 people out of every 100 polled said they would welcome the delivery of *The Bulletin* each month. That meant a print run of more than 300,000 copies and made the paper the largest monthly council newspaper in Britain. It was also confirmed as the Council's most valuable platform for telling Glaswegians what was happening in Glasgow, which was more than the other newspapers did.

Various methods of distributing the paper in Glasgow were tried over the years and for some time it has been given away each month inside the *Herald* and the *Evening Times*, a method which seems to satisfy most people.

In November 1980 Bill Aitken, leader of the Tory group, accused me of using the newspaper for Labour propaganda. I had made great play of the claim that the paper was not to be used for political propaganda but it would be ludicrous to say it was never used for this purpose.

In fact some of the stories we published were blatant propaganda for the Labour administration because they roundly condemned current government policies. Steve Hamilton, the Town Clerk and Chief Executive, expertly articulated my problem in a letter I shall come to shortly.

Bill Aitken told the *Herald* and *Scotsman* that what I was doing was legally questionable and morally indefensible,

'When my group and indeed my party propagate our views we do so by means of the media or at our own cost, and most certainly not at the expense of the city ratepayers. We will not be contributing to the paper, particularly where it is clear that a complete bias in respect of space is given to the Labour administration'.

Bill's tirade was prompted by the impending publication of a report about Labour's opposition to the sale of council houses. I had asked the Tory group for a comment on the story but they had refused. I then wrote to Bill Aitken again offering space in the paper and added that their refusal didn't do much for his group's image. Bill's response was to tell the newspapers that he was preparing to report the whole matter to the local government auditor. 'When the ratepayers see this misuse of public money it is hardly surprising there is talk of rate strikes.'

Unfortunately for Bill the ratepayers were consumed with indifference about this alleged misuse of their money. I don't know whether or not Bill complained to the auditor but nothing ever happened. The incident didn't prevent the Tories from constantly demanding space in the paper to have a go at the Labour group in one way or another but the paper didn't exist for the purpose of letting parties have a go at each other. I was quite happy to print stories about Tory councillors doing something interesting for the city or any of its institutions but as they were not in control they weren't in a position to do anything worth reporting.

Complaints by the Tories went on for a long time. Iain Dyer, another senior Tory, wrote to me at considerable length about allowing myself to be a Labour propagandist and about not getting space in the paper to give the Tory view on the sale of council houses. He repeated that I was 'responsible for illegal expenditure and in the face of a flagrant breach of the public code you also render yourself liable to dismissal.'

I was a bit stung by all this abuse and wrote back, 'I am sorry you have been so deeply wounded by my recent efforts to fulfil my function of keeping the ratepayers of the city informed about attitudes and decisions made in the City Chambers which impinge upon their daily lives. I can only repeat that there exists within our Council very efficient machinery by which complaints against officials may be registered.

I feel I have to add that I can understand the sound and fury of political debate, even on occasion involving officials, but I am grieved that you should think it necessary to attack me personally in such an intense and offensive way.'

Iain Dyer also complained to Steve Hamilton who was not easily intimidated by councillors or anyone else. Steve wrote back, 'I do not share your opinion that the publication of members' views about Council policies is an irregular or improper use of public funds, and I am satisfied that the

Public Relations Officer is operating within the law and in accordance with the best traditions of the public service as well as those of British journalism.'

Then came the punchline.

'I hope that in future you will refrain from threatening and attacking members of the Council's staff who are carrying out their duties to the best of their abilities within the law and in accordance with the Council's policies.'

Four years later the Tories were still hammering at my editorship of *The Bulletin* and writing tortuously long letters of complaint. In March 1984 Bill Aitken again wrote to Steve Hamilton, 'It is quite inconceivable that by any stretch of the imagination the *Bulletin* content can be seen as other than completely partial to the Labour side on a number of issues which are quite frankly party political ... The way in which the department has been used over recent months to feed to the media political views, and restricted political views at that, relating to, for example, the conflict with the Secretary of State regarding the rate rise restrictions and the other aspects of local government legislation, has certainly been a matter for very real concern.'

Steve wrote back, 'The Public Relations Officer has two main responsibilites which are not always totally compatible. Firstly he is expected to project a favourable image of the City of Glasgow as a good place in which to live, work and invest and as an attractive place to visit for a holiday, shopping expedition, for entertainment or a conference.

The other main task is to publicise the work of the Council and to describe its activities and the various initiatives it takes and to explain and to justify to the public its policies and plans, since these involve the expenditure of public money.

In this latter role the Public Relations Department, operating as it does in an environment in which party politics play an important part, cannot but reflect the views, aspirations and policies of the party in power ... The feature on government-imposed cuts concentrated on an aspect of government policy which is clearly very controversial. In promoting its policies the government has used its own powers and influence to attack local government in general in a manner which, in my experience, is quite unprecedented.

The majority view within Glasgow District Council clearly is that the Council and the services it provides, and local government in general, are under threat and against that background it seems to me to be neither surprising nor unreasonable for the Council's newspaper to reflect that view.'

Robert Brown, one of the very few Liberal councillors, also put in his tuppenceworth from time to time. He wrote that he was 'horrified and astonished' at what could only be described as an election manifesto for the Labour administration. Very little notice was taken of him either.

Despite all the tough talk in some of these exchanges we were all quite friendly, or at least gave that impression. Politicians can attack each other, and officials, quite venomously but to see them in the dining room afterwards one would never think they would say a harsh word to each other although that certainly doesn't always apply. Some politicians would cheerfully cut each others throats, or anyone else's, if they could get away with it; and it wouldn't matter if the object of their animosity was in the same political party.

Chapter 20

IT AIN'T WHAT YOU DO ...

ACCORDING to a writer in *Business* magazine in October 1987 it was the opening of The Burrell Collection of more than 8,000 works of art in 1983 that put Glasgow on the international cultural map. Some have claimed that the presence of the collection contributed significantly to the decision to award Glasgow the title of European City of Culture in 1990.

I don't know whether this is true or not but I do know that publicising the opening of the gallery was probably the biggest public relations exercise ever carried out in Scotland for a single event. It will never be known how widely throughout the world the collection has been written about or shown on film and television.

The *New York Times* described the collection as one of the most remarkable assemblages of works of art ever brought together.

A case history of the publicity project is the only one of its kind in the University of Glasgow Library. It was presented to the Principal, Sir Alwyn Williams, by Lord Provost Robert Gray. The project also won me an award in the Institute of Public Relations Sword of Excellence awards scheme.

Barry Gasson, the young architect who led the team who designed the Burrell gallery and who was later appointed an OBE, wrote to me, 'Thank you for all your support in ensuring the gallery's success.'

A letter from Alasdair Auld, Glasgow's Director of Museums and Art Galleries, said, 'Without your expertise we could not have made such an impact on the world.'

It was a strike of postmen in 1972 which made Gasson and two associates famous as the designers of the Burrell gallery, which became known on every continent even before it opened. Less than a year after the opening by the Queen on 21 October, 1983 the millionth visitor passed under the 16th-century archway into the courtyard of the gallery.

The design for The Burrell Collection had been put out to competition but Gasson, a Cambridge lecturer in architecture, John Meunier, and Brit

Andresen, had not finished their submission by the deadline date.

'Then the date was extended because of a strike of postmen and we were able to send in our entry,' said Gasson later.

The gallery continues to be one of Glasgow's major tourist attractions. Nowadays it has about half a million visitors a year. My instruction from the Council at the beginning of 1983 was 'to publicise the opening of The Burrell Collection.' That was it. A few paragraphs would have done it.

After all, the story of Sir William's gift to the city had been written about for decades. And then there were all the stories during the building of the gallery, including some of my own. What else was there to say, except who was going to open it. If it was the Queen as we hoped, that would merit another few paragraphs nearer the opening date.

We already had about five museums and apart from the Scottish news media who would be interested in another one? Then I thought, what the hell, I think I'll try something different. After all, as the old song says, It Ain't What You Do, It's The Way That You Do It.

I decided that here was an opportunity to tell the world that Glasgow had a unique art collection and that the city was a major cultural centre and no longer the grimy, grim-faced, slum-ridden, polluted city of bygone days.

At a special meeting with the Council hierarchy and the Director of Finance in his office I had asked for £10,000 to publicise the opening of the gallery. One councillor, Hugh Macrae, who had always been friendly towards me, said the job couldn't be done for as little as that and that I should get £15,000, although neither of us had the slightest idea how much the operation would cost. I wouldn't be surprised if this was the first time in the history of the world that a Council official had been given more than he asked for. As it happened I didn't spend more than £9,000.

Researching the story involved Council records going back to 1944, newspaper stories throughout the decades, *Hansard* for references to the collection by Members of Parliament, and interviews with current and former members of staff of the museums and arts galleries department.

Material was prepared in four parts:

- The story of how The Burrell Collection was given to Glasgow and the search for a suitable home for it.
- Personalities involved with the collection in the four decades since it was given to the city.
- Previous art collections bought by or given to the city which had contributed to its reputation as an important art centre.
- Description of the Burrell building.

All this turned out to be a press release of more than 3,000 words, breaking every possible rule of public relations which decrees that a press release should nornally not exceed a couple of pages, otherwise no-one would bother to read it. I expect that's quite true because most press releases are rubbish.

One Sunday morning I got up at 7 o'clock and went into the City Chambers to set up a picture of me in the banqueting hall surrounded by 500 press packs, each containing the story, four black-and-white prints and four colour transparencies. Alasdair Auld later sent me a bill for £2,000 for the pictures, which I thought was rather unsporting of him in view of the fact that I was publicising his museum throughout the world.

Alasdair, at all times a gracious and civilised man, told me later that he had only a small promotional budget and he, too, had his priorities, which I suppose was reasonable enough although I was a bit annoyed at the time.

Setting up the picture in the banqueting hall took nearly three hours. Then I went round to the *Glasgow Herald* office and said to whoever was on the picture desk, 'I've got a great picture set up. Can you get someone to come round to the chambers with me?'

'Aw, Harry, give us peace. You and your bloody pictures,' was the response.

'I'm telling you this is a good one. You'll be sorry if you don't get it.'

Eventually the man on the picture desk told Ian Hossack, the photographer on early duty that day, to go with me. After he had taken the picture I said to Ian, 'Would you like to help me pick up the packs?'

'Aye, that'll be right, Harry. I've got more important things to do.' So I spent another two hours picking them all up again.

It would be impossible to track down the number of publications that picture appeared in throughout the world. The press pack went to everyone at home and abroad likely to be interested in the story. A month before the gallery opened I flew a plane load of London-based foreign correspondents to Glasgow to see the gallery, and whatever else the city had to offer.

Among the correspondents were Mary Cronin of Time Life News Service, Gaia Servadio of *La Stampa*, Turin, Su Jinhu of Xinhua News Agency, China, Dan Ehrlich of the *San Francisco Examiner*, Adel Mourad of *At-tadamon*, which circulated in 22 Arab states, Siegfried Helm of the German Springer group of newspapers, Diana Decker of the New Zealand Associated Press, and many others.

During August and September The Burrell Collection was visited by about 250 news media people from newspapers, magazines, and television and radio stations throughout Britain and overseas. Television documentaries and radio features were prepared by most of the major television organisations.

After the opening many of the foreign correspondents wrote to me. Dirk de Villiers of Argus South African Newspapers said, 'It makes the job of the foreign correspondent, or any journalist, so much easier to receive information so clearly and readably set out ... my report will follow it closely!'

Su Jinhu wrote, 'It was an unforgettable experience in Glasgow. It was a great pleasure to meet you and your colleagues'.

Patricia Morgan of the *Herald and Weekly Times*, Australia, said, 'I was extremely delighted to have the opportunity to see such a wonderful collection and its superb new home.'

On 9 January, 1994, just over a decade after the opening of The Burrell Collection, a leader in the *Scotsman* about a National Gallery of Scottish Art which is to be built in Glasgow, said, 'The proven track record of the Burrell in gaining international recognition from a standing start is second to none.'

I think some of that press release in August 1983 is worth reproducing:

Glasgow reveals its hidden treasures

On 21 October in a shaded corner of a field in a 361-acre parkland estate only three miles from the centre of Glasgow the Queen will open The Burrell Collection museum and one of the most difficult problems of its kind any city has faced will finally be resolved.

After almost four decades one of the largest art collections ever assembled by one man and the largest ever given to a single city will at last have a permanent home.

The Burrell Collection has become part of Glasgow's folklore. It contains more than 600 paintings in oils, watercolours, and pastels by French, Dutch, Italian, British, Flemish and German masters.

There are works by Degas, Cezanne, Manet, Rembrandt, De Heem, Kalf, Maris, Bellini, Joseph Crawhall, Thomas Hudson, William McTaggart, John Lavery, Sir Henry Raeburn, McNeill Whistler, Memlinc, and Lucas Cranach.

There are collections of Chinese pottery, porcelain, and jades, Persian pottery and metalwork, gold, silver, bronzes, carpets, furniture, two of the finest collections of stained glass and tapestries in the world, and artefacts from the ancient civilisations of Mesopotamia, Assyria, Egypt, Greece and Rome.

All of this, and much more, was brought together by Sir William Burrell, a Glasgow shipowner, and it took him 80 years to do it. The collection is so large that not even the new art gallery and museum, one of the largest built in Britain this century, occupying 137,241 square feet, is big enough to display more than 40 per cent of The Burrell Collection at one time.

Alasdair Auld, Director of Glasgow's six major civic museums and art galleries, including The Burrell Collection, says, 'It will be years before we are able to rotate items in the collection so that everything will have been seen.'

Auld was a 13-year-old schoolboy in Edinburgh 'with inclinations towards art' when Sir William Burrell gave 6,000 art treasures to Glasgow in 1944 in the name of himself and Lady Burrell. His deed of gift specified that a gallery to house the collection should be built within four miles of Killearn, Stirlingshire, and not less than 16 miles from the Royal Exchange in the centre of Glasgow.

Sir William laid down these conditions because he felt his collection would look better in a rural setting but he was also worried about the harm to the treasures which could be caused by the belching, corrosive fumes of thousands of domestic and factory chimneys which clouded the air over a heavily industrial Glasgow.

But a museum containing an art collection of such importance 16 miles from the city would not have been easy for the City Council to administer. Nor would it have given much pleasure to the people of Glasgow who could hardly have been expected to travel in their thousands so far to see it.

Seven years later in 1951, after considerable persuasion, Sir William relented and agreed to a site at Dougalston estate, Milngavie, which had been left to the city and was only seven miles from the city centre, but the National Coal Board said they were planning to develop coal mining in the area and Sir William immediately banned the site.

Attention then turned to Mugdock Castle, also near Milngavie, but despite endless discussion and volumes of correspondence the problem was still no nearer solution when Sir William died in 1958 at the age of 96, leaving another 2,000 treasures to the city, making the problem even more difficult, if that were possible.

But independent forces were at work which were to rescue Glasgow from its unique dilemma. In 1956 the government had passed the Clean Air Act which compelled the country's cities to tackle the problem of air pollution and in 1959 Glasgow began a campaign which was to make it one of the cleanest cities in Britain.

Then in 1967 another act of munificence from one of the city's daughters this time, paved the way for what will become one of Britain's finest galleries. Mrs Anne Maxwell Macdonald, daughter of the late Sir John Stirling Maxwell, the tenth baronet, gave to the city an estate which had been in her family for 700 years — and it was only three miles from the centre of

Glasgow.

The Trustees of The Burrell Collection agreed that Pollok Estate was an ideal location for the Burrell treasures and plans for a gallery to house it were allowed to be made. A nationwide competition was sponsored by Glasgow Corporation and was won in 1972 by Barry Gasson, a young Cambridge lecturer, and two associates, John Meunier and Brit Andresen.

In June 1977 Glasgow District Council (the name of the authority changed with the reform of local government a few years earlier) agreed to put out to tender the contract for building a home for The Burrell Collection after an agreement from the government that it would make a considerable contribution towards the cost of building the museum.

In January 1978 the council awarded the contract to Taylor Woodrow Construction (Scotland) Limited and on 3 May Miss Silvia Burrell, Sir William's daughter, pressed a button on a bulldozer and a home for The Burrell Collection started to become a reality.

The museum was to cost £12.3 million and take three and a half years to build but as Robert Burns wrote more poetically, the best laid schemes of mice and men often go wrong and the museum took nearly five years to build and cost £20.6 million.

Poor weather, constantly rising prices, the complexities of perfecting a variety of mechanical and electronic systems adequately to store, protect, and display to its best advantage one of the world's most remarkable art collections all contributed to the delay.

Sir William had left Glasgow £450,000 towards the cost of building a gallery for his treasures and the interest from this money helped the Burrell Trustees to buy other treasures to add to the collection. One of these was The Warwick Vase, a second-century vessel unearthed near Rome 200 years ago by the Scots painter and archaeologist Gavin Hamilton. Napoleon Bonaparte said if he had been successful in conquering England the first thing he would have taken possession of was The Warwick Vase.

The vase was bought in 1979 for £253,808 to stop it going to the Metropolitan Museum of New York. The Burrell Trustees were assisted to raise the purchase price by the Scottish Heritage Fund, the National Art Collections Fund, and the Carnwath Trust. It has already been on show in Glasgow's famous Museum of Transport because it had, at the time, the only floor strong enough to support its nine tons.

Thousands of words have been written about The Burrell Collection by newspaper and magazine writers and by radio and television scriptwriters, ironically because Burrell would never talk to a newspaperman about any of his acquisitions. Nearly all of the scribes have insisted on putting a cash value on the collection because it makes good headlines. In recent years the more enthusiastic writers have put figures like £40 million, £60 million, and even £100 million on the collection. The figure of £100 million is the one mostly used by the news media because I gave it to them after countless requests for a figure.

I have to confess that I made it up because the true figure will never be known. The army of specialists necessary are not likely to be assembled to appraise the 8,000-odd treasures, and even if they were their evaluations would be no more than informed guesses.

Richard Marks, Master of Arts, Doctor of Philosophy, author of an 80,000-word thesis on English medieval stained glass, who was appointed Assistant Director of Glasgow's Museums and Art Galleries and Keeper of The Burrell Collection in 1979, says simply, 'I am not a valuer but as far as I am concerned the collection is priceless.'

William Burrell is said to have bought his first painting at the age of 15 with a few shillings his father gave him to buy a cricket bat. He never stopped buying art objects for the next 80 years. He and his older brother George took over the family shipping firm when their father William died in 1885.

For very sound business reasons Burrell sold his shipping firm twice. The first time was in 1899 when he decided to spend some of his spare time as a Glasgow town councillor. He served for seven years during which he naturally took a great interest in the city's artistic affairs but he also served on the Council's sub-committee on housing in which he made rather less impact.

Being the good businessman he was, the Burrell shipping empire was soon restored but he sold it again in 1917 to devote most of his time to his art collection. The shipping business finally closed in 1939.

Because of the size of the collection Burrell could not contain it all at Hutton Castle — so much of it was scattered throughout museums and cathedrals around Britain. Luckily Burrell kept meticulous records so it was not difficult for Glasgow City Council to track it all down.

The Burrell Collection compares favourably with the great American collections of Henry Clay Crick, J Pierpont Morgan, and Andrew Mellon, but Burrell was a canny Scot with an astute eye who paid a lot less than his transatlantic counterparts for his collection. In 1947 for instance he bought a 14th-century Chinese porcelain vase for £85. It is now estimated to be worth £250,000. Other ceramic items Sir William bought for £10 are now valued at £150,000.

Sir John Rothenstein, one of Britain's most distinguished art historians and a former director of London's Tate Gallery, says, 'Burrell was a collector of vast perception. The addition of The Burrell Collection to Glasgow's other museums and art galleries gives the city an honoured place among the great art centres of Europe.'

Sir John reveals that Burrell considered giving his collection to the Tate Gallery, but the Tate, to their 'intense regret' couldn't take it because of its enormous size and range.

Ironically the people of Glasgow, who are the real owners of the Burrell Collection, have never seen much of it. Because of its great value and the lack of a home for it the collection has been hidden in a variety of buildings throughout Glasgow for the past four decades. Items of one kind or another have been included in various exhibitions but not a lot of it has been seen in Scotland at any one time. The biggest exhibition of Burrell treasures was held in London's Hayward Gallery for seven weeks in 1975.

The Burrell Collection is only two or three hundred yards from Pollok House, once the home of a long line of Maxwell baronets, one of whom, William Stirling-Maxwell, the ninth baronet, last century amassed one of the largest and most important collection of Spanish paintings in Britain. This also came to the city from Mrs Anne Maxwell Macdonald in 1967.

The monument to one of Glasgow's greatest benefactors blends an art gallery of the late 20th century with its modern design, space-age technology in lighting, heating, and air-conditioning, with stone arches and doorways and stained glass windows painstakingly fashioned by craftsmen hundreds of years ago. Incorporated in the building are 15 archways which Burrell bought because he thought they would be useful for that very purpose.

Some of them came from the estate of William Randolph Hearst, founder of the American newspaper empire, and had originally been part of Hornby Castle in Yorkshire, but Hearst kept them in a warehouse in Wales because he didn't know what to do with them. One of them, a 12th-century stone archway 15 1/2 feet high cost Hearst £5,000. He shipped it to America, couldn't find a use for it, and shipped it back to Britain. Burrell later bought it for one tenth of what it cost Hearst.

The entrance to the Burrell building is a 13-feet high early 16th-century archway which leads into a glazed courtyard. The entrance to the collection itself is the Hornby portico, a 26-feet high English Renaissance doorway which weighs 26 tons.

The Burrell building incorporates reproductions of three rooms from Hutton Castle, near Berwick-on-Tweed, where Sir William and Lady Burrell moved in 1927. These are the drawing room, hall, and dining room, each furnished in the original manner and with some of the original woodwork.

The building also has storage for the many items not on display, a restaurant, lecture theatre, a room for children's activities, library, photographic studio, and even living quarters for visiting scholars.

Barry Gasson, one of the original designers of the building, now has his own architect's company in Glasgow and has been working closely with the builders of the new gallery in the past few years. Meunier is a professor of architecture in Cincinnatti in America and Andresen is a teacher in Australia.

Gasson, now 43, is a graduate of Birmingham School of Architecture. After a year in private practice he was awarded an English Speaking Union Fellowship to Columbia University in New York for two years. This was followed by two years in the Park Avenue architectural practice of Philip Johnson where projects he worked on included a ballet theatre for the Lincoln Centre, an extension to the New York Museum of Modern Art, and laboratories for Yale University.

He has been working on the Burrell project since 1972.

'A unique experience. I doubt if I will see its like again,' he says.

Whether he does or not his place in the architectural firmament is assured. Six months before the museum was due to open Gasson received the Royal Scottish Academy Gold Medal for Architecture for his design of the Burrell museum.

Admission to The Burrell Collection will be free, despite its enormous cost to build and the estimated £2.8 million a year it will cost to run. Strathclyde Regional Council has agreed to contribute 17 per cent of the annual running costs but this still leaves Glasgow with a great deal of money to find.

The city's Labour administration has rejected a proposal to charge admission to the collection. They take the view that The Burrell Collection is already costing the people of Glasgow enough without charging them money to see it.

Many men played important roles in the story of The Burrell Collection over the decades: Dr Tom Honeyman, Director of Glasgow's museums from 1939 to 1952, who claimed that a phone call to his home in Glasgow from Sir William Burrell in December 1943 started the negotiations which brought the collection to the city, Stuart Henderson, Director of the museums from 1953 until 1972, during whose term of office it was finally decided that a Burrell gallery would be built, and Trevor Walden, who came to Glasgow in 1972 from Leicester confident that he would go down in the appropriate history books as the director who reigned during the building and opening of The Burrell Collection, but who died suddenly in 1979.

Then there were the keepers of the collection whose major task was to ensure that the priceless paintings and other manifestations of man's creative genius were adequately safeguarded in their various hiding places and restored as far as possible to their original artistic glory: Andrew Hannah, who carried out this important task from 1944 to 1956, William Wells 1956 to 1978, and Richard Marks, who supervised the building of the Burrell gallery and saw it opened.

The no-charge policy still applies to the collection although a charge was made at the end of 1993 for an exhibition of Degas bronzes which was said to be necessary because of the high cost of transporting and insuring the exhibits.

I have lost touch with Barry Gasson since these events took place. Perhaps if he reads this he will let us know where he is.

Glasgow runs 12 museums and galleries, more than any other city in in Britain, which are acknowledged to be among the best in the UK for the quality, variety and value of their treasures. These include the Museum of Religion, the only one of its kind in Britain, and the Gallery of Modern Art, an exciting and challenging experience, which opened in March 1996 to the accompaniment of considerable controversy. The National Gallery of Scottish Art and Design, which will occupy the former Post Office building in George Square will be run by the National Galleries of Scotland in Edinburgh.

Chapter 21

THE DOODLE THAT WENT ROUND THE WORLD

JOHN STRUTHERS, a Glasgow advertising man, and his 14-year-old son Mark were doodling, John's own word, on sheets of paper on a flight to London trying to devise a campaign slogan for their native city.

Page after page was discarded as they wrote things like 'GLASGOW TOPS FOR YOU, GET TO KNOW GLASGOW, GROW WITH GLASGOW, THE GLASGOW SMILE'. They still hadn't quite got it when they arrived in London. Then on a train from the airport to the centre of the city John wrote 'GLASGOW'S MILES BETTER'. When they got home that night they substituted a smiling face for the letter 'O'. And so was born the slogan that swept the world.

Struthers took his idea to Lord Provost Michael Kelly, who had the wit and foresight to see its possibilities. He persuaded the City Council to put up £150,000 towards a full-scale promotional campaign for the city. The business community put up £200,000. Kelly persuaded business leaders that what was good for Glasgow was good for them and their businesses too. After all, if a lot more people were attracted to the city because of the things they read they would obviously spend money there.

The Glasgow's Miles Better campaign, which started in 1983, was one of the best promotions ever mounted by a British city. It won the International Film and Television Festival of New York award in 1983, 1984, 1985 and 1987.

145

'The only reason we didn't win in 1986 is because we didn't enter the festival,' says Struthers.

Struthers devised a series of advertisements based on the things we had been publicising over the years: the city's international hotels, museums, parks, restaurants, sporting facilities. Then came badges, car stickers, umbrellas, tee-shirts, and plastic carrier bags, all carrying the miles better slogan.

The slogan, advertisements and promotional items were first-class, but one other ingredient was necessary to make the campaign the success it was — editorial publicity. And this is where my department came in. We injected the miles better theme into almost every story that came out of my office, and many of these stories were published and broadcast internationally.

Even the running, jumping and falling events organised by the parks and recreation department were miles better than anyone else's. The newspaper headline writers also made everything to do with Glasgow miles better. Well ... nearly everthing.

All my international news media contacts gratifyingly took up the miles better story. In addition, radio stations in America, Canada and Australia which regularly catered for people of Scots descent with 'Scottish Hour' programmes were all given up-to-date news about what was happening in Glasgow. That gave us millions of dollars worth of publicity for the cost of the stamps for the press releases.

Before that the programmes had relied mainly on people in Scotland occasionally sending them newspapers from which they gleaned most of their news. Incidentally, during our Californian adventure in 1981 I was astonished at the number of people who regularly put on full Highland dress, organised ceilidhs, and drank enormous amounts of whisky. Many of them had never been anywhere near Scotland and had no intention of going there. They were very good hosts, though!

Two young men, Roger Laing, a lawyer, and David Haig, a scientist, came in one day to tell me they intended to fly to America and back in a single-engined Cessna 210 aircraft to raise money for cancer research.

They said they would like to promote the city, too, so I gave them mountains of car stickers and other items and even arranged for their aircraft to use the call sign Glasgow One. Their flight took in Iceland, Greenland, Baffin Island (in the Canadian Northwest Territories), Boston and Chicago because an aircraft of that size obviously couldn't fly across the Atlantic.

I sent a story about their flight and its purpose to news media everywhere they touched down and they gave out the promotional material. The two young flyers were made a tremendous fuss of in America and in fact flew to quite a number of places not on their flight schedules. The result in publicity terms for Glasgow was incalculable.

My younger son Michael distributed miles better material, including tee-shirts, in the Negev desert of Israel where he worked and my older son Harvie and his Brazilian-born wife Rejane gave out stickers and tee-shirts when they went to Rio de Janeiro on holiday with their children.

Bob Reid, a planning officer, used up two years' leave to go on a six-week expedition to the Himalayas where he and a friend, Edward Farmer, were the first climbers to conquer a 21,000ft mountain. They wore Glasgow's Miles Better sweatshirts, among other things, for the climb and planted a miles better flag at the peak.

No opportunity to spread the word was overlooked. Holidaymakers flying out of Glasgow Airport had the miles better stickers on their luggage in a variety of languages. People like Jimmy Saville and Lulu were recruited for promotions by council departments. Even the Queen was pictured with Michael Kelly under a miles better umbrella.

When two young girls from Italy had their cameras stolen the boss of a camera shop read about the theft and gave the girls new cameras and film. When the newspapers reported the incident they quoted the girls as saying Glasgow was miles better because they had been so well treated there.

At one point John Struthers devised a miles better advertisement to put on Edinburgh buses during the Edinburgh Festival but we were refused permission by the city's transport authority. We had planned to spend about £2,000 on this exercise but the transport authority's refusal was reported worldwide and we received millions of pounds worth of publicity for nothing. I was even quoted on the front page of the *Wall Street Journal*, one of the most influential newspapers in America.

In March 1984 Michael Kelly launched the campaign nationally with a breakfast in the Savoy Hotel in London hosted by Britoil. The list of guests from every walk of life was enormous. One of them was Billy Connolly. Mr Connolly was being what he considered amusing for the benefit of the crowd in a reception area when I approached him quietly at Michael Kelly's request and stopped a few feet away. I waited until he acknowledged my existence by looking in my direction and said, 'Would you mind taking your place at the top table Mr Connolly so that we can get started.'

Mr Connolly looked me up and down and said in a voice that carried to Carlisle, 'Whooo are yoooo? Fuck off.' A few self-conscious titters broke out at this brilliant riposte. Mr Connolly had obviously been misled by my immaculate appearance.

I put my hand under his armpit, assisted him to a nearby wall, and whispered in his ear in the idiom which he apparently understood best,

'Listen pal, Ah'm a Glasgow man an' all and if you talk to me like that again I'll rip yer scruffy fucking heid aff and fling it to all yer admirers out there. Get the message, son?' Mr Connolly was taken aback, abashed and nonplussed. He went in for breakfast.

Michael Kelly would not have been pleased at my inelegant language to one of our guests. He liked to keep Council officials in their place. He once rounded on me angrily when I had the impertinence to ask him for a lift back to the City Chambers from some event we had been at. A newspaper colleague who witnessed Michael's churlishness called to him, 'Stuff your Rolls-Royce, Michael. I'll give Harry a lift.'

Michael has since become, in the minds of many of the lazier news media people, and perhaps even in his own, the ultimate authority on city image-building. He is interviewed regularly on the subject and carefully avoids contradicting any interviewer who mistakenly implies that he invented the miles better campaign and was solely responsible for telling the world about everything good that ever happened in the city.

Many people were disappointed, including John Struthers of course, when the miles better campaign ran out of steam about 1989 and was succeeded by the Glasgow's Alive slogan. David Harris, the designer who devised the new slogan, didn't submit it by the deadline date. He brought it to my office afterwards and I took it to Pat Lally, leader of the Council, and persuaded him to allow the judging panel, of which he was chairman, to consider it along with the rest of the submissions.

After many meetings and much discussion 'Glasgow's Alive' was the winner but despite a considerable amount of money spent on it in the following few years it merely limped along until a meeting of Glasgow City Council's Policy and Resources Committee on 3 November, 1994 resolved to revive the Glasgow's Miles Better campaign at an initial cost of £100,000 with more to come.

The slogan's revival owes a lot to its inventor, John Struthers, who laboured mightily over the years to ensure that the slogan wasn't forgotten. Struthers claims that the original miles better campaign didn't really help him to acquire several more very lucrative clients as he already had them. Maybe, but it certainly didn't do him any harm either. Nor will its revival, especially with the scope provided by the various festivals and other activities planned by Glasgow in the years leading to the millennium.

Chapter 22

A CALL FROM THE DESERT

DURING my years as Head of Public Relations for the city I was asked for advice by a number of cities, both in Britain and abroad. Delegations of politicians and officials came to my office from Liverpool, Stevenage, Bradford, Belfast and Dublin, among other places.

In 1982 we had a visit from Mr Timothy Chirwa, Town Clerk of Blantyre in the East African republic of Malawi. Mr Chirwa spent three days in Glasgow and announced that a public relations department along the lines of ours was one of his town's priorities.

The Town Clerk said they did have newspapers and a radio station but they did not always accurately reflect his Council's views and objectives, a comment which occasioned no great surprise to his Glasgow hosts. He thought it would be a good idea if I could go to Blantyre to help them set up a public relations department, a suggestion that was greeted with some enthusiasm by some of my political masters, notably the Tories, but regrettably it never happened.

A couple of weeks earlier I had received a visit from Dr Harford Onoh, Deputy High Commissioner for Nigeria, who wanted to know how to set up a newspaper like *The Bulletin*. I don't think that ever happened either.

In 1988 I was asked to advise the town of Bhopal in India how to improve its image as it had understandably been badly tarnished by the leak four years earlier of poisonous gas from the Union Carbide factory which killed more than 3,000 people in the world's worst industrial disaster. I forget what my advice was but I doubt if it did any good.

Other people tried from time to time to entice me away from the City Chambers. A firm of executive search consultants asked me to apply for a job with Rolls-Royce at Crewe. I told them I already had the best public relations job in Britain and that during the war I was sometimes stranded at Crewe station with all my army kit and had to lie on a cold, hard wooden bench all night waiting for a train and I resolved that if I survived the war I would never again set foot in Crewe … and I never have.

The last issue of the *Sunday Standard*, an unsuccessful attempt in the early 1980s by the *Herald* group to run a Sunday newspaper, contained a story that I had turned down a highly-paid job with an international conglomerate which offered unlimited expenses and an opportunity to travel the world. The company also had their own executive aircraft. I was quoted as saying I got dizzy looking off the pavement.

I couldn't understand how the *Standard* had got this story as the negotiations had been made in the closest secrecy. It turned out that a reporter had been listening carefully to my conversation with a friend in a restaurant.

An invitation from the township of Dimona, deep in the heart of the Negev desert of Israel, near the biblical town of Beersheba, caused a minor uproar. In August 1986 a letter arrived at the Town Clerk's office from Mr Eli Allali, Mayor of Dimona, saying, 'We have heard of the impressive success of Glasgow District Council in projecting to the citizens of Glasgow and to the world at large the new image of the city as it restores its position as one of the leading conurbations in Britain.

We understand that Mr Henry Diamond has been responsible for publicising the city over the past decade, including the Burrell Collection and the Glasgow's Miles Better campaign and we would ask you to permit us to invite Mr Diamond to visit Dimona for a period of at least a week and to relay to us how your success was achieved so that we may learn from this and employ these lessons in the work we have now commenced.'

Mayor Allali said Dimona had been built 30 years earlier and was known as the Flower of the Desert but had sadly lost much of its initial attraction.

He added, 'We have now embarked on a massive programme of renewal and revitalisation and are seeking to project this to our citizens and the wider public. Mr Diamond is familiar with our country and would we believe make an excellent ambassador for your great city.'

It would be nice to be able to claim that my brilliant work for Glasgow had penetrated deep into the heart of the Negev desert but the truth is that two Glasgow men who had known me for years were responsible for the invitation. Mark Goldberg, Chairman of the Glasgow-based Goldbergs department store group and Geoffrey Ognall, Chairman of Legal and Trade Financial Services, were joint-chairmen of the Joint Israel Appeal Project Renewal Dimona Committee formed in 1986 to establish a partnership between Jews in Britain and Dimona. The project was modelled on a highly successful renewal project in the southern town of Ashkelon. In fact there were a considerble number of renewal projects throughout Israel heavily supported by British Jews.

Mayor Allali's invitation attracted considerable publicity and was approved by my Council's Policy and Resources Committee, which remitted it to the Personnel Committee to decide if I was to be granted paid leave to go to Israel.

The day the committee met a letter appeared in the *Glasgow Herald* from a Mr Jim Lister of the West of Scotland Friends of Palestine pointing out that Glasgow was an anti-nuclear city and should not support Israel's 'aggressive policies' in the Middle East. Mr Lister also referred to Israel's trade relations with South Africa which were anathema to Glasgow's Labour group who strongly condemned apartheid.

The convener of the Personnel Committee, Councillor Maria Fyfe (now Member of Parliament for Maryhill, Glasgow), took fright at the possibility of breaching the Council's policy and continued the proposal until the invitation was looked at again. I thought it was rather odd for an important Council committee to be panicked by a grossly-biased letter in a newspaper, even the *Herald*, but all kinds of odd things influence politicians.

The resultant headlines read 'P.R. CHIEF'S ISRAEL TRIP SPARKS ROW' (*Glasgow Herald*) and 'ISRAELI TRIP TURNS OUT TO BE BAD P.R. FOR LABOUR' (*The Scotsman*).

Surprisingly little was heard of the matter after that and the Council finally agreed that I could go on paid leave to Israel. Pat Lally, the Council leader, told reporters, 'The local council in Dimona have no say in the nuclear policy of their central government just as we don't in this country. We have one of the biggest stockpiles of nuclear arms in Europe on our doorstep and there is little we can do about it.'

Israel's policies continued to disturb Labour groups in Britain and in 1989 Manchester City Council's ruling Labour group vetoed an official visit to Israel by their Lord Mayor, Councillor Pat Conquest, who pointed out that she would have meetings with both Jews and Arabs but it didn't influence her colleagues.

Although I had been authorised to spend a week in Dimona I was there two weeks because I also took a week's holiday I was due. Mayor Allali and his council proved to be very good hosts and I had a series of discussions with councillors and other officials.

One afternoon during a visit to Jerusalem I was standing in Jaffa Road trying to find on a map the street in which Radio Israel was located. A passer-by asked if he could help. I tried to tell him my problem in Hebrew and he said, 'Excuse me, sir. You English?' I didn't want to argue the point so I just said *ken*, yes.

'You speak English, please,' he said. 'Your Hebrew hopeless!'

When I came back to Scotland I made a full report to Mark Golberg and Geoffrey Ognall. There was one vital flaw in my plan. There was no one in Dimona to do the things I had suggested.

My son Michael was wandering about Australia at this time but he returned shortly afterwards. After seeing more than once what the rest of the world had to offer he did not care for the idea of living and working in Glasgow. I told him about Dimona and he said he was willing to give it a try. I told Messrs Goldberg and Ognall that Michael was interested in going back to Israel and after a couple of interviews he was appointed Co-ordinator of the Joint Israel Appeal's renewal programme in Dimona. His job was to progress the programme but of course he did a lot of PR work, too, as he had picked up quite a few of my techniques over the years.

Michael worked with the JIA until 1992, receiving wide praise for his work. His PR efforts reached newspapers in Britain and America. Jenni Frazer, the London *Jewish Chronicle*'s resident correspondent in Israel, wrote a big piece in April 1991 about Dimona in which she said, 'Much of the dramatic improvement in Dimona's fortunes can be credited to the work of the Joint Israel Appeal and its representative in the town, ex-Glaswegian Mr Michael Diamond.'

Michael now works for Ben Gurion University at Beersheba liaising with supporters of the university world wide.

Chapter 23

JACKIE

MY life fell apart at 5 pm on Saturday, 10 October, 1987. Jackie and I were watching television in our bedroom when she said, 'Henry, I'm sore,' in a voice filled with weariness.

I put my arms round her as she slumped back in the bed and said in a panic, 'Jackie, can I get you something, a drink, medicine, anything?'

The pupils of her eyes slid to one side and she was gone. I laid her down gently and walked out of the house and up and down the street in a daze looking for someone to tell. The street was empty so I went back into the house and phoned Harvie.

Joel Lee our family doctor arrived shortly afterwards along with my friend Jack Miller, but I don't remember phoning them. I do remember Jackie's funeral the next day, throwing earth on her coffin as is our custom, walking away from the graveside in a daze, trying to remember what people were saying to me.

I didn't weep a lot in the first few days because the relief of tears wouldn't come, but I've made up for it since. Michael couldn't get home from Israel in time for Jackie's funeral; he arrived the day after. He stayed with me a fortnight but we didn't talk a lot about the only thing I could think about, the all-consuming desolation that filled my soul.

I stayed in the house a week after Jackie's death. Michael did any errands that were necessary. Then I went out for some fresh air. I was shocked to see cars and buses running, people walking in and out of shops, vanmen making deliveries, children playing. I wanted to shout at them, 'What do you mean by carrying on as if nothing has happened? My Jackie has died. Don't you realise that?' I was lonely, cold, bewildered, mentally and emotionally exhausted.

Two or three weeks after Michael went back to Israel I flew out there to stay with him for a while, but we still didn't talk much about anything. He seemed rather withdrawn and preoccupied with his own thoughts. Michael wasn't married when Jackie died so there wasn't anyone to talk to while he was at work. I didn't know anyone else there so I walked about the desert screaming at the heavens and asking unanswerable questions.

Eventually I went back to work but I didn't do anything. I felt that everything I had ever worked for had collapsed in ruins. There wasn't any point in it all any more. My deputy David Bell and Audrey McCormack my secretary and the rest of the staff in my office in the City Chambers carried me for a long time and I shall always be grateful to them for that.

I think a lot about when Jackie and I first met. I saw her dancing with someone at a youth club. I fell in love with her the moment I saw her. During the evening I managed to talk to her and told her I was a newspaper reporter and that sometimes I was sent to the theatre to do a review and please would she come with me next time.

I took her to the theatre a couple of weeks later and she told a friend she wasn't going out with me again because I was boring! I probably was, too. My mind was filled with newspapers and running after stories and I wasn't very good at thinking up things to say to girls. We did go out again, though, for a couple of years.

I vividly remember the first couple of sentences of my speech at our wedding dinner: 'Nine years ago today I left home to serve my king and country. Today I leave home to serve my queen,' turning, smiling, to touch her gently. The guests applauded loudly with delight.

The tears lasted a long time. I can still cry when something triggers me; in fact I'm doing it as I type. I had come to regard myself as quite skilled at what I did for a living. I was confident, independent, and arrogant. Sometimes this arrogance showed more than it should have done. But it was all swept away in one afternoon. I was a heavy smoker for more than 40 years and I put away a fair amount of alcohol but a few days after Jackie died I poured the contents of my drinks cabinet down the lavatory and threw my cigarettes away because I was in great danger of settling into a chair and smoking and drinking myself to death. I didn't want to do that because I realised how hard it would affect Harvie and Michael.

Harvie has phoned me almost every night for years just to ask if I am alright and Michael phones from Israel if he hasn't had a letter or a phone call for a couple of weeks. I am very lucky to have two such sons.

Loneliness is something I never thought much about when Jackie was here. I suppose it was because I was never lonely. I know all about it now, though. I know also that the attitude that nothing matters any more is wrong and destructive but I think everyone has to go through this phase and survive the best way they can. Some people benefit from counselling and some don't. I preferred to bite the bullet and stick it out by myself but I'm not recommending this course to anyone else.

My effort to take counselling wasn't at all successful but I'm not blaming anyone for that. A few weeks after Jackie died I was sitting at my desk in the office when I was overcome with such a sense of desolation that I walked out and went to the office of the Glasgow Council for Voluntary Service in Bath Street to ask about Cruse, a group which helped the bereaved. As it happens there was a meeting that day and I was directed to a room where a number of men and women were gathered having tea. By an interesting coincidence I had written a press release to announce the opening of the then-named Volunteer Bureau in March 1974.

I was offered tea and biscuits but no-one made any kind of fuss about my arrival. Everyone knew why I was there. One woman asked me if I was interested in old-time dancing. Another asked me if I would like to go on a bus-run or was I interested in bingo. It became obvious very quickly that I lived in a different world from these people.

I don't want to be snobbish about it but they came from a different social and professional class from myself and had different interests. It was obvious I was not going to get the kind of help I needed. Maybe I could have got it if I had tried but I was too spiritually beaten to say anything.

I noticed a well-dressed man sitting on a settee not saying anything so I went over and introduced myself. He told me his name and I said, 'I don't think this is for us.'

'No,' he said.

'Let's go somewhere for a coffee.'

That started off my friendship with Bryce Aitken, a civil engineer whose wife had died about the same time as Jackie. We went to the theatre and had dinners together and were friends for two or three years until he, like Jackie, died of cancer. Bryce had introduced me to a neighbour, Bill Allan, a retired banker, who lived two or three doors from him in Bearsden on the outskirts of Glasgow and who was also a fairly recent widower. Bill has been a good friend ever since. About three years ago he married a charming lady named Isobel and both of them are my friends now.

A number of other people helped me through the difficult days and still help me to keep my sanity: Jackie's cousins Marlene and Harry Berkley, Ezra and Susan Golombok, Freddy and Florence Levine, Gerald and Pamela Levin, Gerald Strump, Irene Markson, Kenny and Linda Davidson, Jackie Monk and John McLaughlin.

I am also grateful to my old friend George Todd in whose villa in the south of Spain I spent two holidays during which he listened with patience and understanding to my woes. And then there is Elsie Greig, who worked in the marketing department of the gas industry until her retirement. I haven't seen Elsie since the 1960s but she wrote to me from her home in Angus after seeing an article about me in the *Scots Magazine*. I wrote back and told her Jackie had died a few months earlier and she has been writing words of encouragement to me regularly ever since.

Nearly 200 people wrote to me after Jackie died and in the following few weeks I answered all the cards and letters, some of them from America, Canada, Australia and mainland Europe. I still have a regular correspondence with some of the writers. Other people with whom we had been friends for up to 30 years suddenly seemed to vanish from the planet and I never heard from them again.

Nine years after Jackie's death I can now say there is life after the death of a loved one. It might not be much at times but it's better than the alternative. A lot depends on the individual's determination to survive and be useful again, even to strangers. They won't be strangers for long.

Despite my commitment to my religion I am filled with doubts. I have difficulty in reconciling the existence of a deity with all the misery in the world, the millions who die of starvation, the victims of wars, the so-called free will that human beings are supposed to have when in fact they often have no control of any kind over their lives.

Sometimes I think there isn't much point to it all but the sensible half of me tells me that's wrong. If it were not for my Jackie there would have been no Harvie and Michael to meet Rejane and Yaffa. There would have been no Tiffany and Gideon and Yuval and Ophir, my four grandchildren, to bring brightness and goodness into my life and each other's. Maybe they are the answer to my dilemma.

Some time after my visit to the Cruse session I went to see Dr Philip Millington, a lecturer in the bio-engineering department of the University of Strathclyde, who was Vice-Chairman of Cruse. He told me there were many people like myself, professional men, who had difficulty coping with bereavement.

'We don't have enough of them to form a group,' he said. 'They just don't make themselves known to us. This repression of feelings by men is responsible for all kinds of breakdowns among them. Professional men are particularly vulnerable. Up to the moment of bereavement they are fully occupied with business and social life, self-possessed, confident and secure. Suddenly they find themselves bereft of all these things but pride does not allow them to tell anyone. They don't want anyone to feel sorry for them as that makes them feel diminished as individuals.'

Woman were different, said Dr Millington. 'They tend to form groups easier than men. And if they are over 45 they tend to avoid getting involved in relationships with men. They don't really want to marry again.'

For a while I considered starting a group for professional men but I felt I had enough to cope with. I did speak to one or two people but it was difficult to get them to commit themselves to regular meetings. One man confessed that he felt so lonely one day he tried to think of a way of having a minor accident so that he could be taken to hospital where he would be among people he could talk to.

The problem of loneliness among men was highlighted by a Samaritans report 'Behind the Mask' in May 1995. Mr Simon Armson, the organisation's Chief Executive, stated that more men were committing suicide for a variety of complex reasons. One of them was loneliness and the need for a close supportive relationship.

'Single, divorced and widowed men over the age of 24 have suicide rates three times greater than those of married men,' said Mr Armson.

An earlier report by the Samaritans revealed that the pressures of living in the 1990s, combined with a reluctance to talk about feelings, could be too much to cope with.

Cruse now have more professional men coming to them for help and offer a one-to-one counselling service for professional people and anyone else who wants it, a service which was introduced about five years ago. Men are still a problem, though. Generally they are still reluctant to bare their souls.

Yvonne Alexis, Chairman of the Glasgow branch of Cruse, says there are many one-time responsible, working, family men who become derelicts, sleeping in doorways and under bridges, because they have lost a wife and her companionship, can't talk about it for one reason or another, and no longer have the will to do anything but exist.

I have now left the house that Jackie and I and the boys lived in for so many years and moved into a comfortable little flat. I just couldn't take it any more, wandering round the house where every corner had a memory.

Like so many other people in a similar situation I am reluctant to laugh with the crowd and say I'm alright in case anyone should think I have recovered from losing Jackie and am now enjoying life. Thanks to my family and friends I am alright much of the time but again like so many others I carry a sorrow which is never likely to go away.

Chapter 24

AFTER THE GARDEN FESTIVAL

GLASGOW Garden Festival in 1988 was a marvellous event for the city. It gave Glaswegians such a tremendous boost of morale, attracted so much favourable publicity to the city, brought so many visitors, and generally gave the city an air of excitement and buoyancy.

Eight years later much of the festival site is still derelict although various offices are awash with reports, maps and plans for the 60-acre stretch of land on the south bank of the river Clyde.

In 1995 Miller Developments were given outline planning consent to build a leisure and business complex, national science centre, millenium tower, and Imax theatre on what is now called Pacific Quay and is owned by the Glasgow Development Agency.

Whether or not any of this comes to fruition depends on the Millenium Commission who in 1996 rejected the first application for millions of pounds for the development. All is not lost, though, as BBC Scotland has announced its intention of moving to Pacific Quay by 1999.

The Glasgow Development Agency plans have met with considerable opposition over the years. Various organisations, Clyde Festival Gardens, New Glasgow Society, Clyde Maritime Trust, and Glasgow Chamber of Commerce all wanted to see the site transformed into something like the famed Tivoli Gardens in Copenhagen but with a maritime heritage centre to reflect the Clyde's one-time great shipbuilding industry.

I have often been asked why Glasgow didn't keep the garden festival. There are a number of answers to that. Glasgow claims to have more parks and open spaces than any other city in Britain, perhaps Europe, and has a

158

difficult enough job finding the money to maintain what it has without having to look after another vast acreage. Nevertheless the city Council does own 11 acres of the site which has been designated a park but as the rest of the site is so unttractive no-one goes there.

Glasgow Garden Festival was never meant to be anything than temporary. The buildings were not built to last and the vast number of exhibitors could not have maintained their presence for any length of time. The landscaping could not be maintained and even the drainage on the site could not have sustained a lengthy festival. Besides, the owners of the site, Laing Homes Limited, wanted it back afterwards although they didn't develop it as they originally intended.

In return for the 'loan' of the site Laing were enabled to buy seven offset sites throughout the city so that they could continue their house-building programme. Laing had acquired the site from Clydeport just before the Secretary of State announced it was to be the site of the garden festival. In 1992 Laing sold it to the Glasgow Development Agency. All that has happened on the site is that Laing have built 63 houses and 76 flats there. There is still the highly-expensive Bell's Bridge, which links the festival site with the Scottish Exhibition and Conference Centre, but regrettably no-one uses it.

In 1994 the aptly-named Govan Initiative, a publicly-funded body established in 1986 to regenerate the local economy of Govan, opened a £2.1 million Festival Business Centre on the ground occupied by the garden festival administration building. The centre included a purpose-built nursery to serve the 27 units, all of which were quickly occupied.

Many people were astonished that a place like Glasgow was even considered as a locale for a garden festival. They still had an image of the city as a place of grime, drunks, razor slashers, and gang fights, a perception that was decades out of date although astonishingly there are people in London even now who think Glasgow is a place to avoid.

Glasgow was told in 1984 that it was to host Britain's third National Garden Festival and being the independent thinkers they were my Council hierarchy quickly changed the name to Glasgow Garden Festival just as two years later they changed the official title of European City of Culture to Cultural Capital of Europe.

A Garden Festival Company was formed by the Scottish Development Agency (forerunners of the Glasgow Development Agency), principal funders of the festival, and a great deal of work behind the scenes followed. Imaginative plans for environmental improvements to all the approaches to the festival site were devised by city planners led by director James Rae and

John Watson, one of his deputes.

Eighty buildings and bridges were nominated for floodlighting, British Rail were asked to clean up embankments and even the Scottish Gas Board agreed to paint a gas holder blue instead of the usual depressing slate grey.

By September 1985 we were ready to tell the world about our plans for the great event. The announcement was to be made in London by Lord Provost Robert Gray and Mr George Younger, Secretary of State for Scotland, much to the annoyance of Mrs Jean McFadden, leader of Glasgow City Council, who said later, 'I refused to go because I thought the launch should have been in Glasgow, and I didn't see why I should spend more than five hours travelling to London just to be an adjunct to George Younger doing his thing.'

Mrs McFadden was by no means the only one who thought that if Glasgow was good enough to be Britain's garden festival city it was important enough for the announcement to be made there. After a great deal of murmurings from the City Chambers and elsewhere it was decided to have a simultaneous announcement in London and Glasgow.

Mrs McFadden duly took her place at the top table in the City Chambers with Mr Allan Stewart, Minister for Industry and Education in the Scottish Office, who made the announcement.

Lord Provost Gray flew to London under protest and found when he got to Heathrow airport that the Scottish Development Agency had arranged for him and a Council officer (usher) who was carrying the Lord Provost's £60,000 gold chain of office, to travel to their hotel by underground. The Lord Provost was not amused.

By a stroke of luck I also had some information which gave the festival story a great deal of additional impact. Steve Inch, head of a section of the Council which kept track of investment in the city, had at my request compiled a list of developments which had recently been completed or were in the course of construction. We discovered that these amounted to a billion pounds.

They included a glass-covered shopping complex in St Enoch Square, a hotel near the Scottish Exhibition and Conference Centre, a shopping, leisure and entertainment development in Princes Square off Buchanan Street, a plan to convert Kelvin Hall into a major indoor sports stadium and Museum of Transport, and a plan to build what became the Glasgow Royal Concert Hall. The story of plans for the festival and the billion pounds worth of investments was sent far and wide at home and abroad.

As plans for the festival progressed the Council announced the establishment of a fund of £500,000 to create 900 events throughout the city featuring opera and classical music concerts, children's projects, community events, and anything else that would give the city a festival air and provide a curtain-raiser for 1989 and culture year in 1990.

Two internationally-known figures in the British arts scene were recruited in 1987 to make Glasgow's star shine in the international arts firmament in the following three years: Robert Palmer, Drama and Dance Director of the Scottish Arts Council, and Neil Wallace, Director of Chapter Arts Centre, Cardiff.

Among the productions they were responsible for bringing to the Tramway Theatre in Glasgow in 1988 was the first performance in Britain of Peter Brook's trilogy of plays *The Mahabharata*, billed as one of the most sought-after productions in world theatre. The three plays lasted a total of more than eight hours. Artistes from 20 countries came to the city to dance, sing and make music.

The following year the dynamic duo (apologies to Batman and Robin) brought another Peter Brook first to Glasgow, *La Tragédie de Carmen*, which also played to packed audiences at the Tramway.

Palmer, a slim, dark, fast-talking Canadian, was later appointed Director of the city's Department of Performing Arts and Venues, a post he still holds. Wallace became Artistic Director of the Tramway Theatre but later left to become a freelance producer and reviewer.

In July 1987 Theo Crombie, a Depute Town Clerk and the Council's liaison man with the festival, asked me if I would go with him to see George Chesworth, the festival's Chief Executive, who felt there should be more international publicity for the event. Bill Simpson, the festival's Director of Marketing, and Rob Reid, his Public Relations Manager, were preoccupied with producing vast amounts of material for the British news media but the international media weren't taking enough notice of what was going on.

Crombie knew I had developed an extensive range of contacts in foreign newspapers, magazines and the broadcast media during my years as a daily newspaperman and later as a public relations man so I went with him to see Chesworth, a retired Air-Vice-Marshal and the man who masterminded the first raid on Stanley during the 1982 Falklands War. He is now Lord Lieutenant of Moray.

The result of our talk was that I flew to London shortly afterwards and with the help of Martin Cole, Head of the London Correspondents' Service of the Central Office of Information, arranged for 15 foreign correspondents representing news media in America, Austria, Belgium, Brazil, France, Germany, Israel, Saudi Arabia, and Spain to come to Glasgow to see what all the fuss was about.

They included Jim Perry of the *Wall Street Journal*, who was described by a fellow-American, Timothy Crouse, as one of the superstars of American journalism, Wolfgang Kuballa of the *Rheinische Post*, Dusseldorf, and five other German newspapers, and Arie Zimuki of *Yediot Achronot* (*Latest News*) of Tel Aviv. The result was millions of pounds worth of publicity for the festival and the city.

Heidi Burkline of *Die Welt* in Bonn told a BBC television interviewer, 'Glasgow is fantastic, great! It's amazing what is being done here.'

Punch magazine also sent two writers to take what turned out to be a two-page, good-natured poke at the festival and the *Glasgow Herald* recalled that the day after the opening by the Prince and Princess of Wales of the Glasgow International Exhibition of 1988 Lord Provost Sir James King was elected Chairman of the Glasgow District Board of Lunacy.

My friends Emi (Kaz) Kazuko and her husband Denis Van Mechelen, publishers of *Eikoku* (*Britain*) which circulated widely in Japan and Britain, promised to feature Glasgow just before the start of the festival.

Michael Almaz of the Israel Broadcasting Authority agreed to provide stories about Glasgow for the authority's English, Arabic and Hebrew services covering the entire Middle East.

Newspapers published in Britain for the benefit of visitors from Australia, New Zealand and neighbouring islands in the South Pacific, also agreed to take material about Glasgow, as did the British Tourist Authority's newsletter *Britain Calling*.

Glasgow Garden Festival opened on Thursday, 28 April, 1988. The sun shone and Glasgow quivered with excitement. The world's most talked about, and perhaps envied, husband and wife, the Prince and Princess of Wales, had come to open what newspapers and the promotors described as Britain's biggest consumer event of the year … the most spectacular and exciting event of 1988 … a celebration symbolising the continual quest for improved standards of living.

Just before I left the office to attend the opening a woman phoned my office to complain about the festival's official slogan, 'It's a Day out of This World.' The woman had recently had a bereavement in the family and she thought the choice of words were unfortunate in that once you were out of this world you stayed out permanently, not just for a day. I tried to persuade her not to take the slogan too literally as it was merely a figure of speech meant to convey something exciting and extraordinary, but she was unconvinced.

Attractions of the festival included the Coca Cola Thrill Ride, in which no amount of money in the Bank of Scotland could persuade me to ride, a

250-foot tower celebrating the Clydesdale Bank's 150th anniversary, the Bell's Bridge, the first significant footbridge to be built over the Clyde for 120 years, the biggest teapot in the world, the return of tramcars for the first time since 1962, a railway, 112 gardens, 24ft metal and glass-fibre irises, tea towels made in Pakistan, and six major theme areas: health and well-being, water and maritime, recreation and sport, landscape and scenery, science and technology, and plants and food. Who could ask for anything more?

Figures relating to the cost of setting up Glasgow's festival, the benefits that accrued to the city in terms of investment, creation of jobs, and the redevelopment of the post-festival site rain down like confetti from a variety of sources, including the Glasgow Development Agency, Glasgow City Council, consultants and journalists.

According to *An Evaluation of Garden Festivals* compiled by PA Cambridge Economic Consultants, Cambridge, in collaboration with Gillespies Dudley and published by HMSO, the festival cost £69 million, but after the sale of residual assets, disposal of the site, and festival income this figure came down to £30 million.

I have to admit I didn't much care about the finances of the operation. That wasn't my responsibility. My own feeling was that as long as it gave the people of Glasgow a new pride in their city, enhanced its image nationally and internationally, persuaded people that Glasgow was a good place to invest in, to visit as a tourist, or to live and work in and bring up one's family, it was worth whatever had to be spent.

An Evaluation of Garden Festivals said that although Glasgow had been hailed as a great success it should be recognised that conditions were favourable for image-building and exploitation of tourism. The festival was used to promote Glasgow and the longer term benefits should become apparent through further initiatives such as the city of culture designation.

Glaswegians were asked if they were aware of improvements related to the festival and whether these had affected their attitude to living in the city. Sixty-four per cent gave a favourable answer.

Some reports have claimed that the festival injected £100 million into the local economy. Glasgow City Council announced that £170 million was to be spent in the area in the five years following the festival, £110 million on the festival site and £60 million by private house builders and other developers. The evaluation also pointed out that the festival had resulted in substantial reclamation gains on the offset sites.

Glasgow was lucky to have a festival at all. When the subject was first mooted some Council leaders did not want to become involved because they did not know how the festival was to be funded. Nor did they see what the long-term benefit to the city would be. They believed it would be a short-term Disney-like spectacular that would come and go and leave no permanent mark on the city. The politicians' attitude changed when the Scottish Development Agency said they would fund the event.

Other parts of Scotland complained because, they said, the SDA was spending all its money on Glasgow leaving nothing for them. The answer to that was that the festival would be a gateway to Scotland as a whole.

The opening day of the festival was not the happy day for me it might have been. Many evenings during the previous two years when I sat in a small upstairs room in my house writing stories about the festival Jackie used to tell me how much she was looking forward to the opening. She never lived to see it, having died a few months earlier.

The world's first garden festival took place in Essen, Germany, in 1937 and after the 1939-45 war the idea spread throughout Europe to Vienna, Nice, Nancy, Berlin, and finally to Britain. Its concept was to take a derelict site and build on it in such a way that it could be further developed into something permanent and viable afterwards.

Britain had four garden festivals, Liverpool (1984) Stoke-on-Trent (1986) Glasgow (1988) and Ebbw Vale (1992). In terms of visitors Glasgow's was the most successful with 4,345,820, beating its nearest rival Liverpool by nearly a million, although income fell short of the target. The Scottish news media compared the festival with the great Empire Exhibition in Glasgow in 1938 when 13 million people, including me and my mother, visited Bellahouston Park between 3 May and 29 October.

Chapter 25

CULTURAL CAPITAL OF EUROPE

GLASGOW'S involvement in the performing arts and its many museums and art galleries place the city quite high in the league of European cultural centres. This probably comes as a surprise to many of Glasgow's critics, most of whom come from London as far as I can see. Even more people were surprised in October 1986 when it was announced that Glasgow was to be European City of Culture in 1990.

The year turned out to be unprecedented in the eight centuries of the city's history. There were 3,439 public events, performers and artists from 23 countries, 40 major works commissioned in the performing and visual arts, 60 world premières in theatre, dance and music, 3,979 performances of 656 theatrical productions and 3,122 musical performances, 2,200 of them free, 1,091 exhibitions, and 157 sporting events.

Events involved schools, churches, synagogues, mosques, hospitals, prisons, homes for the elderly, training centres, theatres, galleries, universities, community centres, warehouses, parks and streets.

My own view of the year is conditioned by the fact that I am an unashamed propagandist, if you accept the dictionary definition of propaganda as the organised dissemination of information. I believe our year of culture was a success because when it ended there were few places of importance in the world that did not know Glasgow was a city of major significance.

The European City of Culture concept was introduced in 1985 by Melina Mercouri, Greece's Minister of Culture at the time and one-time actress and singer ('Never on a Sunday'). Athens was the first city to hold the title, followed by Florence, Amsterdam, Berlin, Paris and Glasgow.

If ever a word has been misused and misinterpreted it is the word culture. Hanns Johst wrote at the beginning of this century, 'Wenn ich Kulture höre … entsichere ich meinen Browning!' (Whenever I hear the word culture I release the safety catch on my pistol.) Culture doesn't mean a ballet performance or an opera or a classical concert. It means all of these things and a lot more. It means the total range of the inherited ideas, beliefs, attitudes, values, and activities of a group of people. This is what Glasgow's culture year set out to project.

Work started on publicising the year four years before the event. By the time 1990 dawned my work was virtually finished and a specially-established press office dealt with the world's news media who flocked to Glasgow to find out what all the fuss was about.

My office put out a press release in April 1986 that the city was making a bid for the title of European City of Culture, or Cultural Capital of Europe as we quickly renamed it. Glasgow was competing with Edinburgh, Liverpool, Leeds, Bristol, Cardiff, Bath, Swansea and Cambridge. In October a phone call from the Cabinet Office in London told me that Richard Luce, Britain's Minister for the Arts, would nominate Glasgow for the culture title at a meeting with the 11 other Ministers of Culture of the European Economic Community in Brussels on 13 November. The award to Glasgow would be automatic as it was Britain's turn and Glasgow would receive unanimous approval.

The Cabinet Office also asked me to organise a press conference for 20 October at which Mr Luce would announce the nomination. The excitement was tense as a large number of journalists, some of whom sent their stories worldwide, gathered in the City Chambers to hear the announcement.

Mr Luce said it was an important day in Glasgow's history. All the other cities had put forward interesting nominations but Glasgow had put together the best case. That didn't prevent the Government from declining to give the city much help with its plans for 1990. The Office of Arts and Libraries gave the city only £500,000 which amounted to less than one per cent of the total cost.

The world's biggest advertising agency, Saatchi and Saatchi, was later commissioned to help publicise 'culture year'. Not everyone in the Labour group of the City Council was thrilled about employing the agency which had done so much for Labour's arch-enemy Margaret Thatcher but Pat Lally, the Council leader, was determined that only the 'biggest and best' was good enough to work for Glasgow.

Some of their brightest public relations stars were assigned the task of devising a slogan for the year. The lights burned late night after night in their London office until inspiration settled on the furrowed brows. 'There's a lot Glasgowing on in 1990' was born. My first inclination was to burst into hysterical laughter. Glaswegians had the greatest difficulty in saying it and it was utterly impossible to translate for the benefit of the rest of the world.

The politicians approved the slogan anyway but we also used one we bought for £20,000 from John Struthers, the man who devised the Glasgow's Miles Better slogan. 'The Flying G' as we nicknamed it, didn't mean much either but it was useful enough as slogans go because the success of a slogan depends largely on how well and how often it is publicised. People will get used to anything in time. Saatchi's efforts for 'culture year' cost £2.5 million, most of which was spent on newspaper advertising.

The year, for which the City Council had created a budget of £15 million to subsidise events, provide guarantees against losses by performing groups, and to provide seed money to get projects started, had already been running three months when M. Jacques Chirac, Mayor of Paris, formally handed the culture crown, metaphorically speaking, to Glasgow's Lord Provost Susan Baird. The ceremony took place in the King's Theatre on 2 March, 1990, watched by the Queen and diplomats and politicians from all the European community countries and a galaxy of stars from a variety of other firmaments, including industry and commerce, the church, the visual and performing arts, law, medicine, and the halls of academe.

Because of the number of French speakers in the audience the theatre manager, Billy Differ, anxious to display his linguistic skills, introduced the Queen as La Reine d'Angleterre, the Queen of England. Even the lady herself joined in the laughter.

After the ceremony the Queen went to the McLellan Galleries which had been refurbished at a cost of £3.5 million, to see The British Art Show, the work of 42 artists in their twenties and thirties. The exhibition included dustbin lids, metal filing cabinets, giant fur-covered spoons, and what looked like roof guttering, in addition to more conventional manifestations of man's creative genius. There is no record of what the Queen thought of the exhibition, which was described in its advertising as daring, innovative, and significant.

Highlights of 1990 included shows by the world's great artists, Peter Brook, the Berlin Philharmonic Orchestra, the Dramaten Theatre directed by Ingmar Bergman, Frank Sinatra, Luciano Pavarotti, and the Bolshoi Opera Company. Their success depends very much on whether one looks at them from the perspective of an aesthete, an accountant, or a member of the public who has to find the money for tickets. The Sinatra concert, for instance, cost the city £665,000, of which £575,000 was Ol' Blue Eyes' fee. The Bolshoi Opera cost more than £1 million and Luciano's concert cost £800,000 to mount, but these were covered by ticket sales.

Robert Palmer, our Director of Performing Arts, later wrote an account of what was involved in getting the Bolshoi Opera company to Glasgow:

'Communication with the Soviet Union was not easy. Twenty-three telexes were sent to The Bolshoi Opera in the two-month period following a visit to Glasgow in November 1989 by Aleksander Lazarev, the company's Musical Director.

In January 1990 Valery Levental, Chief Designer of the Bolshoi, Vladimir Taran, Technical Director, and Sergey Selivanov, came to Glasgow, engulfed themselves in technical drawings of the SECC and talked for hours, counting and discounting possibilities.

One evening the Russians came to my office and told me, "We want to perform in Glasgow. It will be difficult but we think it can be done." That was the start of many detailed negotiations. Consultants pored over inventive conversion proposals, seating plans and acoustics and the SECC talked about hires and services. Eventually more than 900 people were involved in helping to make possible the Bolshoi's visit to Glasgow. But it was worth it.'

A number of events featuring Soviet performing and visual arts were held in Glasgow during 1989 and 1990, including New Beginnings, described by Chris Carrell, Director of the Third Eye Centre, as 'the largest season of contemporary Soviet arts ever staged in Britain'. Journalistic hyperbole was a valuable and much-used tool in those days. The Third Eye Centre was reborn later as the Centre for Contemporary Arts and is now directed by the talented Penny Rae.

Neil Wallace, Depute Director of Festivals, and I had a monumental row in my office one day when I was writing a press release to announce that Pavarotti would be among the stars of culture year. Neil said I shouldn't emphasise the Pavarotti involvement as the year was not about him but about hundreds of things that were happening.

I tried to tell him I had to start the story somewhere and the fact that Pavarotti was coming was news. Not being a journalist Neil had difficulty in understanding what I was talking about and we had a real slanging match. Eventually for the sake of peace I didn't start off my story with Pavarotti but when the story appeared in all the newspapers it started off with the Italian singer. That was the last time I let anyone interfere with what I was writing.

Needless to say Neil and I have been friends ever since.

Among the benefits of garden festival year and 1990 is that never again will Glaswegians be reluctant to say where they come from, as was the case in the 1970s. Never again will a writer in one of America's most influential business magazines, *Forbes*, be able to refer to Glasgow as 'Siberia in a kilt'.

Directly because of culture year Glasgow now has the Glasgow Royal Concert Hall, the refurbished McLellan Galleries, making it the finest and largest fully air-conditioned exhibition space outside London, the Tramway, a former tramcar depot, which has won many awards for its high-quality innovative theatre and visual arts programmes, a second studio within the Centre for Contemporary Arts, a second cinema for the Glasgow Film Theatre, and the Arches exhibition and theatre area under the Central railway station.

New festivals were also initiated, including The Glasgow International Early Music Festival, Chorus International, the Tryst Festival and a festival of children's theatre to add to Mayfest and Glasgow International Jazz Festival which had been established earlier.

A variety of other theatre, music and arts groups were spawned by culture year and are still going strong. They include Call That Singing (a choir of 500 voices), and Jewish Arts, the brain-child of Louise Naftalin, wife of a Glasgow lawyer, which organises concerts, recitals, talks by well-known writers, art exhibitions, and children's events.

Successful exhibitions during the year included The Age of Van Gogh, Treasures of the Holy Land, The British Art Show (despite the dustbin lids), Degas' Images of Women, 2,000 Years of Art & Design, Henry Moore sculptures, Camille Pissarro, and many more.

One exhibition attracted about 500,000 visitors, more than all the others combined, and was still considered a disaster. Glasgow's Glasgow, in the Arches, was described as an exposition based on the theme of Glasgow's history demonstrating in a dynamic manner the uniqueness and variety of the city.

Unfortunately it didn't live up to its lofty aspirations, entry was too highly priced, it was too poorly marketed, and too few people could get in at one time even if they did turn up. Instead of being self-financing as was intended it cost the city £4.5 million, the most expensive single event of the year.

Doug Clelland, the originator of the exhibition, made a spirited defence of the event and understandably laid the blame for its loss at a variety of doors. He also claimed it contained within it 16 mini-exhibitions, that a lot of people liked it, that it demonstrated the vitality and versatility of the city, brought tourists, provided a platform for diverse theatrical performances, gave birth to *The Words and the Stones*, one of the most comprehensive books on the city, transported, exhibited and safely returned to diverse owners 3,923 artefacts, and much else.

All of which came as something of a relief to me as Doug Clelland came to me in 1987 with the idea for the exhibition and later wrote asking me to discuss it with Robert Palmer, then Festivals Director, which I did, giving it my enthusiastic support.

Investment in the arts has benefited the economy of the city by increasing tourism, business, and creating jobs. More than 6,500 people, 2.8 per cent of the economically active population, are involved in the cultural scene, more than in the banking sector.

Attendance figures for performances, the growth of cultural industries such as film production, book publishing and design were all given a considerable boost by the 1990 City of Culture initiative.

Robert Palmer is invited 70 to 80 times a year to speak at and chair international conferences in places like Paris, Helsinki, Stockholm, Toronto, Athens, Luxembourg, Harare, Berlin, Moscow, and St Petersburg. All of these cities want to know about the management of festivals, how a city like Glasgow devises urban cultural policy, how the arts relate to urban regeneration, how to manage the arts, and Glasgow's long-term cultural transformation. Foreign journalists constantly ask him about the city's cultural policy.

Compared with 1989 there is a 14 per cent increase in attendances at theatre events, concerts, exhibitions, and events: 4.5 million arts attendances a year. More people attend arts events in Glasgow than any other city in Britain except London. Glasgow is featured prominently in publications throughout the world in articles about cultural capitals.

Glaswegians have had to be very adaptable. Their city has changed many times in the eight centuries of its existence, from a little town with only ecclesiastical significance in the Middle Ages to a prosperous and beautiful city in the 17th and 18th centuries, to a rich but overcrowded industrial sprawl in the 19th century, to a modern business and cultural centre today.

For a time it was the second city of the British Empire, an empire greater than the Romans ever dreamed of. There is no continent which has not benefited from the ingenuity, imagination, enterprise, skill, inventiveness, clarity of thought, and even genius of people born or trained in Glasgow. Its ships sailed every sea, its locomotives pulled the trains on every continent, its fabrics adorned the world's beautiful women, its engines powered the world's industry, and its carpets rolled across the floors of the world's exotic palaces, and a few desert tents.

For more than five centuries Glasgow University has turned out graduates who have gone all over the world to distinguish themselves in every field of human endeavour. The University has the oldest engineering school in the world and a medical school which is the largest in Britain and one of the largest in Europe.

People sometimes talk about Glasgow's culture year as if the city had a brief flirtation with culture in 1990 for the first time in its life. Whatever one might think of Glasgow's civic leaders it doesn't alter the fact that generation after generation of them have done what they could to enrich the cultural life of the citizens, even if they haven't always been conscious of it.

To ensure their continued existence the Corporation of Glasgow bought the Citizens Theatre in 1955 and the King's Theatre from the London-based Howard and Wyndham Limited in 1967. The Citizens is known throughout Europe for the quality of its productions.

The City Halls in Candleriggs were opened in October 1841 as the first concert hall in Glasgow. It was also the venue for important speakers, who have included Charles Dickens, Benjamin Disraeli and William Gladstone.

When St Andrew's Hall was burned down in 1962 the City Hall came into its own as the venue for Scottish National Orchestra concerts. These have now gone to the new Concert Hall but the City Hall is still used for other concerts and meetings.

Glasgow now has the Royal Scottish National Orchestra, the BBC Scottish Symphony Orchestra, Glasgow Philharmonic Orchestra, Scottish Opera, Scottish Ballet, 14 theatres, 28 theatre companies, 150 professional performing arts organisations, almost all of which are heavily subsidised by the Council. In 1988 the Queen Mother opened the new £12 million Royal Scottish Academy of Music and Drama.

In 1990 Glasgow City Council established a £3 million investment fund to acquire works by Scottish and international artists. And there are also a large number of privately-owned studios and exhibition places in addition to the Council's own galleries.

In 1983 the marketing worldwide of the opening of The Burrell Collection was the biggest and most successful operation ever carried out in Scotland on behalf of an exhibition or museum. In 1981 The Realist Tradition exhibition at the Museum and Art Gallery at Kelvingrove achieved the second highest attendance, 118,900, since the museum was opened 81 years earlier.

In 1979 the Exhibition of Jewish Art at Kelvingrove and the Jewish Way of Life exhibition in Hillhead Library achieved record attendances despite what might have been considered a limited, sectarian appeal.

Glasgow School of Art, Scotland's premier art school, has an international academic and artistic reputation in architecture, design and fine art and in its 150 years has influenced major movements in European art, has produced a high number of Scotland's great painters and has had a major influence in Scottish design.

A considerable number of professional artists live, work and exhibit regularly in the city, including many who have achieved international reputations, such as Campbell, Conroy, Currie, Howson, Watt and Wiszniewski.

The last decade has seen the development of considerable artistic activity within the minority ethnic communities in Glasgow who have produced exhibitions and specific projects in collaboration with most of the leading arts organisations.

Glasgow's interest in the visual arts goes back to 1670 when the town council bought from London portraits of Charles I and Charles II for the town's use. At the Council House they joined portraits of James V and James VI, laying the foundation for the city's art galleries.

Many of the men who amassed considerable fortunes when the city was a great industrial and maritime metropolis collected paintings as a hobby and later they or their families gave the collections to the city.

The Hunterian Gallery, originating as a collection left to the University of Glasgow by William Hunter in 1783, has the distinction of sharing with the Freer Gallery in Washington a claim to possessing the world's finest collection of paintings by James McNeil Whistler.

In 1865 the Town Council acquired from the estate of Archibald McLellan, a coach builder, a magnificent collection of paintings and a building which is still known as McLellan Galleries.

In 1874 the city was given the Dutch and British art collections of William Euing, an insurance broker. Three years later John Graham-Gilbert's collection came from his wife. This collection included many paintings by Graham-Gilbert himself, a member of the Royal Scottish Academy. The collection included two of Glasgow's prized possessions, Rembrandt's *Man in Armour* and Rubens' *Nature Adorned by the Graces*.

All of which means it shouldn't really have surprised anyone that Glasgow became Cultural Capital of Europe in 1990. Most Glaswegians benefited from the city's year of culture even if they don't know it; and as I have said, it certainly did a lot for the city's image, which was my major concern.

Chapter 26

MICHAEL HAS A TASTE OF WAR

BAD nights when I can't sleep are all too frequent in my life but one of them was worse than most. It was the night in January 1991 when Saddam Hussein attacked Israel with Scud missiles at the start of the war in the Persian Gulf. Apart from my interest in the survival of the State of Israel I was also worried about Michael and Yaffa in Dimona.

This is how he described in a despatch to the *Glasgow Herald* what it felt like to be under attack. I know it doesn't compare with what the people of Bosnia, Rwanda, and other places had to suffer, but the difference was that my younger son was involved and I had already lost my young sister Sheila and my wife and I didn't need any more misery.

Michael wrote:

'As a 32-year-old Glasgow lawyer I haven't had much experience of war, let alone gas masks, air raids, or Scud missiles. I haven't slept properly for five days. On the first night Yaffa and I were awakened at 2am by a sound I recognised from the Pathé newsreel I last saw when I was about seven at the Waverley Cinema in Shawlands. It was the sound of an air raid siren. It took a few moments to realise that the noise outside was real and that an air attack was expected.

We had been told to prepare a sealed room in each house with taped windows and doors, a flashlight, battery-powered radio, heater, blankets, and of course our gas masks. Our instructions were to close ourselves in the room, switch on the radio, put on the gas masks, and wait for further instructions from the civil guard on the radio. We sat gulping for air through our gas masks for the next six hours. We were waiting to be bombed with chemical weapons. It's a most frightening thing sitting in a sealed room wearing a gas mask just waiting to hear something. People are obviously worried about the situation but the Israelis are fairly resigned to this kind of thing.

In the morning after the all-clear I went out to the supermarket for some items of food and then went straight home. We were told to stay at home and go out only for essential provisions.

During daytime there is relative calm, but with radios on continuously tuned to Army Radio which has been combined with all the other channels. We listen to developments in the war just a missile's throw from our border. Tensions are high.

On the second day my neighbours knocked on the door and asked for my help to prepare the bomb shelter at the foot of the stairs. Last month we were all issued with gas masks and since then we have been watching public service broadcasts on television on how to use them. We have been reminded again and again that the attacks may be chemical or conventional and we should be prepared for both.

On the second night I went to bed at 7pm expecting to be wakened in the middle of the night by the siren. Within an hour it sounded and I ran to my sealed room, grabbing my gas mask on the way. On went the radio. Within 20 minutes we were informed it was a false alarm and I went back to bed.

Instructions to Israelis are to listen to the radio all the time. Often a siren won't be heard in a peripheral area so it is played on the radio, too. Sleeping with the radio on, with the tensions of the moment, is not easy. Despite the fatigue on the second night I manage to doze. At 2am I hear a reference to "staying in a sealed room". My heart leapt. Did a siren sound that I didn't hear? I jump out of bed into the sealed room. The radio announces it is for the citizens of Jerusalem alone. An explosion has been heard there.

Back to bed. At 6am another siren. I'm used to it now. Go to sealed room, gas mask on, radio tuned. I wait, heaving for breath with the windows of my mask steamed up. I look out of the window to see people running from the synagogue across the street, gas masks flying. After half an hour we are told our area can relax, but Tel Aviv should remain alert.

By now TV has started. Israel Radio does not report missile hits until much later than I hear about them on the BBC. Army Radio does not broadcast "unconfirmed reports".

Press reports warn that we are still not free of missile strikes and that more are expected. As dusk approaches each day tension rises. We are waiting for the chemical weapons. School was supposed to start yesterday but was cancelled. Radio reports that the mess of Saturday's attacks has been cleared away and that the homeless are being put in hotels.

Last night the Scud attacks were on Saudi Arabia. On the radio we heard their siren and confused it with our own. For a moment my blood ran cold. To realise it was theirs was no relief; it will be our turn again soon.'

As I lay awake listening to the progress of the war my mind went back 52 years to 1939 when I had the same sickening feeling of dread when the sirens announced waves of German bombers over Glasgow and my highly nervous mother and father hurried across the road to an air-raid shelter in my school. Please keep Michael and Yaffa safe, I murmured.

All kinds of things went through my mind, like the day Michael was born. Jackie poked me in the ribs in the middle of the night and told me to call a taxi. We couldn't afford a car at that time. I helped Jackie gently into the cab holding three-year-old Harvie. The plan was to leave Harvie with my mother-in-law who lived nearby and then go on to Redlands Nursing Home in the West End of the City, but the taxi broke down near my house and I had to push it to a garage and get another taxi. Jackie sat mute in the cab. For some mysterious reason I developed a raging toothache. By the time the second taxi arrived I was in a panic and we went straight to the nursing home. I took Harvie to my mother-in-law on the way home again.

Then there was the Saturday morning I woke up feeling uncharacteristically energetic and said to Michael, who was 12, 'I'll show you the kind of unarmed combat I learned in the army.' We squared up to each other in the hallway and I said, 'Right, you try to hit me.' Some time later I woke up in the Victoria Infirmary staring at an X-ray machine hovering over me. A distraught Michael helped me home with a broken rib.

Michael has always been the most adventurous member of my family. After qualifying as a lawyer he spent two periods in Israel and one in Australia before finally going to Israel again in 1987 to live. His first visit to Israel was in 1979 when he spent a year in a kibbutz, Kfar Hanassi (which means the President's village), founded in the Upper Galilee in 1948 by a group of Glasgow people, among them Michael and Rene Cohen, Joe and Pauline Rifkind (relatives of Defence Secretary Malcolm Rifkind), Joe Cina, Lawrence Marcusson, Noah Shine, Rhoda Goldman, Rose Karnovsky, and Ivan Levine.

Michael is still in Israel and is not likely ever to come back to Scotland. He married Yaffa Maimon, a deputy head teacher in a local school, in 1992. She was born in Beersheba but her family come from Tunis.

I flew to Israel with Harvie and his family for Michael's wedding. The ceremony was held at the poolside of a kibbutz near Beersheba at 8pm to avoid the burning heat of the day. I spent much of the time circulating among the guests, renewing old acquaintances and making new friends.

I went to bed about 2am and was up again at 7am to take a taxi to Jerusalem to attend the wedding of a couple of friends, Jane Moonman from London and Yoav Biran, Israeli Ambassador to Britain.

My older son Harvie and I are not adventurous types although he did spend a few weeks in Israel in 1983 and came back to tell me he wanted to marry a girl from Brazil he met in Jerusalem. They were later married in Tel Aviv. Jackie and I flew out for the wedding which was also attended by a number of former Glaswegians.

Harvie was also born in Redlands Nursing Home. I took Jackie there about 4am and was told to phone at 10am. I walked up and down the floor for four hours and couldn't take it any more so I phoned the nursing home at 8am. A nurse told me I was the father of a beautiful baby boy weighing whatever. I tried to say thank you but nothing would come out I was so choked with emotion. The nurse finally hung up and went to tell Jackie I had phoned.

'What did he say?' Jackie asked.

'Nothing,' said the nurse. 'He fainted!'

'That's my Henry!' said Jackie.

Chapter 27

DEATH OF A NEWSPAPER

THE *Jewish Echo* did not publish a notice of my birth in 1926 because it had not yet appeared, but it published everything else about me, my bar mitzvah, marriage, the birth of my two sons, their marriages, the progress of my career, and Jackie's death.

The *Echo* appeared for the first time on 6 January, 1928 and not once until 29 May, 1992 did it miss a single edition despite illness, staff difficulties, fire and flood, paper shortages, and a world war.

Like many other members of the Jewish community of Scotland I regret its absence, not just because it also published the many stories I wrote about the Jewish community over the years, but because it was such an important cohesive, unifying force in the community.

Its place has been taken by the Manchester-based *Jewish Telegraph*, which has established an office in Glasgow to collect news, advertisements and communal announcements.

The London-based *Jewish Chronicle*, which modestly styles itself 'The World's Leading Jewish Newspaper' made a brief appearance in the arena but quickly withdrew leaving the field clear to its Manchester rival.

Most Scottish Jews don't like buying a Manchester newspaper to read about themselves. Apart from the fact that is is not printed in Scotland it has a tendency to sensationalise the most trivial of stories but if people don't buy it, and many don't, they have to rely on friends to tell them who was married and who died during the week.

When the last edition of the *Echo* appeared on that fateful Friday it proved such a traumatic experience for its readers that the Glasgow Jewish Representative Council published a communal newsletter 'to cut down the serious effect of living without the *Echo*'. But as many others have learned, newsgathering is a time-consuming and expensive business and the communal newsletter lasted only three issues.

Mr Harvey Livingston, President of the Council and director of a bedding company, then called a special general meeting to explain to a baffled community the reasons for the *Echo*'s closure. The meeting was told that despite a massive injection of cash by Glasgow Jewish Community Trust, which had bought the paper's title in 1988, the paper had to close because of ever-spiralling losses.

The 120 people present passed a resolution asking the Council to investigate the feasibility of starting another newspaper in Glasgow to serve the community, a proposal fraught with innumerable difficulties.

Mr Livingston later reported that a special committee he had formed to carry out the feasibility study had concluded that a Glasgow-based Jewish newspaper was a viable proposition and invited anyone who was interested in managing the paper to contact him. The fact that no-one on the committee had the slightest idea how to run a newspaper did not inhibit their conclusion in any way.

Plenty of wannabe press barons volunteered to be members of the board of Jewish Echo 1992 Limited but financial backers were as scarce as pork pies at a bar mitzvah. An appeal for a grant of £40,000 to set up the new *Echo* was made to Community Enterprise in Strathclyde but apart from a few phone calls back and forward not much else happened.

Even if the grant had been approved the Jewish community would still have had the problem of finding money for running costs and editorial staff qualified to run their newspaper, a task which would have been even more difficult than raising the start-up money.

The *Echo*'s founder, Zevi Golombok, was 24 when he arrived in Glasgow from Birzi, a small town in Lithuania, in 1904. He left his native country, like so many others, to escape the pogroms in Europe. He could speak and write Russian, German, Hebrew, and Yiddish (a Judeo-German dialect) but not a word of English.

In the years that followed Zevi worked hard to learn English, reading everything he could lay his hands on. His habit of reading in bed by candlelight late at night almost cost him his life on one occasion when the candle set his bed on fire.

Like many people who conscientiously apply themselves to a foreign language he used words unfamiliar to the native speakers around him. He was fond, for instance, of describing himself as an autodidact, someone who is self-taught.

Zevi worked with his older brother Israel who had preceded him to Glasgow and set himself up as a printer. As a fervent Zionist convinced that the Jews of the diaspora were doomed to extinction without a land of their own in which they could live without persecution, Zevi encouraged his brother to publish a newspaper to spread the Zionist message and in 1914 they brought out the *Jewish Evening Times* in Yiddish.

This lasted only a few issues and then came the *Jewish Voice*, also in Yiddish. This didn't last very long either and eventually in 1928 when Zevi had learned enough English he founded the *Jewish Echo*.

In the early days he went out among his fellow Jews, mainly in Gorbals, to gather the news of what they were doing, went back to the office, laboriously wrote his reports in longhand, set them in type, printed the paper — and then went out to deliver them at a penny a copy.

In the second issue Zevi chided Glasgow Jews for ostentatiously flaunting their wealth by spending large sums of money on bar mitzvahs and weddings. He suggested they reintroduced the old Jewish custom of holding a dinner for the poor to celebrate a joyful occasion. This did not meet with any great enthusiasm.

From June to September in that first year Zevi serialised a book, *Michael's Return*, a bodice-ripper described as 'a romance of absorbing interest'. Zevi himself translated the book from the German.

One of the newspaper's earliest contributors was George Stewart, who founded the Rex Stewart Advertising group for which I once worked. Zevi allowed Stewart to write film notes on the condition that the cinemas' performances were advertised in the paper.

Two attempts were made by others over the years to start another Jewish newspaper in Glasgow, the *Jewish Leader* in 1932 and the *Jewish Times* in 1964. Both lasted only a few months because it was impossible to match the dedication, integrity, skill, and reputation of the men who ran the *Echo*.

Attempts were also made to buy the newspaper but neither Zevi Golombok nor his son Ezra considered the making of money to be their first priority, a nobility of character which did not always appeal to their families. They did not think anyone else could sustain the character and quality of the paper the aim of which had always been to be a serious provider of information not available anywhere else.

Zevi Golombok lived long enough to see come true his dream of the return of the Jews to their promised land but when he died six years later he had still not managed to visit the new state.

His son may have been dedicated to the service of the community but that did not prevent him from refusing personal announcements or advertisements from time to time because he did not approve of their wording, an attitude which sometimes generated some heat among his subscribers, especially the ones who wanted to put a bit of schmaltz into their birth or death notices.

Ezra was a 26-year-old research chemist at the Swiss Federal Polytechnic in Zurich, Switzerland, in 1948 when, at the request of his 70-year-old father, he abandoned the halls of academe and what many think would have been a distinguished career to come back to Glasgow to help him run the *Jewish Echo*.

Two years later the Bachelor of Science and Doctor of Philosophy took over the editorship and guided its fortunes for 42 years. The 64 volumes of the *Echo* are now in Glasgow's Mitchell Library for future generations to study.

Ezra Golombok is now Director of the Glasgow-based Israel Information Office, a facility opened by the Israeli government to keep Scots better informed about the complexities of Middle East politics, the peace process and other aspects of Israeli life, commerce, industry, the arts, technology and medicine.

Chapter 28

FLASHMAN AUTHOR COMES TO ERSKINE

THE generosity of the Scottish public is really something to be wondered at. They never fail to respond unsparingly to appeals from charitable organisations.

Erskine Hospital at Bishopton, near Glasgow, is a good example. People have pushed beds, climbed mountains, run marathons, rowed rivers, laid bricks, gone on diets, and held coffee mornings to raise money for the hospital. For decades, too, they have left large sums of money for the care of the disabled ex-servicemen and women for whom the hospital is home.

Few people, including members of the royal family, have turned down an invitation to visit Erskine but much to the disappointment of many of the patients, Dame Vera Lynn, the 'Forces Sweetheart' in the 1939-45 war, repeatedly declined in the 1970s to come to Bishopton. Some of the excuses sounded rather flimsy to me. Admittedly she hasn't been asked again in recent years but as she is rather older now it is even less likely that she would honour us with a visit.

On 11 October, 1995 the hospital's ruling executive committee approved a proposal to build a new hospital on the Erskine Estate and to create at least two satellite Erskine nursing homes in other parts of Scotland. All of them would meet, and perhaps surpass, the health care standards appropriate to the new millennium. The total cost could be £20 million. The decision was not taken lightly. Groups of executive committee members had spent two and a half years investigating and debating every conceivable option suggested to them by consultants.

My association with the Princess Louise Scottish Hospital, to give it its formal name, began in 1969 when I joined the small advertising agency of D C Cuthbertson, which handled the hospital's advertising. David Black, the Managing Director, asked me if I could do some public relations work for the hospital and I agreed. The hospital had a total of about 400 patients and running costs of £270,000 a year. It now has fewer patients and costs £8 million a year to run.

In 1974 I was elected to the executive committee, on which I still serve. I am also convener of the Publicity Committee. The executive committee members, all of whom work hard and conscientiously for the hospital without any kind of financial gain, are drawn from a wide range of skills and experience from the military, business and professional community of Scotland.

It would only embarrass them if I said any more about them but I have to record that the Chairman and Commandant when I joined the hospital, General Sir Gordon MacMillan of MacMillan and Colonel David Boyle, were men of outstanding ability, dignity and humanity, and their contribution to the hospital is incalculable.

The hospital's Vice-Chairman for 15 years, until his retirement in March 1995 on the brink of his 80th birthday, was Brigadier Alastair Pearson, the most decorated Scottish soldier of the 1939-45 war. He died a year later.

In March 1995 Lieutenant General Sir John MacMillan, Sir Gordon's son, took over the chairmanship of the hospital from Vice-Admiral Sir Thomas Baird. The hospital's Chief Executive is Colonel Martin Gibson, an energetic ex-army colonel of great experience, who also joined us in 1995.

One of my early tasks was to devise the launch of an appeal for £200,000 for an extension to the hospital. I persuaded an old *Glasgow Herald* colleague, George MacDonald Fraser, a former officer in the Gordon Highlanders, to fly from his home on the Isle of Man to launch the appeal at Erskine. The money for the extension was raised in no time. George is author of the famous Flashman books and a Hollywood scriptwriter. I have always been envious of my old colleague, not only because of his success as an author but because he wrote scripts for Raquel Welch.

In 1982 the executive committee approved my suggestion that John Calder, another old newspaper colleague, whose father had once been a patient at Erskine, be commissioned to write a history of the hospital. This excellent book, *The Vanishing Willows*, has proved a steady seller ever since. The willow trees were unobtrusively acquired by Sir William Macewen, a founder of the hospital in 1916, from the grounds of Glasgow University, to make limbs for the patients.

Publicising the work of Erskine Hospital is not difficult. The hospital holds a very special place in the hearts of the Scottish public and often a great deal farther. As a journalist I very quickly realised that the hospital had more human interest stories than I could ever tell and over the years I have told some of them and I would like to think they have given the outside world a better idea of what Erskine is about.

When I first started to write about Erskine David Boyle told me, 'Don't try to excite pity or be melodramatic in whatever you write. Just give the facts and say we need help to carry on our work.' Here then are some of the facts without the journalistic hyperbole.

It was the news media who in 1978 called the following story 'the final chapter in one of the great love stories of the century' when the Lauder-Thomson ward was named at the hospital in memory of the son of Sir Harry Lauder, Captain John Lauder, and Mildred Thomson, who died unmarried in 1975 at the age of 83 and left the residue of her considerable estate to Erskine 'to provide some amenity for the hospital in memory of my late fiancé … '.

John and Mildred, whose families had known each other since they were children, became engaged in 1916 when John was in the army. A few months later, on 1 January, 1917, on the dawn of what had promised to be a joyful year for all of them Harry Lauder was appearing in a highly-successful review 'Three Cheers' at the Shaftesbury Theatre in London when a telegram containing only two words was handed to him at his hotel. It came from his wife in Scotland and said, 'John Killed'.

Harry Lauder was numb with grief. A steady stream of London society came to his hotel to offer him sympathy but the man who had made millions laugh all over the world was unable to see any of them — with one exception, the girl who was to have been his daughter-in-law.

She stayed with him for several days intercepting the many telegrams and letters of condolence delivered to the hotel. Among the sympathisers were Queen Alexandra, wife of Edward VII, Prime Minister Lloyd George, The Earl of Derby, George Robey, Vesta Tilley, Sir Thomas Dewar, Sir Thomas Lipton, founder of the world's first grocery chain, and others from every class of society. Only hours after being given the tragic news Mildred had received John's last letter from France.

Mildred never recovered from her grief. For 58 years she kept a leather bound scrapbook containing 280 newspaper cuttings about John's death. An accompanying book of poems from Lady Lauder was inscribed 'To darling Mildred in loving memory of the dearest boy that once lived, my son Captain John Lauder.'

Harry Lauder's love for his son was legendary. The two embraced emotionally when they met. In December 1911, when John was studying law at Cambridge University, he caught a bad cold while returning to Laudervale, the family's palatial home in Dunoon.

Harry was in pantomime in Manchester and was so anxious to see his son that after a Saturday night show he caught the midnight train north. He arrived at Gourock at 8.30am on Sunday and as there was no steamer or motor boat he paid two fishermen to take him the five miles across the Firth of Clyde.

The weather was so rough they had to turn back, but the anxious father was persistent and persuaded the fishermen to try again later. After a three-hour struggle in heavy seas the three men reached Dunoon numbed by cold and sodden clothing. But father and son were united, which was all that mattered to Harry.

When Harry Lauder was knighted in 1919 for his work for the troops and the Allied cause his wife said, 'How my boy would have rejoiced at this royal recognition of his father's worth and work.' Lady Lauder died in 1927 and her husband in 1950, at the age of 80. But the story of his love for his son and Mildred Thomson's undying devotion to the 22-year-old Argyll and Sutherland Highlander live on.

Understandably this story received massive coverage in the news media throughout Britain. Mary Marquis, anchorwoman on BBC television news in Scotland, had tears in her eyes as the camera moved back to her after a reporter told the story.

Roddy MacLeod is an expert crossword solver and drives about the hospital in his motorised wheelchair. Mr MacLeod has been paralysed from the neck down since 1965. A Bachelor of Science and former physics teacher, he gained an honours degree in mathematics from the Open University within days of his 65th birthday in 1987.

The written work for his degree was done with a computerised typewriter, the keys of which are activated by a highly complex series of sucks and blows into a tube in Mr MacLeod's mouth. The typewriter does not have all the mathematical symbols involved in Mr MacLeod's studies so he did many of the calculations mentally and got someone to write down the answers.

Two years later he started another honours course. Among the subjects were complex analysis, number theory and logic, graph theory and design, and numerical computation. Because of his paralysis all Mr MacLeod's reading is done with the help of automatic page turners. Books are supported on a plastic and metal frame. Two other smaller tubes into which Mr MacLeod blows control the guidance system for his wheelchair.

Mr MacLeod served in the Royal Corps of Signals during the 1939-45 war. He had to give up teaching at Johnstone High School in 1958 because of multiple sclerosis. By 1965 he was completely paralysed and was admitted to Erskine Hospital.

George Collins was 23 in 1972 when an army vehicle in which he was patrolling the border between Northern Ireland and Eire was blown up by a 500lb bomb. He lay in a Belfast hospital for six months sightless, speechless and motionless and was moved to a second hospital before going to Erskine in 1974 where, as he puts it, 'I was brought back to life.'

He now lives in a cottage at Erskine Hospital with his wife Joy and children Lyndsey (11) and Amanda (9). George, a former Argyll and Sutherland Highlander, works in the hospital workshops.

Erskine has looked after something like 60,000 men and women since 1916. Almost two decades ago I wrote that in the year 2000 when man's ingenuity has pushed back the frontiers of human knowledge and hopefully found cures for some of the world's ills, there will still be sick men and women waiting for a place in Erskine Hospital.

I was right, too. I don't know how far the frontiers have been pushed back but I do know there have been 60 conflicts since the end of the 1939-45 war in which British personnel have been involved so there is not likely to be a shortage of patients for a long time to come.

Chapter 29

JOHN STARTS A BUST-UP

JOHN MCLAUGHLIN is a close and valued friend. I first met him when I was doing some voluntary publicity work for the renal unit of Glasgow's Western Infirmary. Suitable kidneys were always in short supply, as they still are, and from time to time I did stories about transplants that had transformed the lives of men, women and children, the idea being to encourage people to carry organ donor cards.

After I had been doing this for some years I wrote to the Chief Rabbi in London to ask if Jews were allowed to donate organs as it seemed illogical, if not downright immoral, for me to try to persuade others to donate organs if I couldn't do it myself when the time came.

The same evening I wrote to Maureen Lundie, Matron of Erskine Hospital, accepting her invitation to the dinner dance she hosts every year for members of the executive committee and others who have an interest in the hospital. I told her I would not be bringing Anne Lorne Gillies, the beautiful and talented singer, again because on the way home the previous year Anne had given me an impressive and comprehensive list of my failings as an ideal partner.

Next morning Mrs Lundie phoned to say she had received a letter addressed to the Chief Rabbi. With mounting dread I waited for another phone call and sure enough it came shortly afterwards. The soft voice of Rabbi Dr J Shindler, Director of Rabbinic Liaison, said, 'Mr Diamond, this is the Chief Rabbi's office. We have received a letter which I think should have gone to Erskine Hospital.'

Later I received a considerable amount of literature from Mrs Rhoda Goodman, Assistant Executive Director of the Chief's Office, in response to my question. The answer is far too complicated to go into here but my interpretation was 'yes, under certain very strict circumstances.' My own solution to the problem is much simpler, 'Don't ask … '.

One of the stories I wrote about successful kidney transplants was that of a young girl named Pauline McLaughlin. Before she received a new kidney in October 1985 she had had years of misery, always tired, always dependent on a dialysis machine.

She had a boyfriend but they couldn't make any plans for the future as Pauline wasn't sure she would even have a future. A week after her successful transplant 22-year-old Pauline and Wilf Burling decided there was no longer any reason for them to fear the future and they made plans to be married.

Pauline's father, John McLaughlin, came to me and asked me if I would tell the story of Pauline's return to health and renew the appeal for organ donors. He was desperately anxious to give hope to other sufferers. As a result of the story I wrote there were almost as many news media people as guests at the wedding in Our Lady of Lourdes Church at Bishopton, near Glasgow, on Easter Monday 1986.

The guests included Mr Malcolm Brown, who performed the transplant on Pauline, Dr Douglas Briggs, Consultant Physician in the renal unit, Ruth Stewart, the transplant co-ordinator and other doctors and nurses from the Western Infirmary. It was one of the happiest weddings I've ever attended. John McLaughlin and I dreamed up the idea of making it a condition of attendance that each of the almost 400 guests must sign a donor card. Even some of the press complied!

The donor campaign was assisted by the publicity department of the *Glasgow Herald* which produced a poster I designed featuring a smiling Pauline and the headline 'THANKS FOR SAVING MY LIFE'.

Pauline has since had a second kidney transplant but is quite healthy and the mother of two healthy boys, and John is still persuading people to carry organ donor cards. The Western Infirmary renal unit has performed more than 1,500 kidney transplants since 1968 and there is an ever-increasing waiting list for kidneys suitable for transplant. The government ruling that seriously ill patients must not be kept alive merely so that their organs may be used for transplant cuts down their availability even further.

The donor card campaign was joined in 1991 by Councillor Jean McFadden whose husband John had died earlier in the year despite two successful kidney transplants. John was the prime mover in the setting up of Second Chance, whose function was the promotion in Scotland of the organ donor scheme through a computerised register of potential donors. A national computerised register is now in operation in Bristol.

John McLaughlin has not come through all the anxious periods entirely unscathed. Six years ago he had a heart attack and was told to stop climbing buildings with the roof skylights his company in Govan manufactures and take up some light work, so he left the heaving and carrying part of the business to two of his four sons, Andrew and Stephen, and started to carve chairs to help pass the time. Most of the chairs are heavier than the roof skylights he used to carry but that doesn't prevent him from taking them all over the country to show at special events. Most of the work is done by John in a basement workshop in his house in the middle of the night because he's a bad sleeper.

You can't buy a McLaughlin chair. John will make one only out of love and thankfulness for the life of his daughter Pauline and for his own survival from the heart attack. He makes them for people he considers have made a worthwhile contribution of some kind to the life and times of his native city and so far has made about 80 chairs for clergymen, politicians, businessmen, footballers, policemen, officials of the city, and friends.

A couple of years after I retired, but without telling me, John tried his carving knife at producing a bust of me from pictures he found in various newspapers and offered it to Julian Spalding, Director of Glasgow's Museums and Art Galleries, for display at the Council's flagship gallery at Kelvingrove. John was inspired to make his offer after reading that Julian had bought a bust of Council leader Pat Lally for £10,000 earlier in the year.

After he had recovered from the shock Julian wrote to John, 'Much as I am an admirer of Harry Diamond's contribution to the city, I'm afraid that your bust, though very lively, is not a good enough work of art to enter the city's collections on loan.'

An indignant John got his own back by turning a large area of his factory into an exhibition for his carvings and inviting the Lord Provost to open it. Among the works is my bust, carved from a piece of the mast of the sailing vessel *Carrick*, alongside one of Mother Teresa!

John was a regular visitor to the Victoria Infirmary where I spent a couple of weeks after my retirement. Since then his first words on his regular telephone calls are, 'How's your wee body!' I got up one morning and collapsed in agony with a pain in the groin. I managed to dab myself with some water, get half-dressed, and drive painfully to my doctor's surgery. He poked and prodded and gave me a note to give to the receiving surgeon at the Victoria.

The receiving surgeon poked and prodded, sent me for X-rays, poked and prodded again, and said to someone standing by, 'Admit him to ward five.'

I said my car was in the street and my computer at home was on and the surgeon put a form in front of me and said, 'If you refuse to stay here please sign this form absolving us from any blame when you drop dead in the street!'

'OK, OK I'm staying!'

Minutes later I was installed in a side room of ward five with none of the things one takes into hospital. I left a message on Harvie's answering machine and he brought me my toothbrush and other supplies in the afternoon.

A couple of days later I was operated on for a strangulated hernia, whatever that is. After a few days I was transferred to an annex where where there was a fine collection of shattered humanity.

One guy had both legs cut off above the knees. Of course he singled me out for a graphic description of the operation and what led up to it. Two guys had cancer. Two had emphysema and made breathing noises like some primeval monster dragging its way though a tunnel in the bowels of the earth. One was mute and retarded and walked about with a permanent vacant grin.

One gaunt, silent type gave the impression of being engulfed in suppressed fury. He was very tidy and obedient to the nurses, ate every meal with enthusiasm and talked very little. If he did, his badly articulated comments were generously sprinkled with the F-word. He was a classic example of someone who has been subjected to prison discipline over fairly lengthy periods. He even held cutlery in an odd way, reminiscent of old films with Humphrey Bogart in Sing Sing.

The guy with no legs went on at great length about the lousy effing food. 'Ah wiz aw right till Ah came inty this fucking place and hud tae eat this fucking rubbish. That's how Ah hud to get ma legs cut aff, frae eatin this fucking rubbish.'

At this point I looked up and announced, 'I like the food here. I think I'll come here for my holidays.' There was no response from my companions.

A woman came into the ward one day with the frame of a wooden stool and some cord and asked me if I wanted to weave a seat! I told her to come back in 30 years when I might be into that kind of thing.

An attractive lady in a white coat came into the ward quite regularly and used to look at me intently from a few yards away but she never came any nearer or spoke to me. One day I said to the ward sister, 'Who is that lady who looks at me so intently but never speaks to me?'

'Oh, that's Madelaine, Mr Diamond. She's after your body.'

I thought, Harry son, you've done it again. They just can't keep away from you. Then the ward sister added, 'She's a pathologist.'

Chapter 30

CRAZY HORSE AND QUEEN KONG

THREE people dominated the affairs of Glasgow City Council during my years there: Dick Dynes, Jean McFadden, and Pat Lally, and they all had a hearty dislike of each other, which did nothing for the harmony and unity of the Labour group or its image among the citizenry. All were leaders of the Council, able, strong-minded people who enjoyed their power. All gave long hours to their work and did it in their own individual way.

I had my differences with them from time to time but our disagreements were never very serious. Disagreements is perhaps not the right word. I never disagreed with anything they said. I just stood quietly and let them rebuke me for some imagined transgression or omission on my part. Dynes had a tendency to rant, but didn't take long to cool down. McFadden could be irritatingly querulous, and Lally was quiet-spoken but deadly serious.

It's not a good idea for an official to argue with a Council leader because there is no way the official can win. On the whole, though, I have little complaint. Most of the time they were approachable and helpful in whatever I wanted to do, if it coincided with their interests.

It's not a good idea either for an official to be too friendly with any elected member, the convener or a member of the committee which dictates the policy of the official's department, because it is inevitable that some time or other a councillor will attack the official when it suits his or her purpose. The elected member will never take the blame for anything that goes wrong. It's an interesting fact that when a politician scores a success of any kind he invests himself (or herself) with astuteness, charm, intellect and political skill, but if the project or whatever doesn't go too well his officials who advised him are all fools and knaves.

Dick Dynes and Pat Lally lost their seats in an election in 1977, undoubtedly because of internal and public disenchantment with their frequent squabbles. Dynes disappeared without trace, which was a disappointment to many people, including myself. He could enliven any debate and was a formidable opponent. He could dish it out and take it too, but to be rejected by the electorate was apparently just too much for him. He came into my office to say hello a few weeks after his defeat in 1977 and never set foot in the City Chambers again. He died of a heart attack in October 1994.

Lally worked quietly and persistently in the political backwoods and made a comeback to the Council in 1980. Six years later he took the leadership from his arch-rival Jean McFadden. She got it back in 1992 and lost it again to Lally in 1994. The reform of local government again in 1995 created an interesting situation when Mrs McFadden, a resilient and persistent lady, was elected Convener of the new City of Glasgow Council, narrowly beating Lally for the post and putting Jean in the running for the post of Lord Provost when the new council took over the running of the city on 1 April, 1996.

Jean's elevation to the post was by no means automatic as was proved by a meeting of the Labour group on 18 March when Pat won the post of First Citizen by 52 votes to 25 over Jean, which convincingly confirms the old saying 'You can't tell the result of an election until the votes are counted.'

Mrs McFadden did, however, retain the post of Convener (or Chairman) of the Labour group which was traditionally held by the leader of the Council but the perceived wisdom now is that the convener of the group should be impartial, like the Speaker of the House of Commons. My only comment on that is Aye, that'll be right.

The leader of the new City of Glasgow Council is Bob Gould, who was leader of Strathclyde Regional Council, which disappeared on 31 March, 1996. The new city council has 83 members, 41 of whom were also members of the old city council, 21 from Strathclyde Regional Council, and 21 new councillors. Confused? Don't be discouraged. Most of the electors of Glagow have been confused since the reorganisation of local government two decades ago despite heroic attempts to abduct them. The political make-up of the new council is Labour 77, Conservative three, Liberal-Democrat one, Militant Labour one, Scottish National Party one.

It is difficult to say whether Dynes, McFadden or Lally made the greatest contribution to the affairs of the city because in the end it's really only a matter of opinion. I daresay each of their followers would be able to list many achievements, real or imagined.

Pat Lally had the highest public profile when I retired in 1991. He led the council during garden festival year, culture year, the bid for the title of City of Architecture and Design 1999, and is credited with ensuring that the Glasgow Royal Concert Hall was built before the end of culture year in 1990. As the Lord Provost Pat will now have a further opportunity to make an impact on the life of the city.

McFadden was the intellectual one of the trio, a one-time teacher of Latin and Greek who later studied in whatever little spare time she had as an active politician, graduated in law with honours and became a lecturer at Strathclyde University. Lally was a product of Gorbals and formally unschooled but an intelligent man and a skilled politician.

Unlike many other councillors McFadden never wanted to be a Member of Parliament because a Council leader, or even an influential committee convener, can do more for his or her constituents than an ordinary back bench MP, whose primary function, even if they don't always fulfil it, is to vote the right way with the rest of the party.

Perhaps an even more important consideration prevented McFadden from going to Westminister: the fact that her husband John suffered from kidney failure for a number of years and wasn't able to move far from their home and hospital.

People often ask me is who was the best Lord Provost in my time, a question I find difficult to answer. Best at what? Creating a friendly image of the city? Attracting investment? Generating innovative ideas? Inspiring respect for the city?

Six of them reigned during my 18 years with the local authority. They are elected from among the ranks of the majority party after a municipal election. Understandably there is keen competition for the job as the holder has one of the best jobs in Britain for four years, entertaining visitors of every rank of society from Britain and overseas, travelling extensively abroad, being indulged by an army of councillors and officials, and being treated with respect by the world at large.

The Lord Provost also holds the title of Lord Lieutenant and as such is the reigning monarch's representative in the city with the pleasant task of welcoming members of the royal family to the city.

'He must be a clever man to be made Lord Provost' is a comment I've heard from time to time, an uninformed judgment if ever I heard one. People are made the city's First Citizen for a multiplicity of reasons: some to prevent others from getting the job, some to get them out of the political mainstream because they were a nuisance, and some because they were harmless and wouldn't offend anyone. Now and again someone is elected because he or she has personality or real ability but that doesn't happen all that often.

More often than not three or four candidates put themselves up for election. If anyone gets 51 per cent of the votes at the first ballot he/she is home and dry. If not, the person with the least number of votes drops out and his supporters give their votes in the next ballot to someone else. Eventually the person with the most votes is elected. One of his tasks is to chair meetings of the full Council, which must be one of the most soporific occupations known to man, judging by the standard of most debates.

The post of Lord Provost is a ceremonial one and although they have considerable influence they have no real power. The influence comes from the fact that people respect the office and pay deference to the occupier because he or she is the city's First Citizen. A Lord Provost cannot order anyone but Council lower ranks to do anything. He can complain to the leader of the Council about someone who would then be told off but that's about all, unless of course it was something really serious.

One Lord Provost repeatedly complained about me to the leader of the Council, but as it was well-known that this particular Lord Provost seemed to have an unreasoned hatred of me no-one took any notice of his complaints.

The Lord Provost is a member of all the Council's committees but rarely goes to any of them. It is true that a particularly determined and imaginative Lord Provost can sway people to his or her way of thinking, but the real power in a local authority lies with the Leader of the Council, who presides over the Policy and Resources Committee, and conveners of committees such as Finance, Housing, Planning, Economic Development, Education and Social Work.

All the Lord Provosts I knew contributed what they could, some more than others. I am no great respecter of persons because he or she holds an important job. To me it depends on how they do that job and their attitude to the people around them that earns respect.

All Lord Provosts complain about the burden of office but they don't like to leave it behind just the same. *Herald* columnist Brian Meek declared in January 1988, 'You would be crazy ever to give up the job of Lord Provost willingly.' He quoted an unnamed First Citizen's secretary as saying, 'I can show you the marks on the wall where they dug in their nails on the last day.' This could only have come from Eric Hamilton, who served a considerable number of Glasgow's Lord Provosts with consummate skill and humour until his tragically early death from a heart attack.

Meek was commenting on a rumour that one Lord Provost of Glasgow, Robert Gray, had let it be known that he would not be averse to serving a second consecutive term, something that no First Citizen has ever done because the job is too popular and a lot of other people want it too. A hundred years ago another Lord Provost wanted a second term but he didn't get it either. Meek described Gray as 'a gentle and humorous soul'. Maybe it was Bob's sense of humour which prompted him to say to me the day he was elected Lord Provost, 'Right, Harry, from now on I want the credit for everything and the blame for nothing.'

My attitude to Lord Provosts was entirely influenced by how they co-operated with me as the city's propagandist and what they did for the city. The man who drives the Lord Provost around the city and who has to wait hours outside while the First Citizen enjoys an elegant and expensive dinner, or the Council officer who has to be obedient and respectful to a Lord Provost who is lording it for the benefit of an important visitor, may have a different opinion from me.

Some Lord Provosts made more demands on my office than others although all of them asked us to prepare background notes or public speeches for them. One or two of them used to phone me every time they had someone of importance in their office and ask me to come down and take their photograph together. It wasn't my job to take photographs but as it wasn't possible for me to commission a photographer every time we wanted a picture my staff and I often took them ourselves.

I carefully posed the Lord Provost and his guest and flashed off my camera several times and everyone was happy. More often than not there was no film in the camera because neither the Lord Provost nor his guest ever asked for a copy of the photograph.

Most Lord Provosts were appreciative of my efforts, even if they didn't embrace me fondly after a successful project. Sir William Gray, a lawyer, lent dignity and authority to the post and worked very hard to attract Civil Service departments and jobs to the city in the early 1970s. Bob Gray was amiable enough but tended towards the pompous, Susan Baird was friendly, photogenic and good-humoured, most of the time anyway, and popular with everyone with whom she came in contact. I was particularly impressed with her performance when I accompanied her and her husband George to Israel in 1990.

I had been trying for years to get the Israeli government to invite a Lord Provost because there were many in the Labour group who had no liking for Israel, even if they didn't know anything about it, and others who were active in the West of Scotland Friends of Palestine, a body whose anti-Israel propaganda was consistently distorted and destructive.

Eventually an invitation came from the Israel Labour Party, with which it was felt the City Council could identify more easily than with a government that was 'subjugating the dispossessed Palestinians.' There weren't any Jews in Susan's ward and I doubt if she had much to do with them in her working or political life. Susan and her husband George and I flew to Israel in June 1990 and in the seven days she was away from the City Chambers she did a round air trip of almost 6,000 miles, travelled more than 700 miles within Israel in a minibus, cars and taxis, met mayors, generals, diplomats, Arabs, Glaswegians, doctors, Russian immigrants and a whole lot of other people — and won the respect of all of them.

I don't know how much Susan managed to persuade her political colleagues that the Israelis were not the oppressors they imagined but at least she gained a greater understanding of the country's many problems.

Michael Kelly was educated and manipulative, a formidable combination. He was also very lucky that certain things happened during his term of office that enabled him to show how clever he was. On his last day in office he sent me a note say, 'I'll get out of your hair now!', which was his way of acknowledging that he had made good use of my office and its staff for four years.

Although he didn't devise the Miles Better campaign he certainly knew how to use it. Holding a Miles Better umbrella over the Queen during one of her visits to Glasgow was an inspired piece of showmanship. He was also politically astute.

The ill-fated marriage of the Prince and Princess of Wales in 1981 put Michael in a quandary. The City of Glasgow had to give the royal couple a wedding gift but the ruling Labour group of Glasgow City Council, who had elected Michael to the office of Lord Provost, didn't approve of giving royalty expensive gifts, especially in times of recession when the city needed all the money it could get.

'We had to give the couple a gift worthy of them, which reflected well on the city, and which didn't anger the Labour group and get the city a lot of bad publicity,' he told me later. 'They would have gone mad if I had suggested giving them something like a silver tea service costing hundreds of pounds.'

Benevolent forces were obviously on Michael's side. Not long before, a Glasgow general medical practitioner, Anne Gilmore, a lady of vision and single-mindedness, had come to him to ask him what help he could give her to set up the New Glasgow Hospice in the city. Michael said he would think about it.

Then he had a brainwave. He phoned the Queen's private secretary at Buckingham Palace and asked if a hospice named after the Prince and Princess of Wales would be acceptable as a wedding gift from the city. Royal approval quickly followed and Michael phoned Anne Gilmore, who could hardly reject the idea. The day in August 1981 that my story of the gift appeared in Britain's news media, a Buckingham Palace spokeswoman was quoted as saying, 'It is a marvellous present. The Prince and Princess of Wales approve enormously that the money is going to such a good cause.'

A *Glasgow Herald* leader said, 'An impressive array of royal wedding presents is now on display in London but there could be no more significant gift than yesterday's announcement that Glasgow's contribution will be a hospice for the terminally ill to be opened in the city within the next two years. The plan meets the criteria for the perfect royal gift in times like these: it gracefully honours the royal couple in a way that is also eminently useful to the community.'

Michael Kelly was appointed President of the hospice trust and for the next few years I wrote stories for the news media about every development in the project. Help for the new hospice came from all directions, including of course the District Council whose City Estates Surveyor, Remo Verrico, drew up a list of 23 properties which the hospice might convert to its use. Eventually the council gave the hospice three adjoining properties in Carlton Place, on the south bank of the river Clyde, which had been unused for years. They were originally elegant terraced houses owned by industrialists in the last century when Glasgow was one of the world's great industrial and maritime cities. They later became offices and then fell into disuse.

Funds were urgently needed to convert the Carlton Place houses and in December 1983 I went to Sir Hugh Fraser, who had inherited the Fraser store group from his father and was a trustee of the Fraser Foundation, and asked him if he could help the hospice. He picked up the phone and called his friend David Walton, Chairman of Scottish Metropolitan Properties and a founder trustee of the Isadore and David Walton Charitable Trust.

'Harry Diamond is in my office looking for money for the Prince and Princess of Wales Hospice,' Fraser said. 'I'll give £50,000 if you give the same!'

'It's a deal,' said David Walton.

I vividly recall that day worrying about the gas bill in my pocket.

Money continued to come in from emigré Scots in Europe and America who had read about the hospice. One gift of $500 came from the Saint Andrew's Society of the State of New York to whom I had written. The offical handover of the hospice to the royal couple did not take place until a visit to the city in May 1990.

Since the hospice, which now occupies four buildings in Carlton Place, was opened it has cared for more than 2,500 patients, and given support to their families. At the time of writing the hospice costs £1.4 million a year to run and has 22 beds, but only 14 are occupied because of a shortage of funds.

The day Michael Kelly demitted office a laudatory leader in the *Glasgow Herald* said, 'He willingly admits to being the beneficiary of luck and sound support from his public relations advisers in the City Chambers.' Other Lord Provosts had the same support but would rather go to the stake than admit it.

An outsider could be forgiven for believing that anything I did to attract favourable publicity to the city would be applauded by all my political masters. After all, officials and politicians were all put there for the specific purpose of doing everything we could for the people who lived and worked in Glasgow.

The truth is a little different. Over the years I suffered periodic verbal muggings from politicians of all parties. On balance I think the Tories were more critical than the Labour members, although I think they were a decent bunch really. The reason was simple enough. The city was ruled for 16 of my 18 years by a Labour administration and the projects I devised tended to reflect credit on the ruling party.

The Tories soft-pedalled a little when they took the administration after an election in 1977 although they won only 25 seats. The Labour group won 30 seats but they declined the administration because the Scottish Nationalists took 16 seats and Liberals one, which meant that the Labour group weren't likely to be able to implement their policies if the others ganged up on them, which was very likely.

The Tories hadn't had power in the city for years so they thought it was time for them to have a go. As it turned out no-one could really do anything with the Scottish Nationalists holding the balance of power. No-one knew what their policy was, except perhaps to sabotage anything that anyone else wanted to do. Through a series of wins at by-elections the Labour group took power again in 1979.

The Tories used to taunt me by telling me, 'When we get back into power again you're the first one to go.' After the 1977 elections the Tory group leader, John Young, came into my office smiling broadly.

'Right, John, I'm just clearing out my desk!' I said, to which John responded, 'Oh, don't worry Harry. You're not going anywhere. We want you to do the same job for us that you did for the other lot! I was only joking anyway.' Joking or not you can't get rid of senior officers quite as easily as that.

The previous year when Bruce Millan, Secretary of State for Scotland, asked the Council to make a massive cut in its spending, one of the money-saving options suggested by my friend Bill English, Director of Finance, was the abolition of the public relations department, a suggestion that was enthusiastically supported by John Young who told the newspapers, 'We've never found out what this department is supposed to be doing.' What he really meant was that his group didn't approve of what we were doing because it made the Labour administration look good.

More often than not the Tories' criticism backfired because they sounded like a miserable, unimaginative lot. Actually I thought they weren't such a bad bunch although they could sometimes be astonishingly petty.

Not long before I retired John Young complained that I had sat at his place in the council dining room. Bob Gray, Chairman of the General Purposes Committee, under whose jurisdiction the dining room operated, came into my office one day to tell me about John's complaint. I have to admit he looked very sheepish about it and apologised for having to complain about such a triviality. John himself looked rather sheepish when I tackled him about it later.

Early in the life of the City Council I had the idea of having ties carrying the city's coat of arms made for councillors and chief officials. Men's outfitters in the city wanted to sell them but I told them the Council held the copyright on the design and wouldn't allow anyone else to use it although I doubt if the Council would have taken action against anyone who decided to do it anyway.

The ties came in three colours, blue, maroon and brown. In 1977 when John Young was leader of a short-lived Tory administration he and other Tories and some Scottish National Party members complained that the maroon ties looked very like the Labour Party's red tie. I shrugged off the complaint and then the lady members complained that they hadn't got anything so I produced scarves for them, in maroon.

The Glasgow *Evening Times* reported one day, 'Robert Brown, MP, Minister for the Army, boarded a train in Edinburgh at the week-end for his constituency in the West Division of Newcastle proudly wearing an elegant maroon tie bearing Glasgow's Coat of Arms.

He got it from that irrepressible propagandist on behalf of Glasgow, Harry Diamond, the city's Chief of Public Relations, at the launch of a publicity campaign for the Territorial Army Volunteer Reserve.

In front of a delighted throng of Army hierarchy in Scotland and Ministry of Defence officials Harry persuaded the Minister to swop ties.'

The story didn't say I gave Brown a beautiful new tie and his Ministry of Defence tie looked like it had been through the battle of Waterloo. I put it in a litter bin.

Councillors thought up the most bizarre reasons for needing another tie: the dog chewed it up, the baby vomited on it, I lost it, I sent it to my brother in Canada, I want to give one to an important business contact. One committee convener went as far as to say, 'I think you should give me another tie, Harry. You may want something from my committee one day!'

John Young once accused me of helping the Labour group to dream up anti-government stunts. One alleged suggestion of mine was a papier-mâché effigy of Mr George Younger, Secretary of State for Scotland, with an axe in his head. A fake funeral procession to the City Chambers, with the Secretary of State as the central figure, was something else I was supposed to have suggested. What the point of all this was supposed to be, I don't know.

Once I persuaded John to speak at a seminar on public relations and he told his audience, quite rightly, that there were not nearly enough people in local government qualified to cater for the information needs of Scotland's 3,837,000 electors. This was generous of John as judging by their votes not many of them were interested in the part the Tories played in local government in Scotland.

When I told him in 1994 that I was writing my autobiography and intended to tell of some of our encounters he laughed delightedly. Next day he sent me a membership form for Cathcart Conservative Association. When I declined to join he followed up with an invitation to a dinner at which the guest speaker was Mr Malcolm Rifkind, Secretary of State for Defence. I told Alastair Mackenzie, Chairman of the Cathcart Tories, that I had spent much of my working life listening to politicians making speeches and much as I was an admirer of Mr Rifkind I did not intend to pay £20 of my meagre pension to hear him tell his followers what a great job they were all doing.

John Young didn't think they were all doing a great job. Several times during the year he had voiced his concern over certain party policies and the attempt to impose a 17 per cent rate of Value Added Tax on domestic fuel was the last straw. John declared he would be standing in the 1995 municipal election as a Cathcart Conservative. He would still be a member of the Conservative Party but would take an 'independent stance'. Bill Aitken decided to take a similar independent stance as a Kelvindale Conservative. Not that their declaration of independence was such a dramatic move as neither of them had any national ambitions and were not likely to be ousted by any official Tory candidates standing against them.

One Tory leader in the City Chambers did have a genuine complaint against me although to his credit he treated my seeming transgression as a great joke. Iain Dyer, a law lecturer, came into the City Chambers one morning to find that overnight he had become a member of the Labour group. An inattentive typesetter had typed Labour under his picture in a brochure I had produced about the council's services. The brochure was hurriedly reprinted.

Local authorities are not popular institutions and councillors are not held in high esteem by the public they serve: a rather blinding flash of the obvious. Some of them ask for the criticism poured on them, but I really don't think they are all that much worse than any other group of fallible humans.

There are myriad answers to the question of what motivates people to go into politics. It is not always the craving for power, because most of them never achieve any, although it is true that people of very modest achievement and intellect can chair committees which dictate the policies of departments with budgets of millions of pounds.

Politics is such an absorbing activity, like bridge or golf or football, and there is always something to talk about, someone to criticise, someone to sneer at. Almost anyone can participate in politics. For most politicians, local or national, the only qualification required is the ability to talk at great length without really saying very much that has not already been said a hundred times before. And if one talks long enough, loudly enough, or outrageously enough one can get on radio or television and become a media personality.

Councillors are drawn from various levels of society. Some of mine were conscientious and honest, some devious, some ineffectual, some witless, some unemployed, and some of doubtful value to any employer. They really weren't all that different from people in other professions and disciplines with the difference that everything they did was done in the harsh glare of public scrutiny. No-one can appear selfless, pure, and unsullied in the constant light of flashbulbs and with microphones thrust in their faces.

Inevitably we had nicknames in the best Damon Runyon tradition for many of the elected members. Some of the more memorable were the Six Dollar Man (a play on the television series The Six Million Dollar Man), Crazy Horse, The Budgie, Yogi Bear, Miss Piggy, and Lazarus. One councillor whose favourite reading matter was 'pull ring to open' was known as The Tank and a large lady councillor was known as Queen Kong.

Some councillors made life difficult for me in the City Chambers. There were a number of ways this could be done, some subtle and some quite boorish. Some would criticise almost everything I tried to do and others would be continually sarcastic.

Sometimes they would ask questions at a committee meeting which could only be answered in such a way as to imply that the councillor was half-witted to ask the question. Now and again I would get my own back by giving a councillor who was not overburdened with brains a letter from one of his or her constituents containing a complaint of some kind. I would tell him, 'I've told the writer I have given his complaint to his local councillor. I think you should sort this one out; it wouldn't look at all good in the newspapers.'

Some councillors and the officials whose departments they oversee have a good working relationship. Others don't. Councillors have a tendency to want to show their authority, especially if they are nonentities outside the Town Hall as so many of them are.

Often there seems to be a love-hate relationship between councillors and officials. I think this is because elected members have to appoint officials to jobs paying a lot more than the politicians can ever aspire to. This makes them jealous and as soon as they appoint a well-paid official they immediately try to make him look incompetent. The politician will of course plead that he or she is merely making sure the Council gets value for the taxpayers' money but I don't see it that way.

Just after my retirement was announced I was approached by a newspaper and offered quite a lot of money (well, it was to me anyway) to 'lift the lid off the City Chambers'. I turned down the offer, not because I am such a noble-minded fellow but because the 'inside stories' hardly compared with Watergate or Camillagate; more like Gardengate ...

They were so trivial and tawdry they weren't worth writing about, Besides, I had always considered it an honour to be allowed to work for the city and I didn't feel any compulsion to bite the hand that had fed me and my family for so long. Working for Glasgow was exciting, challenging, rewarding, nerve-wracking, and frustrating, and I enjoyed it all.

There were, however, some things that worried me all through the years. There were councillors and officials who did not always seem to be conscious of the fact that every single person in the authority, from the Lord Provost and leader of the Council, and the Town Clerk to the labourer in the parks department, were there for only one purpose: to serve the needs of the people of Glasgow, not to provide themselves with safe seats or comfortable jobs. From time to time I found it necessary to remind people of this fact, especially petty bureaucrats behind counters who treated members of the public as if they were a nuisance.

Another thing that worried me was the enormous number of Glaswegians who had difficulty in communicating with their fellow human beings, especially anyone in authority however minor. Many times I found members of the public wandering about the corridors of power looking for an office. Some of them didn't even know what office they were looking for. They clutched letters they didn't understand, not always because the letters were unintelligible but because their powers of comprehension were undeveloped, and were desperately seeking someone who could solve whatever problems they had.

Occasionally I had to spend some time in poorer areas of the city where I met people whose articulation and use of language was so bad I could not understand anything they said. I had to ask them time and time again to repeat what they had said and they always answered in mumbles with eyes cast down as if afraid to look anyone in the eye. They were unable to communicate with anyone outside their tight little circle. The outside world was somewhere to be feared. This worried me because they were unable to articulate their needs, aspirations, fears, and problems. This inability to communicate made it difficult, if not impossible, for them to defend themselves against large bureaucracies like the local authority, big companies, public utilities, or any other organised institutions who visited indignities or injustices upon them.

Once upon a time we in Scotland were able to boast about the superiority of our educational system. It would be difficult to persuade me of its superiority now. Unfortunately I can only articulate the problem; I do not know the solution, although I do think discussions on education are made at too lofty a level, prone to intellectual debate rather than the practicalities of the classroom.

One night at a dinner given to a very influential group of business men in the very elegant Satinwood room of the City Chambers one of the guests engaged me in polite conversation over the brandy and cigars.

He asked me what I did and when I made the mistake of telling him he asked me a lot of questions which I answered with considerable and uncharacteristic patience … spanning in 15 tortuous minutes a career of 50 years in journalism and public relations.

Eventually my inquisitor leaned across the table and asked in a voice dripping with sincerity and the thirst for knowledge, 'Tell me, is it possible for someone like you to work yourself up to be a councillor?'

When I told some of my political masters they said, 'You should have told him it would take you 20 years to work yourself DOWN to be a councillor!'

Chapter 31

CAN YOU GET MY NAME IN THE PAPERS?

PUBLIC relations is an odd trade. You don't need a single qualification to call yourself a practitioner, an executive, or even a consultant, despite heroic attempts by the Institute of Public Relations to improve standards and gain chartered status. One problem is that not every PR person belongs to the institute, which makes it impossible to impose its standards on every self-styled practitioner of the 'black art' as my old friend Arnold Kemp, former Editor of the *Herald*, calls it. Another problem is that many clients don't seem to care whether or not their PR people are members of the IPR.

Nevertheless the profession has come a long way since I went into it in 1962. Nowadays there are courses on the subject in colleges and universities in addition to private companies which run courses and seminars.

Some of these companies claim to tell the students in two or three days and for a few hundred pounds everything there is to know about catering for every type of news media, which may be the bargain of the century in view of the fact that it took me nearly half a lifetime to master this trick. Maybe I was a slow learner.

In a speech to the Confederation of British Industry Scotland in April 1980 I made a plea for public relations to be taught as a degree course at university. Eight years later Stirling University started Europe's first postgraduate Master of Science degree course in public relations, lasting one year. The following year a four-year BA honours programme was introduced at Bournemouth Polytechnic, now Bournemouth University, and in 1991 Stirling introduced a two-and-a-half year MSc, by distance learning programme.

An ever-increasing body of opinion opposes the view that training in journalism is a necessary prerequisite in public relations, or that catering for the news media is the principal function of public relations. Perhaps not, but there is absolutely no doubt about the dependence by public relations people on the news media to spread their message because that is the cheapest and most effective way of reaching the most people at one time. Nor can it be denied by the news media that they depend heavily on PR people to give them stories they would otherwise not hear anything about.

Public relations people now claim to be able to help clients do almost anything, go public, go private, cope with crises, or make a better mousetrap, but in my opinion, and experience, writing for the news media is still of critical importance because clients want to see favourable mention of themselves in newspapers, and if that mention is also on radio or television so much the better.

Many public relations people fail dismally in this area. They may learn from seminars how newspapers and radio and television news programmes are produced but writing for them is utterly beyond them because the writing skill takes years of experience to acquire and young people don't want to spend years learning to write. Nor do many of the executives already in public relations jobs, which is why they spend their days dreaming up stunts to attract attention to their clients or employers, the implication being that the client doesn't have a story worth telling until something is cooked up by a public relations consultant.

I have found over the years that among the things which can make news or feature articles are:

- How much of a product is made.
- Where it is made.
- Who makes it.
- The personalities involved.
- How many people are employed to make it.
- Where it all goes.
- How it gets there.
- Facilities available to employees to keep them happy at their work.
- How the product benefits the people who use it.
- How it can benefit others if they use it.
- How it benefits the community in which it is made.
- The extensive use of other people's goods or services.
- New products or ranges of products.
- Large orders received or placed.

- Changes in management or staff.
- Increase in number of employees.
- Visits by important or interesting people (not necessarily the same!).
- How the product's export earns revenue for Britain.
- Overseas travel by executives.

The list is virtually endless, and it may all be presented in a way that reflects credit on the company, its management, its employees, its product and on the wisdom of its customers in buying that particular product. And that's all the routine material. There are also dozens of other stories which emerge in the course of a year's trading.

Public relations in local government is different from commercial PR because there is a service rather than a product involved. Often it's more difficult because the news media would much rather criticise local government, often with good reason, than praise it, but despite all the difficulties it is also true to say that the news media will always take positive stories from local government if they are any good and the way to make them good is to research and write them properly.

The man or woman who can write for the news media in a way that is acceptable and intelligible to them in their terms has an infinitely better chance of publication or broadcast than the stunt arranger or the 'fixer' type of public relations practitioner although I admit they have a place in the great scheme of things.

There is no substitute for being able to write a series of simple, consecutive, intelligible, informative, unambiguous sentences in one's native language. Words properly used can do the most miraculous things. They can make us laugh or cry, love or hate, they can make us envious, fill us with admiration or wonderment, change our attitude, create a good impression or a bad one, make people think we are well-informed or ignorant, make us sympathetic or antagonistic, make us fall in love or out of love, influence what people think about our product or services, or someone else's. Think of the effect Shakespeare's words have had upon the world, or the words of the Bible, or the Koran, or the Torah.

It also helps to know about modern printing techniques, photography, research, marketing, how to interview and be interviewed, making films and other visual aids, the design of brochures, pamphlets and house journals, and the organising of exhibitions and other special events.

Public relations is not a cheap form of advertising. They are different forms of communication, just as televsion is different from radio. No amount of promotional and sales literature, no matter how expensively produced, serves the same purpose as material prepared specifically for editorial use.

Despite its increasing importance in public, business and institutional life and its contribution to the greater understanding of what goes on around us, and despite stars in the public relations firmament like Peter Gummer, Roddy Dewe, Sir Tim Bell, Lynne Franks, Sir Bernard Ingham, Mike Hingston and others, public relations is still regarded by many as a trade for dilettantes, dabblers and bright young things.

And no wonder. An example of the drivel that public relations consultancies produce is this statement by one of Scotland's leading consultancies in September 1991 when making a proposal to Glasgow City Council: 'Glasgow is faced with an immediate challenge to raise its image … by overcoming a past negative image and aligning it with the existing progress and revitalisation.' This was after the opening of The Burrell Collection, the Garden Festival, Culture Year, and almost two decades in which Glasgow's merits and virtues had been consistently and regularly publicised throughout the world.

In February 1995 BACUP, a national cancer-counselling service launched its first office in Scotland and was advised by a promotions company that a good way to interest the press was to release 1,800 balloons from the centre of Glasgow. A card attached to each balloon carried the name BACUP but did not say what it was or give the organisation's address or telephone number, which meant that anyone retrieving one of the balloons would not have the slightest idea what it was meant to tell them.

Two or three young people I know are in various stages of learning about public relations. When they came to me for advice I told them to choose another profession. I pointed out that in the time it would take them to become competent in public relations they could qualify as a doctor, a lawyer, an architect, a chartered accountant, a computer systems analyst, an engineer, or an airline pilot and everyone would know what they did for a living, and would respect them for it, whereas public relations could mean anything and was understood by very few. Of course they ignored my advice.

We are still at the stage when people look rather doubtful when you say you're a public relations person because it can mean almost anything. A friend of mine who advertised for a public relations executive once received an application from a retired butcher who said that after dealing with the public for 30 years there was nothing he didn't know about public relations. He wouldn't have applied for a post as a surgeon because he spent 30 years cutting beef.

I never made any secret of the fact that I approached public relations as a journalist looking for news or feature stories about my clients because that's wanted they wanted above all else. Rightly or wrongly that's the way they thought.

In the November 1994 issue of the *Journal of the Institute of Public Relations* Mr Neville Wade, a former president and a respected member of the fraternity was quoted as saying, 'In the job we do what PR means to employers and clients is lots of press cuttings. Learned books on the practice and theory of PR are a million miles from what many clients want. They just want to know can you get my name in the papers.'

Gordon Beattie, a journalist who runs a very successful public relations consultancy in Lanarkshire, incensed a large number of PR people when he claimed in an article in *Scotland on Sunday* in August 1995 that journalists make the best PR practitioners.

In June 1991, a few months before I retired, Pat Lally asked me to write something about the direction I thought the public relations department should take in the future. Here are some of the points I made in a report I produced. I don't know what Pat did with it but I do know my department's name was later changed to the Marketing and Public Relations Department.

Marketing Glasgow, or it's the way you tell 'em

1. The main functions of the Public Relations Department are to:
a) Heighten public awareness of the functions, workings, and services of the Council.
b) Publicise decisions of the Council and the implications of thesedecisions for the lives of the people who live and work in Glasgow, who invest in it, and who visit it for whatever purpose.
c) Publicise the work of the Council's departments and explain how their activities serve the interests of the public.
d) Help institutions in the city and the private sector to publicise any project which reflects credit on the operator or developer and the city.
e) Publish *The Bulletin*, the Council's newspaper.

2. The department's objectives must be to keep Glasgow, Scotland, Britain and the rest of the world constantly informed of anything of a positive, constructive nature that is happening in the city, using whatever media of communication are appropriate or available.

3. An essential ingredient in the marketing of Glasgow is 'editorial marketing', a continuous flow of information to the news media in Britain and abroad written in a way that is intelligible and acceptable to news and feature editors and producers.

4. Everything that happens in the city must be assessed for its value as a means of publicity. This is a matter of judgment based on experience and should therefore be carried out by the Public Relations Department.

5. Experience has demonstrated that there are few of the more positive aspects of the city's life that cannot be made interesting to the print and broadcasting news media, either in Britain or abroad or both.

6. Every possible outlet for information about what is happening in the city must be explored. In the past two decades the Public Relations Department has enlisted the co-operation of the Scottish Information Office, Scottish Tourist Board, British Tourist Authority, Central Office of Information, British Council, Press Association, Associated Press of America, Reuter, Agence Presse (France), Xinhua News Agency (China) Argus South African Newspapers Limited, At-Tadamon (Middle East), Chambers of Commerce, embassies, personal contacts at home and abroad, newspapers, magazines, airline in-flight magazines,. radio and television stations in Britain and overseas. All of these are still prepared to publicise Glasgow if the material is supplied to them in a form they in turn can market.

7. Public relations staff may of course glean much information about decisions of the Council and the activities of departments from Council minutes but it is essential that directors should liaise closely with the Public Relations Department and keep it informed of projects from the day they are planned. Nothing is issued to the news media without the agreement of the department concerned.

8. Time and time again directors have allowed their own staffs to send out what they call press releases which failed to interest the news media because they did not conform to even the most fundamental rules for catering for the news media. There is a reluctance to recognise the fact that promotional literature, no matter how expensively produced, does not serve the same purpose as material prepared specifically for editorial use.

9. There are times when an element of showbusiness may be injected into the Council's activities and projects (or stunts) may be devised to attract attention, but one must be careful not to rely too heavily on activities like these as they tend to be very expensive for what they achieve.

10. In an organisation like Glasgow City Council which has an influence on

the daily lives of so many people who live and work in the city it must be acknowleged that the day-to-day activities of the Council and its departments, and the myriad activities of the business community and the visual and performing arts should yield most of the material necessary for marketing the city without having to resort to artificial devices or stunts.

11. Although currently there are no high-profile 'glamour' events like the Glasgow Garden Festival or GLASGOW 1990 it is my belief that there are enough things happening or at the planning stage to persuade the world that Glasgow did not close down on 31 December, 1990.

12. It is beyond the wit of man to list the number of publications and radio and television stations throughout the world which have featured the more positive aspects of the life and times of Glasgow since 1975 but it is certainly true to claim that almost all of this exposure has been achieved through editorial marketing.

13. An effective marketing operation must of course also make use of advertising and when appropriate, films, videos, logos, books, brochures, pamphlets, conferences, exhibitions, and even trinkets like key fobs, pens and drinks coasters, but it is unchallengeable that the most effective marketing operation also contains an editorial element, which is often the most cost-effective way of spreading the city's message.

Many groups of London-based foreign correspondents were persuaded to visit the city over the years. This was quite an achievement because as far as their news organisations were concerned London was where everything happened in Britain and there was rarely any need to go elsewhere for a story. Other news people came from their home bases overseas. All of them were prepared to publicise Glasgow when material was supplied to them in a form they in turn could send home.

One of our overseas visitors was Jack Webster, a Glasgow-born man who had become one of Canada's leading television broadcasters. Jack claimed that his father, Willie Webster, an iron-turner, fitted pumps on every battleship, destroyer, and merchant ship built on the Clyde between the two World Wars.

Jack flew in with a crew of producers and technicians in the Spring of 1981 to do a 30-minute documentary about his birthplace but he was so fascinated by the changes in the city that the documentary was extended to two 30-minute slots on British Columbia Television. Some months later I was told by a relative in Vancouver that he saw me in a lengthy discussion with Webster on the revitalisation of Glasgow.

I enjoyed my working life. Maybe it took up too much time sometimes when I should have been with Jackie and the boys but many men have regrets of this kind. It is difficult for an ordinary mortal consistently to be a good and conscientious son, brother, husband, father, employee, employer and friend all at the same time. I look back on some of my adventures with wonderment and think did I do that? What was I trying to prove? I'm not sure what the answer to that is, unless I just wanted to show how clever I was.

I was a bit anxious when I retired about passing my time productively. My old friend and colleague Tony Meehan, founder of TMA Communications, came to my rescue and gave me a part-time consultancy job, but I had difficulty in adapting to Tony's way of working, which is very successful, and we parted company amicably after a few months.

Then I decided to do some consultancy work and my first client, John Smith, a Cambuslang roofing contractor, started a golf club manufacturing company, Scotgolf Europa (Marketing) Limited, and asked me to publicise it internationally, which I did. At the end of the exercise I sent Mr Smith a bill for £1,800, which included £600 I had spent on translations and other services, but Scotgolf Europa had gone into liquidation and I never got paid. I did get a cheque from Mr Smith for £600 but this was returned by my bank as there were no funds to honour it. My bank also charged me for processing the cheque! I found all this a bit discouraging so I gave up consultancy work and now I concentrate on communal and charity work.

I've often been asked which career I enjoyed most, as a journalist or a public relations man. The answer is I enjoyed them both, but I would like to think that in the years I spent with Glasgow City Council, in addition to enjoying myself, I did leave my mark on the city, even if it was such an intangible thing as helping to change people's perception of the place. I didn't go crazy working for politicians as some of my friends predicted but if you have a propensity in that direction a Town Hall is a good place to start the process.

I enjoyed meeting so many people in every stratum of society and people who had only their 15 minutes of fame; and I enjoyed my own moments of glory when occasional recognition came for my work. In 1978 I was the first person in local or national government in Scotland to be elected a Fellow of the Institute of Public Relations and in 1989 I received the Stephen Tallents medal for 'exceptional achievement' from the then President of the Institute, Reggie Watts. Harvie was too heavily committed with his law work to go to the presentation dinner in London with me so Michael flew from his home in Israel to share the occasion with me. It would have been good to have

Jackie with me but it was decreed elsewhere that this was not to be.

In the 10th anniversary supplement of *PR Week* in September 1994, three years after I retired, I was described as one of the most influential public relations industry players over the previous decade, but I think the biggest compliment came when letters arrived at the City Chambers addressed merely to Harry Diamond, Glasgow. I knew I had arrived then.

A few months before I retired I got a note from the personnel department asking me if I would like to go to a pre-retirement course at Langside College to learn how to cope with not having to go out to work for a living any more. As this meant a whole day in class each Monday for six weeks I decided it might be fun so I signed up for the course.

The chairman of our course was Doug Randall, who had retired from his job as an income tax officer eight years previously and had been enjoying life ever since.

'The secret of successful retirement is to be properly organised,' he said. 'Do something you like, make your new life worth while.'

Doug told the class about all the advantages of retirement — the freedom to do what you want, not having a boss to make your life a misery, not having to dig the car out of the snow to go to the office, concessionary travel, cheap holidays, the opportunity to meet new friends and new challenges, time to develop hobbies, cheaper tickets for recreational facilities. There were about 15 of us in the class. In the weeks that followed we were told about things like accident and fire prevention, how to wire an electric plug, how to make lentil soup, sensible eating, saving money, music and art appreciation, and a whole lot of other useful things I had known for decades. As a special treat in art appreciation we were taken to The Burrell Collection. I kept my mouth shut during the tour, which wasn't easy.

All the lecturers were experts in their subject, but the first-aid speaker was so dull my eyes got heavy and I almost went to sleep. Suddenly I heard a stern voice saying, 'Are you paying attention?'

'Why, will you give me the belt?' I said. 'Get on with it.' He was not amused.

A lady from the Citizens Advice Bureau told us she and her colleagues could find an answer to any question. One worried caller had difficulty with a job application which asked her for two referees. 'I don't know anything about football,' she complained.

We were told about pension rights by a Department of Social Security video featuring my old friend actor Ian Cutherbertson, and the merits of libraries and books. We also got a pile of literature telling us how to avoid a large number of health hazards from fallen arches to a heart attack. Exercise was very important, we were told. As a college student I was entitled to use the college car park, the refectory (very good soup and spaghetti bolognese for about £1.50), the library, and even the swimming pool.

In a diversionary moment Doug Randall depressed us all by telling us we were born before televison, penicillin, polio shots, antibiotics, frozen food, nylon, radar, computers, dishwashers, clothes dryers, electric blankets, yogurt, Batman, instant coffee, tape recorders, video recorders, word processors, DDT and vitamin pills!

What I really wanted was for someone to tell me that old guys like me were a valuable asset to society with a lifetime of experience and confidence and that the minute it was announced I was retiring I would be bombarded with requests for my expertise which would bring me in at least twice my salary.

I also had a fantasy about finding a wealthy, young, beautiful widow who was prepared to keep me in indolent luxury for the rest of my life, but regrettably that never happened. A number of well-meaning wives of friends went through a period of trying to find a mate for me as if I was a giant panda or something. They've now given up the seemingly impossible task. I have had a couple of lady friends in the past few years but our friendships didn't lead anywhere. I went as far as to go on holiday with one of them. As we walked about in Venice I told her, 'Robert Benchley was once sent to Venice by Harold Ross, the Editor of the *New Yorker* and when he got there he sent Ross a telegram saying, "Streets full of water. Please advise." '

My lady friend said, 'Did he not know that before he went?'

'Eh?'

'Did that man not know Venice was covered in water?'

'Robert Benchley was a very clever humorist. That was a joke.'

'Oh.'

'Have you never heard of Robert Benchley?' I asked.

'Tell me about him.'

'He was an editor, writer, drama critic, humorist, and even a film actor. He died in 1945.'

'I was only a little girl then,' said my lady friend. 'Of course you're older than me. You'll know about people like that.'

I tactfully refrained from saying I wasn't born when Napoleon, Shakespeare, and Moses lived but I still knew about them.

One evening I took the same lady to a concert in Glasgow Royal Concert Hall and we met that marvellous man Sir Alexander Gibson, who did so much for the musical life of Scotland, and his charming wife Veronica at a reception afterwards. Alex wasn't performing that night and I said to my lady companion, 'Meet a couple of friends of mine: this is Alex Gibson and his wife Veronica.'

My lady friend said brightly to Alex, 'Oh, hello, do you like music? Do you come here often?' I wanted to drop through the floor but Alex smiled indulgently and muttered something innocuous like the gentleman he was.

My first meeting with Alex took place in 1974, not long after I joined the city council. I had what I thought was a brilliant idea so I phoned Alex to ask his advice about it and he invited me to his home.

'What do you think of the idea of the city commissioning a piece of music named after it, like the *Glasgow Symphony* or *Concerto*?' I said. 'After all, other cities have musical works named after them; the *London Symphony, Paris Suite, Warsaw Concerto, Symphony of San Francisco, Leningrad Symphony.*'

Alex told me there was even an *Edinburgh Symphony*, written by the Edinburgh-born composer and conductor Guy Warrack, and first performed at the Royal College of Music in London in 1932. Alex thought it was a great idea to have a *Glasgow Symphony* and we even talked about what a grand occasion we could make the première, but my political masters thought it was a rotten idea.

'It will cost us a helluva lot of money and then we might not like it,' they said. I tried to argue that it would be a magnificent public relations exercise for the city and that there was hardly a piece of music of any kind that some people didn't like, but it was no use.

I recalled this story in a letter to the *Herald* when Sir Alex died in January 1995 and several readers, including my old friend ex-Lord Provost Michael Kelly, indignantly pointed out that there were two or three pieces of music inspired by the city, but most of them came after 1974 and had never been heard of by most people.

It took more than a decade and the appointment of Robert Palmer as Festival Director before the city commissioned about 40 musical works, but even with Palmer's heroic efforts there still isn't a major work of music instantly identifiable to the world, or even the rest of Scotland, as Glasgow's own symphony. Not long after Palmer was appointed Director of Performing Arts and Venues I inadvertently referred at a committee meeting to the Department of Performing Lions. Jean McFadden was not amused.

I am happy to be away from the anxieties of being the city's propagandist and I don't really mind being an old-age pensioner, not that it make any difference whether I mind or not. A lot of people don't like the phrase old-age pensioner or even senior citizen but no-one has so far been able to think up an acceptable name for us. In America we're called retirees! There are 10 million of us in Britain, including 865,000 in Scotland.

I still do some communal work and am still very much involved with Erskine Hospital. In 1995 I handled the publicity for the visit to Glasgow of Madame Jehan Sadat, widow of President Anwar Sadat of Egypt who was assassinated by Islamic fundamentalists in Cairo in 1981 because he had signed a peace treaty with Israel a couple of years earlier. She spoke at a Joint Israel Appeal dinner in Glasgow.

I spoke to her briefly at a press conference I arranged and found her a dignified, charming, warm-hearted woman. She got a standing ovation at the dinner for a very moving speech about her husband and about the Prime Minister of Israel who had been assassinated only a week earlier. I was surprised to learn that her mother was born in Sheffield. Small world.

Some years ago when I had achieved what I thought was a certain amount of status, authority and respect in my profession a relative asked me to see a friend of hers whose 20-year-old son had not yet found a meaningful role in life. He had had a number of jobs but had not found fulfilment in any of them.

After some persuasion I allowed this young man's mother into my large, elegantly appointed office and listened for 20 minutes to her sad tale. Eventually she leaned forward and said in an earnest, concerned, and confidential tone, 'The truth of the matter is Mr Diamond, George's father and I don't think he is very bright, but we think he would do well in your kind of work.'